The
Geography Bee
Complete
Preparation
Handbook

The Geography Bee Complete Preparation Handbook

1,001 Questions & Answers
to Help You Win Again and Again!

Matthew T. Rosenberg
Jennifer E. Rosenberg

THREE RIVERS PRESS
NEW YORK

Published by Three Rivers Press, New York, New York.
Member of the Crown Publishing Group, a division of Random House, Inc.
www.randomhouse.com

THREE RIVERS PRESS and the Tugboat design are registered trademarks of Random House, Inc.

Originally published by Prima Publishing in 2002.

Printed in the United States of America

Design by Melanie Haage
Illustrations by Nathaniel Levine

Library of Congress Cataloging-in-Publication Data
Rosenberg, Matthew T. (Matthew Todd).
    The geography bee complete preparation handbook :
    1,001 questions & answers to help you win again and again /
    Matthew T. Rosenberg, Jennifer E. Rosenberg.
        p.   cm.
    Includes index.
    1. National Geographic Bee—Handbooks, manuals, etc. 2. Geography—
Competitions—United States—Handbooks, manuals, etc. 3. School contests—
United States—Handbooks, manuals, etc. I. Rosenberg, Jennifer E. II. Title.
G74 .R67 2002
910'.79'73—dc21   2002025216

ISBN 0-7615-3571-3

18 17 16 15 14 13 12 11

First Edition

To Kiefer, Laura,
John, and Megan

Contents

Acknowledgments

We would first like to thank our family for their love and encouragement. We owe our parents—Ken, Leslie, and Barbara—a debt of gratitude for everything they've ever done for us. We thank our siblings—Kiefer, Laura, John, and Megan. They hold a special place in our hearts. For their years of encouragement, we'd like to thank our grandparents: Patricia and Mark, Eleanore, Abbott and May, Fred and Mary Lou, and Marvin. Our aunts and uncles are very special to us: Willeta and Bruce, Pat and Bob, Marsha and Gary, and Shelli and Alan. We appreciate the love of our cousins: Brian, Pam, Amanda, Kelly, Kevin, Tina, Bailey, Josh, Jaime, Jeremy, Jaclyn, and Rachel. We remember and love Joel, Poppy, Marjorie, and Jerry.

Our friends and neighbors are wonderful—Marc; Layne and Gabrielle; Caroline, Dave, and Wiley; Todd, Michelle, and Lauren; Kevin and Christina; DeRees, Liz, and Haley; Don; Jenneen and Scott; Caitlin; Rick; Robin; Avram; Rich; and Kris.

Matt would like to thank Jean and Candy, who deserve special praise for their continued guidance and support. Matt would also like to thank his team of amazing volunteers who make such a difference in the lives of others every single day—thank you!

We thank Michael Knight and Todd Haverlock for their ideas and extensive contributions. Jamie Miller and Tara Joffe from Prima Publishing are to be commended for their flexibility and assistance.

Introduction

Each year, millions of students participate in the Geography Bee. For most students, the competition ends on the same day it begins, as only one student from each classroom will compete at the school level. Fewer still will compete at the state level, and only fifty-seven (one from each U.S. state and territory) will have the opportunity to participate in the national-level Geography Bee.

Would you like to be one of the students who makes it to the national level of the Geography Bee? Then you need to prepare. This book includes hints, tips, and shortcuts that will help you be prepared for the Geography Bee.

Why You Should Buy This Book

Save Yourself from Embarrassing Moments

Learn how the Geography Bee works so you don't answer in the form of a question, miss a question about your own state's capital, or blurt out an answer that was not one of your two choices.

Why You Should Move to Wyoming

Well, unless you are a Geography Bee fanatic, you really shouldn't move just for the Bee. However, this book explains why it is easier to get to the national level from Wyoming than from California and why you aren't necessarily going to the state level just because you won your school Geography Bee.

Where on Earth . . . ?

Knowing the locations of U.S. states, countries of the world, major waterways, physical features, and other geographic wonders will help you answer many of the Geography Bee questions. Using blank maps will help you fill in what you don't know.

Basic Training

Don't get bogged down in unneeded details. This book contains quick guides for U.S. states and the countries of the world so you can quickly study what you will need to know.

You Can't Dig a Hole to China

Besides the fact that you can't dig a hole that deep, you wouldn't reach China because China is not the antipode of the United States. Learn more about antipodes, volcanoes, earthquakes, clouds, caves, and more from almost three hundred physical geography terms.

"Bee" Super with Superlatives

Which country is the largest by area? Which country is the smallest? This book contains list after list of important geographic superlatives for you to study.

1,001 Attempts to Stump You

Boy, have we tried to stump you! We have 1,001 Geography Bee–style questions divided into eight chapters. You can use them to practice and study. If you can answer all of these, you are a geography master!

Our Disclaimer

The data in this book is not guaranteed to be accurate and the interpretation of answers in a Geography Bee is at the discretion of the judges. Geography changes, and thus facts in this book may become out of date. Verify information through updated atlases and sourcebooks.

Part One

About the Geography Bee

1

The National Geographic Bee

Do you have a fondness for the world around you? Have you ever wondered what it would be like to walk along the Great Wall of China or swim in the Great Salt Lake in Utah? Have you ever wondered why they speak Portuguese in Brazil or how anyone can understand each other in Papua New Guinea with more than seven hundred indigenous dialects? All these questions can be answered with geography. So, are you interested in geography? Do you want to know more about the world around you? Great! Then you are a perfect candidate for the National Geographic Bee.

What Is the National Geographic Bee?

In 1989, the National Geographic Society commissioned a Gallup Poll to investigate the geographic knowledge of students in countries around the world. To many people's surprise and chagrin, Americans

in the eighteen to twenty-four age category (the youngest group sur-
veyed) scored the lowest of the ten countries measured. Even worse,
many Americans could not even locate the United States on a blank
map of the world!

Obviously, geography had taken a back seat to many other subjects in the classroom for too many years. Concerned about this
widespread lack of geographic knowledge, the National Geographic
Society established the Geography Bee to reintroduce the subject of
geography into classrooms. The Geography Bee was to be a fun and
rewarding way for students in grades 4 through 8 to learn about geography. The National Geographic Society held the first national-
level Geography Bee in 1989, the same year as the Gallup Poll was
conducted, and students have been learning geography ever since.

The Geography Bee tests students on much more than just U.S.
states and their capitals. Students must know in-depth information
about U.S. states, countries of the world, human geography, physical
geography, economic geography, political geography, and much
more. For all students, the Geography Bee competitions begin in
their classroom. For those students who are geographically literate,
the competitions continue to the school, state, and national levels.

The Levels of Competition

The National Geographic Bee is run on five different levels: classroom, school, state qualification test, state, and national.

Classroom Competition

For most students, the classroom competition is their first and only
exposure to the National Geographic Bee. The classroom competition is quite informal and takes place any time from November to
early January, usually only a few days to a week prior to the school
competition.

Though the format can vary from school to school, the classroom
competition often consists of a single round of elimination. Each stu-

dent is asked a question. If a student answers incorrectly, the student is out of the competition. This continues until a classroom winner has been determined. Often, when there are only two or three students left, the teacher begins a final round. Here, an incorrect answer eliminates a student only if the other finalists answered their questions for the round correctly. The classroom champion then goes on to the school competition.

School Competition

The purpose of the school competition is to select one student who will take the state-level qualification test to earn one of the hundred spots at the state competition. The school level is a bit more organized than the classroom competition and is similar to how the state- and national-level Bees are run. The questions are mailed to the school principal directly from the National Geographic Society, whose rules must be followed at the school level to determine who will take the state qualification exam.

The preliminary competition consists of seven rounds. Each classroom champion is asked one question per round and must give an oral answer within 15 seconds. Students can ask for the question to be repeated or for a word to be spelled out. A correct answer earns the student one point. At the end of the seven rounds, the students with the top ten scores advance to the final competition. A tiebreaker may be used to narrow the number of remaining students to ten.

The final competition is divided into a final round and a school championship round. In the final round, a student is eliminated if he or she answers two questions incorrectly. This round alternates between individual oral questions and questions given to all students that require written answers. When only two students are left, the school championship round begins. Incorrect answers from the previous round do not carry over. Both students are asked three questions and are given 15 seconds to write down the answer to each. Whichever student answers the most questions correctly is the champion. In case of a tie, an additional question is given, with both students writing down the answer. This continues until one student answers correctly and the other does not. The school champion then goes on to the state qualification test, and the second-place winner serves as a backup in the event that the school champion cannot take the test.

Is That a Fact?

Although the competition is open to students in grades 4 through 8, students are not divided into grade levels at the school, state, or national competitions. Therefore, a fourth grader could be competing against sixth or even eighth graders during the competition. Older students do have an advantage, but it is not uncommon for younger students to win.

State Level Qualification Test

To qualify for the state-level competition, each school champion must take a standardized written test, which in the past has consisted of seventy multiple-choice questions that a student must complete in one hour. In addition to typical geography questions, such as those asked during the classroom and school Bees, there are also analogy and map-reading questions. The analogy questions can be difficult, because students have to look at the relationship between the first two subjects and then determine an answer for the second set of subjects. Here is an example:

Mississippi River : Gulf of Mexico :: Nile River : ?

To answer this question, students must first find the relationship of the Mississippi River to the Gulf of Mexico. Because the Mississippi River empties into the Gulf of Mexico, the relationship between the two features is that a river empties into a body of water. Therefore, the student must read the second part of the question as, "The Nile River empties into what body of water?" The answer is the Mediterranean Sea.

The completed qualifying tests are mailed to the National Geographic Society, and the top one hundred students in each state and territory are invited to participate in their state-level competition. Students who qualify for the state competition receive a letter approximately one month before the competition to congratulate them for winning and to provide information about the location and time of the state competition.

State Competition

All state and territory Geography Bees take place on the same day, typically a Friday in April. Students from around each state travel to the state competition, which is often held on a college campus. Students, parents, and teachers must pay their own expenses for travel, meals, and lodging. There is often a get-together dinner or event the evening before the Bee so that students from around the state can meet each other and have fun.

Because each state and territory uses the same question booklet for the state competition, the National Geographic Society typically schedules East Coast competitions later on the same day as those conducted on the West Coast, so that students compete at approximately the same time. This is to prevent students from calling or e-mailing each other to discuss answers or questions in the Bee.

During the state competition, the one hundred students who have qualified are evenly divided into five classrooms for a practice round (which is not scored) and seven preliminary rounds. In each classroom, there is a moderator who reads the questions, a judge who determines if an answer is correct, a scorekeeper who keeps track of each student's winning answers, and a timer who ensures that each student does not take more than fifteen seconds to answer a question. In some cases, one person may fulfill more than one role, so a moderator may also be a judge.

At the end of the preliminary rounds, the top ten scoring students then advance to the final competition. At the state competition, there is often a tie among those who have answered six out of seven questions correctly. Those students involved in a tie are taken to a separate room for a tiebreaker round.

Once the ten finalists are selected, the final round begins in a large auditorium so that parents, teachers, and other students can watch. The ten finalists are given an opportunity to introduce themselves, and then the competition begins. Some questions in the final round are asked of individual students, while others are asked of all ten students, with each student writing his or her answer on a piece of paper shown to the judge after time has been called. Student by student is eliminated until a state champion, second-place, and third-place winners are chosen. Each state winner receives a gift of $100 and an all-expenses paid trip to Washington, D.C., for the student and his or her teacher escort.

Fifty state winners and up to seven territory winners are represented at the national-level competition. The seven territories include the District of Columbia, Guam, Puerto Rico, American Samoa, the Northern Mariana Islands, the U.S. Virgin Islands, and the Department of Defense Dependents Schools. Thus, as many as fifty-seven students may be competing each year in Washington, D.C.

National Geographic Bee Championships

Millions of students at approximately eighteen thousand schools across the country (and around the world) compete in the National Geographic Bee, but only fifty-seven students make it to the national championship level. The champion from each state or territory is invited to participate in the national competition in May. It is held in Washington, D.C., and is moderated by Alex Trebek, the host of the television game show *Jeopardy!* This competition is televised on some PBS stations and is often Webcast on National Geographic's Web site at www.nationalgeographic.com.

The competition takes place over two days. In addition to the Bee, the event also includes sightseeing and fun activities for all the state champions. The final Bee is much like the state competitions in that the competition is narrowed down to ten finalists who know their geography very, very well. Each of the ten finalists wins $500, but the winner is awarded $25,000, the runner-up receives $15,000, and the student placing third wins $10,000. The first-place winner also receives a lifetime membership in the National Geographic

Society, which ensures that the yellow-bordered magazine will arrive at his or her home every month for the rest of the champion's life.

Past National Geographic Bee Champions

As this book goes to print, there have been thirteen national competitions. Let's take a quick look at the winners of each of these National Geographic Bee Championships and the question that he or she answered correctly but the second-place winner did not. The questions will give you a sense of the level of difficulty at the national championship.

1989

Name: Jack Staddon

Home State: Kansas

Grade: 8

Winning Question: Name the flat intermontane area located at an elevation of about 10,000 feet (3,050 meters) in the central Andes.

Winning Answer: Altiplano

1990

Name: Susannah Batko-Yovino

Home State: Pennsylvania

Grade: 6

Winning Question: Mount Erebus is a volcano on which continent?

Winning Answer: Antarctica

1991

Name: David Stillman

Home State: Idaho

Grade: 8

Winning Question: What type of landform is commonly associated with orographic precipitation?

Winning Answer: Mountain

1992

Name: Lawson Fite

Home State: Washington

Grade: 8

Winning Question: Many coastal countries have established so-called EEZs—areas extending 200 nautical miles from shore over which countries have sovereign rights for resource exploration. What do the initials EEZ stand for?

Winning Answer: Exclusive Economic Zone

1993

Name: Noel Erinjeri

Home State: Michigan

Grade: 8

Winning Question: Tagalog is one of the three main native languages of which island country in Asia?

Winning Answer: Philippines

1994

Name: Anders Knopse

Home State: Montana

Grade: 8

Winning Question: The Tagus River roughly divides which European country into two agricultural regions?

Winning Answer: Portugal

1995

Name: Chris Galeczka

Home State: Michigan

Grade: 8

Winning Question: Pashtu and Dari are the official languages of which mountainous, landlocked country in southwestern Asia?

Winning Answer: Afghanistan

1996

Name: Seyi Fayanju

Home State: New Jersey

Grade: 7

Winning Question: Name the European coprincipality whose heads of state are the president of France and the bishop of Urgel.

Winning Answer: Andorra

1997

Name: Alex Kerchner

Home State: Washington

Grade: 7

Winning Question: Asia's most densely populated country has about three million people and an area of less than 250 square miles (402 square kilometers). Name this country.

Winning Answer: Singapore

1998

Name: Petko Peev

Home State: Michigan

Grade: 8

Winning Question: More than eighty million people live in the European Union's most populous member country. Name this country.

Winning Answer: Germany

1999

Name: David Beihl

Home State: South Carolina

Grade: 8

Winning Question: The condition characterized by unusually cold ocean temperatures in the equatorial region of the eastern Pacific Ocean is known by what Spanish name?

Winning Answer: La Niña

2000

Name: Felix Peng

Home State: Connecticut

Grade: 8

Winning Question: Name two of the three largest sections of Denmark, which include its mainland peninsula and two largest islands.

Winning Answer: Jutland, Sjélland, and Fyn

2001

Name: Kyle Haddad Fonda

Home State: Washington

Grade: 8

Winning Question: Below the equilibrium line of glaciers there is a region of melting, evaporation, and sublimation. Name this zone.

Winning Answer: Zone of ablation

Getting the Geography Bee in Your School

If you would like to have your school participate in the National Geographic Bee, talk to your school principal about registering. The principal must write a letter on school stationery requesting to register the school in the competition. A fee (currently $40) must be included with the letter. Check the National Geographic Bee Web site (www.nationalgeographic.com/geographybee/) for deadlines. Send the letter to the following address:

> National Geographic Bee
> National Geographic Society
> 1145 17th Street NW
> Washington, D.C. 20036-4688

The Society will then send out materials to the school so that it can host its own competitions and possibly qualify a student for the state competition.

2

Tips for Competing

Before you go to your competition, make sure you read through these tips and hints about the Geography Bee.

It's an Unfair Competition

Although we think the Geography Bee competitions are the best thing since sliced bread, they are inherently unfair. The following are a few of the ways in which the Geography Bee puts some students at a disadvantage.

The Grade Differential

The most obvious unfairness is that the competition pits fourth graders against eighth graders. That is a four-year age difference! Because of the additional years of life experience and possibly of study, an eighth grader has a serious advantage over a fourth grader. That does not mean, however, that only eighth graders can win the national championship. If you browse through the listing of past winners in chapter 1, you will notice that three of the past champions were not in the eighth grade and one was even in the sixth grade.

Knowing Your Own State

Would you be embarrassed if you missed a question asking for your own state's capital? Of course you would be. If you received a question about your own state, you would probably have an advantage over an opponent who lives all the way across the country. Although living in the state doesn't guarantee that you will know the answer to the Geography Bee question, you might have a better chance of knowing about the location because maybe you visited there, or know someone who lives there, or learned about it in school.

In addition, students who have traveled more have an advantage over those who have not. This may seem unfair, but it is the nature of this competition.

Almost a Know-It-All

Beware, the following might happen to you. During a competition, you listen as every other student gets what you consider to be an easy question—or at least one for which you know the answer. Then comes your turn. You feel confident. You feel that you know it all. Then you hear the question. That wasn't what you were expecting! There is no hint, it isn't about your state, and you have never heard of the place that they are asking about, so you get the question wrong. This can happen and often does.

Although hundreds of questions are asked at each Geography Bee, you as a participating student will only be asked eight questions before the final round, and these questions vary greatly in difficulty.

You may know the answer to every question other than yours, but the only questions that will count are the ones asked directly to you.

Population Affects Probability

We assume you are reading this book so that you can do better in the Geography Bee. Many of you are probably hoping to get to the national championship level. Did you know that if you live in Wyoming you have a better chance of getting to the national level than if you live in California? This is because your state's population can affect your chances of getting to the state and national levels. For example, Wyoming has only 500,000 people living in the entire state, while California has 34 million people. Because you are competing against your peers for the one hundred spots at the state competition and for the one position from your state at the national competition, you would have fewer competitors if you lived in Wyoming than in California. Now think about your odds if you lived in American Samoa, a U.S. territory, with a total population of only 57,000 people. American Samoa gets to send one student to the national level. It is similar in size to a small town in the continental United States, containing only two junior high schools.

Of course, this does not mean that students from larger states necessarily win the championships. If you look at the past national champions, none have been from the largest states of California or Texas. Maybe, by the time you get to the national level, it all evens out and each student has a fair chance at winning the championship.

Getting Ready for Competition

Everything you do to get ready for the Geography Bee competition should have the purpose of making you relaxed at the Bee. Stress, tiredness, and nervousness can hinder your thinking process. Be on your toes by following these tips:

- **Get a good night's rest.** Make sure you go to bed at a reasonable time the night before the competition so that you can get a good night's rest. Competition is tough enough without having to think while drowsy. Plus, yawning can certainly be annoying and distracting if you are trying to pay attention to the questions.

- **Don't cram.** The Geography Bee is a test of your overall knowledge. As with most tests that you will take in your life, cramming right before the test will most likely hinder you more than help. Maybe glance over a map one more time, but then put away all your study materials, take a deep breath, and relax before the Bee.

- **Eat breakfast.** Eat a good, nutritious breakfast. Foods with a lot of sugar will give you a sugar high early in the day but then leave you tired and drained.

- **Dress comfortably.** Though you don't need to wear a suit and tie or fancy dress at the competitions, it is nice if you dress up a little. The most important aspect about your outfit, however, should be that it is comfortable and not distracting. If you are more worried about your outfit than about your questions, you are not going to be able to focus on what is truly important at the Bee.

- **Be on time.** Although you can't necessarily help make sure your parents are on time for the state and national Bee, you can help them be timely. Find out how long it will take to get to the location, even with traffic, and where you will need to register. Plan on being a little early so you have plenty of time to register, meet people, and perhaps use the restroom before competition begins. Being late or near late can cause you unneeded stress.

- **Bring family.** Bring family and friends who can offer you support. It is always nice to have a cheering section.

Answering the Questions

No matter how well you prepare or how much you know, it all comes down to how well you do when answering the questions at the Geography Bee. From our experience, the number one reason why most students get the questions wrong is not because they did not know the answer; rather, it was because they blurted out an answer without even thinking about the question. Use the following tips to help you listen to and answer questions correctly.

Clues

Many questions at the Geography Bee, especially at the school and state levels, give you multiple clues in the questions. This is a huge advantage because you don't need to know both pieces of information to get the question right; you only need one.

For example, what if you were asked, "What European country, with a capital city of Madrid, occupies most of the Iberian Peninsula?" This question actually gives you three clues. First, it tells you that the answer is a country in Europe. So you can immediately rule out all other countries besides the ones that are in Europe. Then it tells you the country's capital city. If you know your country capitals, you should already know the answer. If you can't quite remember, there is still a third clue. The country lies on the Iberian Peninsula. Clue 1 helps you narrow down the countries; clues 2 and 3 help you answer the question. The answer is Spain.

Think About It!

Take your time. You have fifteen seconds in which to answer the question, and if need be, you can ask to have the question repeated. Though that may seem like a short period of time, it should be enough for you to analyze, think, and then answer. Too many people blurt out an answer immediately following the question, when if they thought about it at all, they would have known the answer.

When you hear the question, analyze it for clues. Then take a moment to think about the clues you found. And only after you have done those two things, give an answer.

Guessing

There is no penalty for guessing. However, only guess after you have decided that you really don't know the answer. Guess wisely. Many students just say whatever country comes to mind rather than making an educated guess. For instance, in the example question earlier, you might not have known which country has a capital city of Madrid and lies on the Iberian Peninsula. However, you still know it has to be a country in Europe. So don't guess South Africa! Take the information that you do know from the question and make an educated guess.

Multiple Choice

Several rounds in a Geography Bee can be multiple choice. For example, you might be asked, "Which capital city is farther west—Salem or Boston?" Notice that they will give you two answer choices. Think about the question. This particular question *appears* to rely on your knowledge of both capital cities' locations. Not true.

Often in multiple-choice questions, one answer is the correct one and the other is completely not true. For instance, if you knew that Salem was the capital of Oregon, then you would realize that you could not get much farther west than Oregon. If you did not know which state has a capital city of Salem, you would then need to think about the second answer choice. Since Boston is the capital city of Massachusetts, you should realize that you could not get much farther east than the state of Massachusetts. Therefore, Boston could not possibly answer the question, and Salem must be the correct one.

Remember to analyze the question, think about it, and then give your answer. Also, for the multiple-choice questions, remember that if you need to guess, give an answer that is one of the choices given.

What If You Lose?

Fourth Through Seventh Graders

If you are in grades 4 through 7, our motivational speech for you is simple; it begins and ends with the phrase "next year." Did you take a few minutes and browse through the list of past national winners listed in chapter 1? If so, you will notice that nearly all the past national champions were in the eighth grade when they won. What that list does not show is that nearly all of the past champions competed in previous Geography Bees before they won the national competition. As you gain experience, understand the process better, and know what you need to study to do better, you will be ready to prepare for next year. At the end of each year, take a short break, congratulate yourself on what you have already learned, and then get started studying for next year.

Eighth Graders

If you are an eighth grader, it is probably time we tell you a little historical secret. It's not something we're proud of, but it may help you understand a little more about the Geography Bee and its contestants. The National Geographic Society created the Geography Bee because of U.S. ignorance, not knowledge, about geography. In 1989, students and adults alike did very poorly in a poll about the world around them. Thus, the National Geographic Society created the Geography Bee for students in grades 4 through 8 to help U.S. students learn more about the world around them. Thus, every student who learns a little bit of geography for a Geography Bee is a winner. Remember, only one student out of millions can be the national champion; everyone else is *not* a loser. Everyone who participates and has fun goes home a winner.

Part Two

Bee Prepared

3

What You Need to Know

The National Geographic Society created Geography Bees in the hope that students would learn more about geography. So, what will you be tested on? Geography. But what is geography? Unlike history, which is the study of the recorded past, or biology, which is the study of living things, or geology, which is the study of the Earth's processes, geography is an extremely broad subject with little to no boundaries. In many ways, it includes all of these sciences plus more.

The word "geography" can be broken into two parts: *geo-*, which comes from the ancient Greek meaning "the Earth," and *-graphy*, which comes from the ancient Greek meaning "to write" or "to describe." Thus, *geography* means "to write or to describe the Earth." To us, to you, and to the writers of the Geography Bee questions, geography can be anything in the past or the present that has had to do with the Earth, whether that be human civilizations, cloud formations, rain forests, water trapped below ground, or erupting volcanoes. The questions can nearly be about *anything* and *everything*. So where should you begin studying? Why not start with our "Bee Prepared" chapters?

How to "Bee" Prepared

Are you overwhelmed by what you need to know? Don't give up! Although anything can show up in Geography Bee questions, some information is more likely to appear than others. We have gathered some of the essential information that you will need to know for the Geography Bee and placed it in the rest of part two. Each chapter in this part is a level of learning, numbered 1 through 6. The chapters are listed in order of importance.

Instead of just reading the sample questions yourself, have someone else read them to you out loud. Questions will be read out loud to you at the Geography Bee, so practicing in this way will give you added ability during the real competition.

Plan; Don't Cram

Before you begin the Bee Prepared levels, you must first analyze your time and balance that with what you need to know. How many days until the Geography Bee? How much time can you set aside for studying? Will you have time to read and study all the levels of learning or just a few? Before you begin, plan how long you will spend at each level. It won't help you to just study levels 1 (locations) and 2 (U.S. states) and not know anything contained in level 3 (countries of the world). Planning and following a study schedule means time will be your friend; waiting until the very last minute to cram will definitely make time your enemy.

Levels 1 Through 3

Levels 1 through 3 contain detailed information about U.S. states and the countries of the world, which can help you in many rounds of a Geography Bee.

Level 1: Location, Location, Location—A large part of geography consists of knowing where things are located. Use blank maps to chart U.S. states, countries, and other major physical features of the world.

Level 2: This Land Is Your Land—Geography Bees often contain an entire round devoted exclusively to the United States. Knowing specific information about each state, especially capital cities and interesting facts, can help you conquer this round.

Level 3: We Are the World—Many rounds include information about some aspect of a country or countries. Knowing a country's capital, physical features, history, and culture can give you an edge.

Levels 4 Through 6

Levels 4 through 6 include information helpful to you for specific rounds.

Level 4: I've Got a Little List—This level contains list after list after list of superlatives, religions, ancient civilizations, and more. Knowing these basics of cultural geography can help with many questions. This level also encourages you to go online and learn more.

Level 5: Earthworms to Earthquakes—Geography Bees often include one round devoted exclusively to physical geography. Knowing these key terms and their definitions is essential for the physical geography round.

Level 6: Extra! Extra! Read All About It!—Rounds of the Geography Bee include questions that test your knowledge of current events and your map-reading skills. Prepare with these tips.

Who Has the Answer?

There's probably no wrong way to use the 1,001 questions we have included in part four. (Well, there probably is, but we just can't think

In Training

An athlete, no matter what sport he or she competes in, spends hours and hours of hard work practicing and training for each minute of competition. The higher the level of competition, the more training needed and the greater amount of dedication and discipline required. The same is true for competitors of the National Geographic Bee. At the lower levels, most students do very little preparation before competing. It may not be too tough to win in the class competition or even at the school level. There is a big jump, however, from the school level to qualifying for the state Geography Bee. This is where competition begins to get fierce. Only students who score in the top one hundred in the written test will be invited to compete at the state level. There is another jump in the caliber of the competition at the national level, and only the most intensely prepared have a chance of becoming the National Geographic Bee champion.

If you want to compete at state and national levels, you need to start early and work hard on a regular basis. You'll need to be familiar with a wide variety of topics and information, so it will be much more profitable to learn at a constant rate rather than trying to cram it all in at the last minute. Make sure you set aside a certain amount of time each day to study.

of it right now.) No matter how much or how little time you have to study, we highly recommend that you try at least a few of the questions in each of the sample question chapters every time you study.

Don't try to do an entire chapter of questions at once! Instead, spread them out by attempting about ten to twenty questions in one sitting. When you are done with each set of questions, make sure you look up any answers that you didn't know. The question chapters in part four can be as great a resource for studying and learning as the Bee Prepared chapters, but only if you study and learn what you didn't know.

What You Will Need for Preparation

Okay, now that you know what you need to study for the Geography Bee, you're ready to sit down and get started. But with an empty desk in front of you, how can you start? You need to collect some materials so you can be ready for serious study.

An Atlas

The primary item you will need is a world atlas. Geography is the study of the world, so you're going to need to know what that world looks like. Although atlases can be expensive, they are well worth the investment. Libraries do have atlases, but these are often kept in the reference section and are not available for checkout. Besides, you will need an atlas for more than a few weeks, and it is always good to have one on hand for reference. You will need a good-

Worldly Tip

A world globe is a great resource to have at home. It gives you a better understanding and visualization of the world than do flat maps. However, you will still need the flat maps of an atlas for their greater detail.

quality world atlas that includes ample coverage of the United States. It should also show political boundaries and natural features, such as lakes, mountains, rivers, and topography. Though we can recommend both the *Times Atlas of the World* and the *Goode's World Atlas*, many other good atlases are available. Whichever atlas you purchase, be sure it was published within the past year or two. The world is constantly changing, and if you study from a fifteen-year-old atlas, you will be learning about countries that no longer exist.

Additional Books

An atlas is an essential reference, but it might not be the most inspiring book from which to study. Therefore, you might also consider purchasing or checking out from a library additional books to use for reference and for fun geography facts.

Reference Books

For this book, we consider "reference books" to be books in which you would look up answers to your specific questions, rather than books that you would read through from cover to cover. Here are a few of our favorite geographical reference books:

Merriam-Webster's Geographical Dictionary: Similar to a dictionary, but for geography. Contains every major feature, waterway, country, territory, and much more. (This is Jen's favorite reference.)

The National Geographic Desk Reference: Contains in-depth chapters about the topics covered in the Geography Bee.

Oxford Encyclopedic World Atlas: Provides lengthy entries about every country of the world, accompanied by a colorful map.

The World Almanac and Book of Facts: Includes tons of information, much of which you don't need to know for the Geography Bee. However, Matt loves this book because it contains lists of superlatives and fantastic resources about states and countries.

Other good reference books include geographical dictionaries and introductory college textbooks on human and physical geography.

Fun Geography Fact Books

Since reference books can seem very dull if you try to read them from beginning to end, you might want to gather a few fun geography books. To use these as effective study guides, first read about a fact in the book, and then look up the country, city, or feature in your atlas and reference books. This allows you to have fun with the trivia while gaining a mental picture of the place's location. Our favorite fun geography fact book is *The Handy Geography Answer Book*. It's hard for us to say too many good things about this book, since we wrote it, but it is filled with interesting geographical tidbits in a question-and-answer format.

Get Started!

What are you waiting for? Start by making a study plan, then tackle Level 1 in chapter 4. Don't forget to intersperse a few rounds of sample questions throughout your hours of studying. Good luck!

4

Level 1: Location, Location, Location

Have you ever heard someone say the most important aspect of real estate is location, location, location? Well, the same is true for geography. You can tell a lot about a country just by knowing where it is located. For example, you can be pretty sure that France is not going to have a border dispute with South Africa because they are not even on the same continent. And you can be confident that Mongolia isn't going to have a big shipping industry since it doesn't lie near a sea. And Ecuador won't have freezing winters because it lies along the very temperate line of the equator.

But most important, knowing the location of every country, U.S. state, major body of water, and physical feature can help you answer many of the questions at the Geography Bee.

How to Study Locations

To study for the Geography Bee, you need to begin by learning the locations of every U.S. state, every country, and every major physical feature on the planet—that's more than four hundred different places! Sounds a little overwhelming, doesn't it? Don't worry—we'll help you get through this. The best way to learn geographical locations is by using blank maps.

Perhaps you are wondering how blank maps can help you if they are blank. It does sound strange, but bear with us. Begin by photocopying the blank maps of the continents found in this chapter. (You may want to enlarge the maps when you photocopy them to make it easier to write on them.) Choose just one continent to begin with. Then sit down at a desk and use an atlas to look up the locations of each of the places we have listed in this chapter. Label them on your blank map. After only a few minutes, you're blank map should look a lot less blank.

Worldly Tip

Get creative when filling in your blank map. Use colored pencils to distinguish the different countries so that you can easily and clearly see their borders. Use blue for the lakes, rivers, bays, and oceans. Write an upside-down "V" to indicate a mountain or a string of "V"s to create a mountain chain.

Once you have all the information written on your map, study it. Memorize it. Then study it some more. Once you feel comfortable with your map, take out another blank map of the same continent and again sit at a desk, but this time without an atlas. Using the list of places found in this chapter, label your fresh, blank map from memory. Can you do it? Did you remember the location of each place? Check both your previous map and the atlas for accuracy. Did you miss any? That's okay. Study the ones you missed a little more thoroughly and then try again later with another fresh, blank map. Soon, you'll find the locations of countries like Guinea-Bissau, Singapore, and Suriname without hesitation.

Creating a Mental Map

When drawing and studying your map, remember to think about which countries lie north, south, east, or west of another. Often Bee questions ask you to relate one place to another. For example, a question could ask, "Which African country is located just north of Sudan?" To answer this question, you need to be able to visualize the countries of Africa. Can you see them in your mind? If so, that is called a "mental map." You need to study the locations of these geographic places thoroughly enough so that if you get a similar question, you will be able to use your mental map, rather than your physical map, to answer the question.

UNITED STATES

United States

STATES

Alabama	Louisiana	Ohio
Alaska	Maine	Oklahoma
Arizona	Maryland	Oregon
Arkansas	Massachusetts	Pennsylvania
California	Michigan	Rhode Island
Colorado	Minnesota	South Carolina
Connecticut	Mississippi	South Dakota
Delaware	Missouri	Tennessee
Florida	Montana	Texas
Georgia	Nebraska	Utah
Hawaii	Nevada	Vermont
Idaho	New Hampshire	Virginia
Illinois	New Jersey	Washington
Indiana	New Mexico	West Virginia
Iowa	New York	Wisconsin
Kansas	North Carolina	Wyoming
Kentucky	North Dakota	

OTHER FEATURES

Appalachian Mountains	Great Salt Lake	Missouri River
Cascade Range	Lake Erie	Rio Grande
Colorado River	Lake Huron	Sierra Nevada Mountains
Columbia River	Lake Michigan	Washington, D.C.
Four Corners	Lake Ontario	
Grand Canyon	Lake Superior	
	Mississippi River	

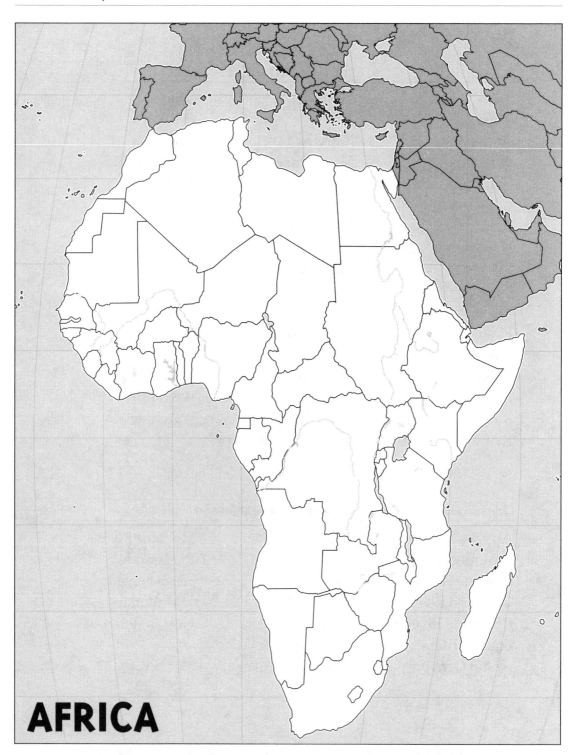

AFRICA

Africa

COUNTRIES

Algeria	Equatorial Guinea	Niger
Angola	Eritrea	Nigeria
Benin	Ethiopia	Rwanda
Botswana	Gabon	São Tomé and
Burkina Faso	Gambia	Principe
Burundi	Ghana	Senegal
Cameroon	Guinea	Seychelles
Cape Verde	Guinea-Bissau	Sierra Leone
Central African	Kenya	Somalia
Republic	Lesotho	South Africa
Chad	Liberia	Sudan
Comoro Islands	Madagascar	Swaziland
Congo, Democratic	Malawi	Tanzania
Republic of the	Mali	Togo
Congo, Republic	Mauritania	Tunisia
of the	Mauritius	Uganda
Côte d'Ivoire	Morocco	Zambia
Djibouti	Mozambique	Zimbabwe
Egypt	Namibia	

OTHER FEATURES

Atlas Mountains	Lake Tanganyika	Red Sea
Cape of Good Hope	Lake Victoria	Sahara Desert
Congo River	Mount Kilimanjaro	Sinai Peninsula
Kalahari Desert	Mozambique	Suez Canal
Lake Nyassa (Lake	Channel	Western Sahara
Malawi)	Nile River	Zambezi River

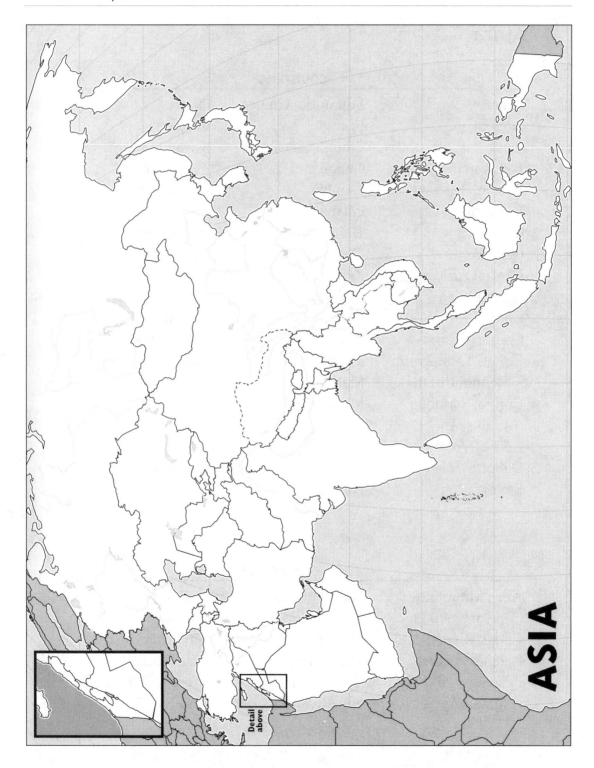

ASIA

Detail
above

Asia

COUNTRIES

Afghanistan	Japan	Qatar
Armenia	Jordan	Russia
Azerbaijan	Kazakhstan	Saudi Arabia
Bahrain	Korea, North	Singapore
Bangladesh	Korea, South	Sri Lanka
Bhutan	Kuwait	Syria
Brunei	Kyrgyzstan	Tajikistan
Cambodia	Laos	Thailand
China	Lebanon	Turkey
Cyprus	Malaysia	Turkmenistan
East Timor	Maldives	United Arab
Georgia	Mongolia	Emirates
India	Myanmar	Uzbekistan
Indonesia	Nepal	Vietnam
Iran	Oman	Yemen
Iraq	Pakistan	
Israel	Philippines	

OTHER FEATURES

Arabian Peninsula	Gaza Strip	Sulawesi (Celebes)
Arabian Sea	Gobi Desert	Sumatra
Aral Sea	Himalaya, The	Taiwan
Asia Minor	Indus River	Tibet
Bay of Bengal	Java	Tigris River
Borneo	K2	West Bank
Caspian Sea	Lake Baikal	Yangtze River
Dead Sea	Mount Everest	Yellow River
Euphrates River	Persian Gulf	(Huang River)
Ganges River	Sea of Japan	Yellow Sea

EUROPE

Europe

COUNTRIES

Albania	Greece	Poland
Andorra	Hungary	Portugal
Austria	Iceland	Romania
Belarus	Ireland	Russia
Belgium	Italy	San Marino
Bosnia and	Latvia	Slovakia
Herzegovina	Liechtenstein	Slovenia
Bulgaria	Lithuania	Spain
Croatia	Luxembourg	Sweden
Czech Republic	Macedonia	Switzerland
Denmark	Malta	Ukraine
Estonia	Moldova	United Kingdom
Finland	Monaco	Vatican City
France	Netherlands	Yugoslavia (Serbia
Germany	Norway	and Montenegro)

OTHER FEATURES

Adriatic Sea	Black Sea	Mont Blanc
Aegean Sea	Bosporus	Mount Elbrus
Alps	Caucasus Mountains	North Sea
Apennines	Corsica	Pyrenees
Mountains	Crete	Sardinia
Azores	Danube River	Scandinavia
Balkan Peninsula	English Channel	Sicily
Baltic Sea	Gibraltar	Ural Mountains
Barents Sea	Mediterranean Sea	Volga River

NORTH AMERICA

Detail at left

North America

COUNTRIES

Antigua and
  Barbuda
Bahamas
Barbados
Belize
Canada
Costa Rica
Cuba
Dominica

Dominican Republic
El Salvador
Grenada
Guatemala
Haiti
Honduras
Jamaica
Mexico
Nicaragua

Panama
St. Kitts and Nevis
St. Lucia
St. Vincent and the
  Grenadines
Trinidad and Tobago
United States

OTHER FEATURES

Alberta
Aleutian Islands
Baffin Bay
Baffin Island
Baja California
Beaufort Sea
Bering Sea
Bering Strait
Bermuda
British Columbia
Cape Morris Jesup
Caribbean Sea
Great Bear Lake
Great Slave Lake
Greater Antilles
Greenland
Gulf of California

Gulf of Mexico
Hispaniola
Hudson Bay
Lake Nicaragua
Lake Winnipeg
Lesser Antilles
Manitoba
Mount Logan
Mount McKinley
Mount Whitney
New Brunswick
Newfoundland
North Magnetic Pole
Northwest Territories
Nova Scotia
Nunavut
Ontario

Panama Canal
Prince Edward
  Island
Puerto Rico
Quebec
Rocky Mountains
Saskatchewan
Sierra Madre
  Occidental
Sierra Madre
  Oriental
St. Lawrence Seaway
Vancouver Island
Virgin Islands
Yucatán Peninsula
Yukon Territory

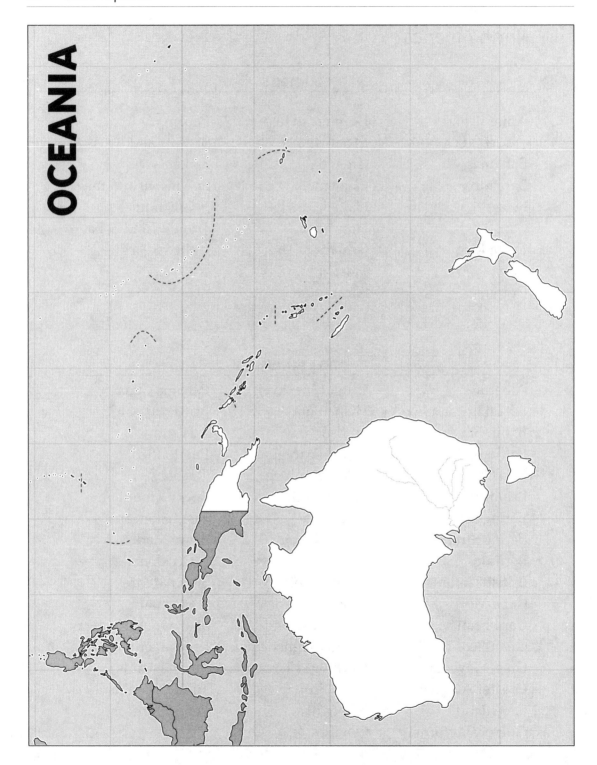

Oceania

COUNTRIES

Australia	Nauru	Solomon Islands
Fiji	New Zealand	Tonga
Kiribati	Palau	Tuvalu
Marshall Islands	Papua New Guinea	Vanuatu
Micronesia	Samoa	

OTHER FEATURES

American Samoa	Micronesia	Pitcairn Island
Great Barrier Reef	Midway Islands	Polynesia
Guam	Northern Mariana	Tasmania
Melanesia	Islands	

SOUTH AMERICA

South America

COUNTRIES

Argentina	Colombia	Peru
Bolivia	Ecuador	Suriname
Brazil	Guyana	Uruguay
Chile	Paraguay	Venezuela

OTHER FEATURES

Amazon River	French Guiana	Lake Titicaca
Andes	Galapagos Islands	Rio de la Plata
Easter Island	Gran Chaco	Strait of Magellan
Falkland Islands		

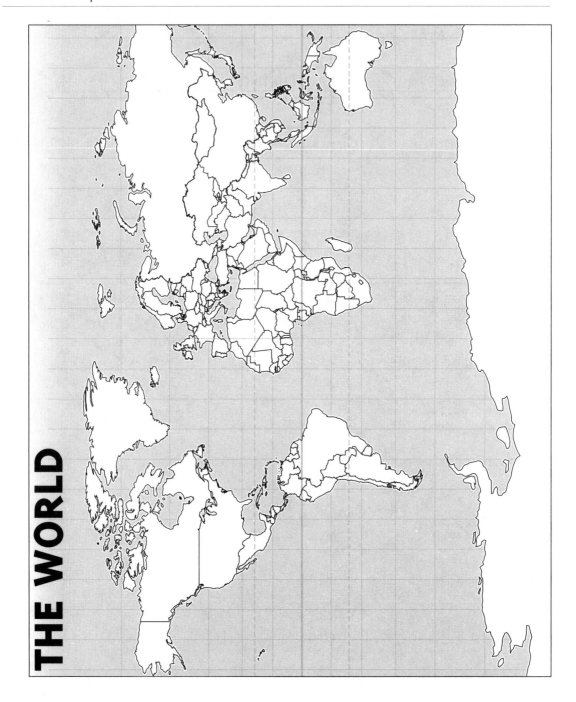

THE WORLD

The World

Antarctica	Indian Ocean	Pacific Ocean
Arctic Ocean	International Date	Prime Meridian
Atlantic Ocean	Line	Tropic of Cancer
Equator	Marianas Trench	Tropic of Capricorn

5

Level 2: This Land Is Your Land

A Guide to Studying the United States

Welcome to Level 2! By now, having completed Level 1, you should know the location of every state, country, and major feature on Earth. In this chapter, you will learn detailed information about each of the fifty U.S. states.

Many rounds of the National Geographic Bee focus on the geography of the United States of America. You'll need to know each state capital, major cities, important topographical features, key products, important facts, key historic dates, national parks, and, of course, the location of the state in respect to the states around it.

Outline Maps

The best way to learn the location of places within each state and, most important, to associate places with a state is to label blank outline maps

with the places we mention in this chapter (capital, major cities, topography, waterways, and national parks). You can find printable outline maps for each country and state online at Matt's site (geography .about.com) and at the National Geographic Society's Xpeditions site (www.nationalgeographic.com/xpeditions/atlas/index.html). Also, some school supply stores sell books of outline maps that can be photocopied and labeled. We strongly encourage you to take the time to label blank outline maps of each state to help you learn the geography. Like you did in Level 1, use an atlas along with this book to label your blank map correctly.

Take your time—don't try to memorize the facts and label the places of more than a few states each day. Focus on each state as you label your blank map, including the facts you won't be labeling (nicknames, products, history, and other facts), so that you develop a clear picture in your mind about the state.

Some rounds in the Bee are called Geography of the United States, but you might also find rounds such as National Parks of the United States or Economic Geography of the United States. This chapter will help you prepare for all of these questions.

If you have extra time to prepare for this level, study detailed maps of each state and look up additional information in almanacs and books about the fifty states. Some online resources for the U.S. states can be found in Bee Prepared 4.

The Quick Guides

This chapter provides quick guides to each of the fifty states as well as the District of Columbia. Each quick guide includes the following information:

Nickname: A phrase used to promote the state. Remembering this phrase may help you remember other aspects of the state, such as history, key products, or topography.

Capital: The name of the state capital, which is also often a major city. Most students learn this information in elementary school, so if you don't know it yet, it is important to know now.

Major Cities: The largest cities in the state. The major cities might be used as part of a question and will give you a hint to the answer.

Topography: Major mountain ranges and other geographic features.

Waterways: Rivers, lakes, and seas within or on the borders of the state.

National Parks: A listing of the national parks that lie within the state. Two national parks—Yellowstone National Park and Great Smokey Mountains National Park—lie in more than one state; find out which ones!

Key Products: The economic activities for which the state is best known.

History: Very important dates in the history of the state.

Interesting Facts: Information that you might hear in a Geography Bee question.

Alabama

Nicknames: Heart of Dixie, Camellia State

Capital: Montgomery

Major Cities: Birmingham, Mobile, Huntsville

Topography: Appalachian Mountains (northeast), Cumberland Plateau (northeast), Piedmont (east-central), East Gulf Coastal Plain (southern half)

Waterways: Tennessee River, Mobile River, Mobile Bay on the Gulf of Mexico

National Parks: None

Key Products: Cotton, peanuts

History

1540: Hernando de Soto explored this area.

1819: Became twenty-second state.

1861: Seceded from the Union.

Interesting Facts

The U.S. Space and Rocket Center is located in Huntsville.

In December 1955, Martin Luther King Jr. began the famous civil rights bus boycott in Montgomery after Rosa Parks was arrested for not giving up her bus seat to a white passenger.

Alaska

Nickname: The Last Frontier

Capital: Juneau

Major Cities: Anchorage, Fairbanks

Topography: Brooks Range (north), Aleutian Range (southwest), Alaska Range (south-central), Aleutian Islands (southwest, extending toward Russia)

Waterways: Yukon River, Kuskokwim River. Alaska is surrounded by water on three sides: Arctic Ocean and Beaufort Sea (north); Bering Sea, Norton Sound, the Chukchi Sea, and Bristol Bay (west); and Gulf of Alaska and the Pacific Ocean (south).

National Parks: Denali NP, Gates of the Arctic NP, Glacier Bay NP, Katmai NP, Kenai Fjords NP, Kobuk Valley NP, Lake Clark NP, Wrangell–St. Elias NP

Key Products: Petroleum, fishing, forestry, tourism

History

1741: Vitus Bering explored Alaska for Russia.

1867: United States bought Alaska for $7.2 million from Russia. Known as "Seward's Folly" or "Seward's Icebox" after Secretary of State William H. Seward.

1890: Klondike Gold Rush began.

1959: Became forty-ninth state.

1964: One of the United States' largest earthquakes (9.2) struck Alaska.

1989: Oil tanker *Exxon Valdez* dumped huge amounts of oil in the Prince William Sound, causing an environmental disaster.

Interesting Facts

Within Alaska, most travel is by sea or air. There are no highways to the state capital.

Mount McKinley is the highest point in the United States at 20,320 feet; also known as Denali.

Alaska has the largest number of lakes in the United States, more than three million.

Juneau is the largest city in the country, measured by area (more than 3,100 square miles).

Northern Alaska is tundra, and only plants like mosses and lichens can grow in the cold.

Arizona

Nickname: Grand Canyon State (formerly known as the Copper State)

Capital: Phoenix

Major Cities: Tucson, Mesa, Glendale, Flagstaff, Tempe, Yuma

Topography: Colorado Plateau (north), Painted Desert (north-central), Grand Canyon (northwest), Sonoran Desert (southwest)

Waterways: Colorado River, Gila River

National Parks: Grand Canyon NP, Petrified Forest NP

Key Products: Copper and mineral production

History

Early civilizations included Anasazi and Hohokam.

1848: Treaty of Guadalupe Hidalgo granted Arizona north of Gila River to United States and ended the Mexican War.

1853: Gadsden Purchase gave remainder of Arizona to United States.

1912: Became forty-eighth state, last of the conterminous states.

Interesting Facts

The London Bridge is now located in Lake Havasu City.

Arizona does not observe daylight saving time.

Hoover Dam is the highest concrete dam in the country (but only the second highest of all dams in the United States).

The Grand Canyon is more than 200 miles long and 1 mile deep.

Arizona's deserts are covered with the stereotypical saguaro cacti.

The Navajo Indian Reservation occupies the northeast of the state.

Arkansas

Nicknames: Land of Opportunity, Razorback State, Natural State

Capital: Little Rock

Major Cities: Fort Smith, Pine Bluff, Fayetteville

Topography: Ouachita Mountains (west-central) and Boston Mountains (north)

Waterways: Arkansas River, Mississippi River, Red River

National Park: Hot Springs NP

Key Products: Soybeans, cotton

History

1541: Explored by Hernando de Soto.

1836: Entered Union as twenty-sixth state.

1861: Seceded from the Union.

Interesting Facts

Arkansas has many therapeutic mineral hot springs near Hot Springs and Hot Springs National Park.

Diamonds are mined at Crater of Diamonds, North America's only diamond mine.

Former president Bill Clinton hails from Arkansas.

California

Nickname: Golden State

Capital: Sacramento

Major Cities: San Francisco, Los Angeles, San Diego, San Jose, Oakland, Stockton, Fresno, Bakersfield, Long Beach

Topography: Sierra Nevada Mountains (east), Central Valley (central), Coastal Range (west), Mojave Desert, Death Valley (southeast)

Waterways: Sacramento River, San Joaquin River, Colorado River, Salton Sea, Lake Tahoe, San Francisco Bay

National Parks: Channel Islands NP, Kings Canyon NP, Lassen Volcanic NP, Redwood NP, Sequoia NP, Yosemite NP

Key Products: Oranges, grapes, and wine; movies and television; computers; tourism

History

1769: Father Juñipero Serra founded first mission in San Diego.

1848: Ceded to United States after Mexican War; Gold Rush began.

1850: Admitted into Union as thirty-first state.

1906: Earthquake and subsequent fire devastated San Francisco.

Interesting Facts

England, Spain, and Russia all had claimed parts of California.

California has the largest population in the United States.

San Andreas and other faults pose a serious earthquake threat to much of California.

Death Valley contains the lowest point in North America (282 feet below sea level) and the highest temperature ever recorded in the United States (134° Fahrenheit). Fewer than 100 miles away is the highest peak in the lower forty-eight states—Mount Whitney at 14,494 feet.

Colorado

Nickname: Centennial State (because it was admitted to the United States as a state in 1876)

Capital: Denver

Major Cities: Boulder, Pueblo, Colorado Springs

Topography: Rocky Mountains (central north-south), including Sangre de Cristo Range and San Juan Mountains

Waterways: Several important rivers begin in the state, including the Colorado, North and South Platte, the Arkansas, and the Rio Grande.

National Parks: Mesa Verde NP, Rocky Mountain NP

Key Products: Skiing, livestock

History

1806: Zebulon Pike explored state for United States.

1858: Gold was discovered at Cherry Creek (Denver).

1876: Admitted into the Union as the thirty-eighth state.

Interesting Facts

Prehistoric cliff dwellings are located at Mesa Verde National Park.

The U.S. Air Force Academy is located near Colorado Springs.

The North American Air Defense Command is located inside Cheyenne Mountain.

Denver is known as the "Mile High City."

Climax is the highest settlement in the United States at 11,302 feet.

Colorado has the highest mean altitude (6,800 feet) and more mountain peaks above 14,000 feet than any other state.

Connecticut

Nicknames: Constitution State, Nutmeg State

Capital: Hartford

Major Cities: Bridgeport, New Haven, Waterbury, Stamford

Topography: The Connecticut Valley lowlands (center north-south)

Waterways: Connecticut River, Housatonic River, Thames River, Long Island Sound

National Parks: None

Key Products: Insurance, submarines

History

1614: Region around Connecticut River claimed by Dutch.

1788: Fifth state to ratify Constitution.

Interesting Facts

The U.S. Coast Guard Academy is located in New London.

Groton is famous for submarine construction, including the USS *Nautilus,* which was the first nuclear-powered submarine.

Hartford is considered the insurance capital of the United States.

Delaware

Nicknames: First State, Diamond State, Blue Hen State

Capital: Dover

Major City: Wilmington

Topography: Atlantic Coastal plain with flatlands through most of state

Waterways: Delaware River, Delaware Bay, Chesapeake and Delaware Canal (connects Chesapeake Bay and Delaware River)

National Parks: None

Key Products: Chemicals, nylon

History

1609: Henry Hudson discovered Delaware Bay.

1787: First state to ratify U.S. Constitution.

Interesting Facts

Delaware has the lowest mean elevation (60 feet) in the United States.

Wilmington is known as the "Chemical Capital of the World."

Second smallest state in area. Also has the fewest number of counties (3) in United States.

District of Columbia

Nicknames: Nation's Capital, America's First City

Waterways: Potomac River, Anacostia River, Tidal Basin

Key Product: Federal government

History

1791: Selected by George Washington as site for new capital.

1800: Government moved to D.C. from Philadelphia, Pennsylvania.

1814: British captured and burned D.C. during War of 1812.

1847: One-third of D.C. returned to Virginia.

Interesting Facts

Residents can vote in presidential elections but elect a nonvoting member of Congress.

City designed by Pierre Charles L'Enfant.

Florida

Nickname: Sunshine State

Capital: Tallahassee

Major Cities: Jacksonville, Miami, Tampa, St. Petersburg, Orlando, Fort Lauderdale, Pensacola

Topography: Mostly flat plain, the Everglades, and Big Cypress Swamp (south)

Waterways: St. Johns River, Lake Okeechobee. State is surrounded by water on three sides: Gulf of Mexico (west and south), Atlantic Ocean (east).

National Parks: Biscayne NP, Dry Tortugas NP, Everglades NP

Key Products: Citrus fruits, tourism

History

1513: Ponce de León landed in Florida searching for the "fountain of youth."

1819: Spain ceded Florida to United States.

1845: Became twenty-seventh state to join the Union.

1861: Seceded from Union.

Interesting Facts

Kennedy Space Center, where space shuttles and most manned missions have launched, is on Cape Canaveral.

Alligators inhabit areas in and around swamps.

World's busiest theme park, Walt Disney World, is near Orlando.

Founded in 1565, St. Augustine is the oldest continuously occupied European-settled city in North America.

Georgia

Nicknames: Empire State of the South, Peach State

Capital: Atlanta

Major Cities: Macon, Columbus, Savannah, Albany, Augusta, Athens

Topography: Appalachian Mountains (north), Piedmont (central), coastal plains (south), Okefenokee Swamp (southeast)

Waterways: Savannah River, Chattahoochee River

National Parks: None

Key Products: Peanuts, peaches, pecans

History

1733: James Oglethorpe established penal colony at Savannah, thus establishing Georgia as a buffer state.

1788: Fourth state to ratify Constitution.

1861: Seceded from Union.

Interesting Facts

Largest state east of the Mississippi.

Last of the thirteen colonies to be founded.

Hartsfield Atlanta International Airport is one of the two busiest airports in the world.

CNN and Coca-Cola are both headquartered in Atlanta.

Hawaii

Nickname: Aloha State

Capital: Honolulu

Major City: Hilo

Topography: Consists of 122 islands, 8 of which are considered main islands. Each island formed by volcanic activity due to a "hot spot" under the Pacific Plate.

Waterways: Pearl Harbor (Oahu), Pacific Ocean

National Parks: Haleakala NP, Hawaii Volcanoes NP

Key Products: Sugar, pineapples, tourism

History

1778: English Captain James Cook visited Hawaii and named the islands the Sandwich Islands.

1790s: King Kamehameha I united most islands.

1893–1894: Queen Liliuokalani overthrown and republic of Hawaii formed.

1898: Annexed by United States.

1941: Japanese attacked Pearl Harbor.

1959: Admitted to the Union as the fiftieth state.

Interesting Facts

Does not observe daylight saving time.

Mauna Loa, on the island of Hawaii, is the world's most active volcano and the world's largest mountain by cubic content (19,193 cubic miles).

Mount Waialeale is the wettest place on Earth.

Only state that is not part of the North American continent.

Mauna Kea, on the island of Hawaii, is the world's tallest mountain, beginning on the sea floor and rising 33,380 feet (only 13,796 of which are above sea level).

The island of Hawaii is the largest island in the United States.

Hawaii contains nearly 2,500 species of plants, some of the most exotic in the world.

Idaho

Nickname: Gem State

Capital: Boise

Major Cities: Pocatello, Idaho Falls, Coeur d'Alene

Topography: Rocky Mountains make up most of the state; Salmon River Mountains (central), Bitterroot Range (northeast)

Waterways: Snake River, Salmon River, Pend Oreille Lake

National Park: Yellowstone NP (but it's mostly in Wyoming)

Key Product: Potatoes

History

1805: Meriwether Lewis and William Clark explored area.

1860: Mormons established first European settlement at Franklin.

1890: Admitted to Union as forty-third state.

Interesting Facts

The Continental Divide lies along a portion of the Idaho and Montana border.

Hells Canyon is the deepest canyon in North America.

Illinois

Nickname: Prairie State

Capital: Springfield

Major Cities: Chicago, Peoria, Moline

Topography: Plains throughout most of state, Shawnee Hills (southern corner)

Waterways: Lake Michigan, Mississippi River, Wabash River, Ohio River

National Parks: None

Key Products: Corn, manufacturing

History

1673: Louis Jolliet and Father Jacques Marquette explored area.

1818: Twenty-first state admitted to Union.

1871: Great Chicago fire destroyed much of city.

1974: Sears Tower opened in Chicago as the tallest building in the world, though today it is just the tallest building in the United States.

Interesting Facts

Chicago O'Hare International Airport is one of the two busiest airports in the world.

President Abraham Lincoln is buried in Springfield.

Indiana

Nickname: Hoosier State

Capital: Indianapolis

Major Cities: Gary, Fort Wayne, South Bend, Evansville

Topography: Flat plains in the north and center, rough hills and valleys in the south

Waterways: Wabash River, Ohio River, White River, Lake Michigan

National Parks: None

Key Products: Corn, steel

History

1816: Indiana became nineteenth state.

1911: Indianapolis 500 car race first run.

Interesting Facts

Indiana's Lost River travels underground for 22 miles.

Parts of Indiana do not observe daylight saving time.

Iowa

Nickname: Hawkeye State

Capital: Des Moines

Major Cities: Cedar Rapids, Davenport, Sioux City, Waterloo

Topography: Most of state is flat plains.

Waterways: Mississippi River, Missouri River, Big Sioux River, Des Moines River

National Parks: None

Key Products: Corn, hogs

History

1803: Became U.S. territory with Louisiana Purchase.

1833: First permanent settlement founded at Dubuque.

1846: Admitted to the Union as twenty-ninth state.

Kansas

Nickname: Sunflower State

Capital: Topeka

Major Cities: Wichita, Kansas City

Topography: Great Plains that gradually rise from east to west as they approach the foothills of the Rocky Mountains

Waterways: Missouri River, Kansas River, Arkansas River

National Parks: None

Key Products: Cattle, wheat

History

1803: Part of Louisiana Purchase.

1861: Admitted to Union as thirty-fourth state.

Interesting Facts

In the 1930s, Kansas was the center of the Dust Bowl, which was caused by a severe drought.

The geographic center of the 48 states is near Lebanon, in Smith County.

Kentucky

Nickname: Bluegrass State

Capital: Frankfort

Major Cities: Louisville, Lexington, Bowling Green, Owensboro

Topography: Appalachian Mountains (east), Bluegrass region (north-central)

Waterways: Mississippi River, Ohio River, Kentucky River, Cumberland River, Tennessee River

National Park: Mammoth Cave NP

Key Products: Tobacco, bourbon whiskey

History

1792: Became fifteenth state in the Union.

1875: First Kentucky Derby was held in Louisville.

Interesting Fact: The U.S. Gold Bullion Depository is at Fort Knox.

Louisiana

Nickname: Pelican State

Capital: Baton Rouge

Major Cities: New Orleans, Shreveport, Lafayette

Topography: Flat Gulf Coastal terrain covers the entire state. Part of New Orleans is below sea level and susceptible to catastrophic flooding in a major hurricane.

Waterways: Mississippi River, Red River, Sabine River, Atchafalaya River, Lake Pontchartrain, Gulf of Mexico

National Parks: None

Key Products: Cotton, sugarcane, petroleum products

History

1803: Became part of United States with Louisiana Purchase.

1812: Admitted as eighteenth state.

1815: War of 1812's final battle at New Orleans, after the end of the war.

1861: Seceded from Union.

Interesting Facts

The world's longest bridge (24 miles long) crosses Lake Pontchartrain.

The bayous are home to alligators and pelicans.

New Orleans is famous for its annual Mardi Gras celebration and jazz music.

Louisiana is the only state with parishes instead of counties.

Maine

Nickname: Pine Tree State

Capital: Augusta

Major Cities: Portland, Lewiston, Bangor

Topography: Coastal lowlands (southeast), White Mountains, Appalachian Mountains, and fjords in the south

Waterways: Penobscot River, Kennebec River, St. John River, St. Croix River, Moosehead Lake, Atlantic Ocean

National Park: Acadia NP

Key Products: Potatoes, lobster, blueberries

History

1820: Became twenty-third state.

Interesting Facts

Maine was part of Massachusetts before becoming a state.

Eastport is the easternmost city in the United States.

Maryland

Nicknames: Old Line State, Free State

Capital: Annapolis

Major City: Baltimore

Topography: Coastal plain, Blue Ridge Mountains, Appalachian Mountains, Delmarva Peninsula (named for Delaware, Maryland, and Virginia)

Waterways: Potomac River, Patuxent River, Chesapeake Bay, Atlantic Ocean

National Parks: None

Key Products: Chickens, dairy products, crabs

History

1634: Lord Baltimore established settlement at St. Mary's.

1788: Seventh state to be admitted to Union.

Interesting Facts

Maryland ceded land to create the District of Columbia.

Maryland was the only Catholic colony and the first to pass a religious toleration act.

Although Maryland was a slave state, it remained in the Union.

Antietam battleground was the site of the bloodiest single day during the Civil War (26,000 casualties).

Fort McHenry is located near Baltimore. The British bombardment of it during the War of 1812 was the inspiration for the "Star Spangled Banner."

Near Hancock, the state is only 1 mile wide, the narrowest point of any state.

The U.S. Naval Academy is located in Annapolis.

Massachusetts

Nicknames: Bay State, Old Colony

Capital: Boston

Major Cities: Worcester, Springfield, Lowell

Topography: Cape Cod and coastal plain, Berkshire Hills

Waterways: Connecticut River, Merrimack River, Charles River, Massachusetts Bay

National Parks: None

Key Products: Cranberries, clams, oysters, lobsters

History

1620: Pilgrims established colony at Plymouth.

1636: Harvard College established—the oldest in the United States.

1775: Revolutionary War began at Lexington, following the Boston Tea Party and Boston Massacre.

1788: Sixth state to ratify Constitution.

Interesting Facts

Salem is infamous for the witch trials.

The Boston Common is the oldest public park (1634) in the United States.

Michigan

Nicknames: Great Lakes State, Wolverine State

Capital: Lansing

Major Cities: Detroit, Grand Rapids, Flint, Ann Arbor

Topography: Two peninsulas, the Upper Peninsula and the Lower Peninsula. Most of the state is plains.

Waterways: Grand River, Lake Superior, Lake Michigan, Lake Huron, Lake Erie, Green Bay, Saginaw Bay

National Park: Isle Royale NP

Key Products: Motor vehicles, dairy products, cereal

History

1783: At end of Revolutionary War, the British refused to give up control of Michigan until 1796.

1837: Became twenty-sixth state in the Union.

Interesting Facts

Henry Ford established his auto company in Detroit, making the state the country's leading auto producer.

Kellogg's cereal company was founded in Battle Creek.

Minnesota

Nicknames: North Star State, Gopher State

Capital: St. Paul

Major Cities: Minneapolis, Duluth

Topography: Plains, with the Mesabi and Vermillion ranges in the northeast

Waterways: Source of the Mississippi River, St. Croix River, and Red River; Minnesota River; Lake Superior; thousands of lakes, including Red Lake and Lake of the Woods

National Park: Voyageurs NP

Key Products: Oats, corn, soybeans

History

1783: United States took control of Minnesota east of the Mississippi.

1803: United States took control of rest of Minnesota with Louisiana Purchase.

1858: Became thirty-second state.

Interesting Fact: Angle Inlet, on Lake of the Woods, is the northernmost point of the conterminous forty-eight states.

Mississippi

Nickname: Magnolia State

Capital: Jackson

Major Cities: Biloxi, Hattiesburg, Vicksburg

Topography: Mostly plains with low hilly terrain in the east

Waterways: Mississippi River, Pearl River, Yazoo River, many oxbow lakes along the Mississippi River, Gulf of Mexico

National Parks: None

Key Product: Cotton

History

1817: Became twentieth state.

1861: Second state to secede from the Union.

Missouri

Nickname: Show Me State

Capital: Jefferson City

Major Cities: St. Louis, Kansas City, Springfield, Independence, Branson

Topography: Mostly plains with rolling hills and low mountains in the south (Ozark Plateau)

Waterways: Mississippi River, Missouri River, Lake of the Ozarks

National Parks: None

Key Products: Soybeans, corn, lead

History

1803: United States took control after Louisiana Purchase.

1821: Admitted to Union as twenty-fourth state.

Interesting Facts

The Pony Express began at St. Joseph in 1863.

Both the Santa Fe and Oregon Trails began in Independence; thus the state was known as the "Gateway to the West."

The Gateway Arch, the nation's tallest monument, is located in St. Louis.

Branson is a popular resort for country music fans.

Montana

Nickname: Treasure State

Capital: Helena

Major Cities: Billings, Great Falls, Missoula, Butte, Bozeman

Topography: Great Plains (east), Rocky Mountains (west)

Waterways: Missouri River, Yellowstone River

National Parks: Glacier NP, Yellowstone NP (but it's mostly in Wyoming)

Key Products: Wheat, barley

History

1803: United States acquired Montana as part of Louisiana Purchase.

1846: United States took control of northwestern Montana from Britain through the Oregon Treaty.

1889: Admitted into Union as forty-first state.

Interesting Facts

Little Bighorn, site of Custer's Last Stand, is in the southeastern part of state.

Yellowstone National Park is the largest and oldest in United States.

The headwaters of the Missouri River are in the state.

Nebraska

Nickname: Cornhusker State

Capital: Lincoln

Major Cities: Omaha, Grand Island

Topography: Great Plains, Sand Hills (north)

Waterways: Platte River, Mississippi River, Missouri River

National Parks: None

Key Products: Cattle, corn, wheat, meatpacking, alfalfa

History

1803: United States took control after Louisiana Purchase.

1865: Union Pacific Railroad began building transcontinental railroad west from Omaha.

1867: Admitted into Union as thirty-seventh state.

Interesting Fact: Nebraska has a unicameral legislature, which means that at the state government level, there is only one house of representatives. In other states, there are two.

Nevada

Nicknames: Silver State, Sagebrush State, Battle Born State

Capital: Carson City

Major Cities: Reno, Las Vegas, Winnemucca, Elko

Topography: Basin and Range province, the Sierra Nevada Mountains (west), along border with California

Waterways: Colorado River, Humboldt River, Pyramid Lake, Lake Tahoe, Lake Mead

National Park: Great Basin NP

Key Products: Gambling, tourism, mining

History

1848: United States took control per Treaty of Guadalupe Hidalgo at end of Mexican War.

1859: Gold and silver discovered in the Comstock Lode.

1864: Admitted to Union as thirty-sixth state.

Interesting Facts

Gambling is the state's leading industry.

Hoover Dam forms Lake Mead.

Nevada has the highest marriage rate in the United States, due to the many couples who marry in Las Vegas.

New Hampshire

Nickname: Granite State

Capital: Concord

Major Cities: Manchester, Nashua

Topography: White Mountains, Merrimack and Connecticut River Valleys, rolling hills and mountains throughout state

Waterways: Connecticut River, Merrimack River, Lake Winnipesaukee, Atlantic Ocean

National Parks: None

Key Products: Dairy products, apples, maple syrup

History

1623: First settlements near Portsmouth and Dover.

1788: Ninth state to ratify Constitution.

Interesting Facts

New Hampshire holds the first primary during presidential elections and is thus in the national limelight every four years.

Mount Washington holds the record for the highest recorded winds on Earth.

New Jersey

Nickname: Garden State

Capital: Trenton

Major Cities: Newark, Jersey City, Atlantic City, Paterson, Camden

Topography: Coastal Plain (east), Pine Barrens (southwest), Piedmont (central), Kittatinny Mountains (northwest)

Waterways: Delaware River, Hudson River, Delaware Bay, Atlantic Ocean

National Parks: None

Key Products: Chemicals, pharmaceuticals, nursery plants, tomatoes

History

1618: Dutch settlement established.

1664: English took control of colony.

1787: Third state to ratify Constitution.

Interesting Fact: George Washington crossed the Delaware River and attacked the British at Trenton on Christmas Day, 1776.

New Mexico

Nickname: Land of Enchantment

Capital: Santa Fe

Major Cities: Albuquerque, Las Cruces, Los Alamos, Roswell

Topography: Great Plains, Rocky Mountains, San Juan Mountains, Sangre de Cristo Mountains

Waterways: Rio Grande River, Pecos River

National Park: Carlsbad Caverns NP

Key Products: Cattle, mining

History

1845: Eastern part of state annexed to the United States.

1848: Western New Mexico granted to United States by treaty of Guadalupe Hidalgo.

1853: Gadsden Purchase increased size of state.

1912: Admitted into Union as forty-seventh state.

1945: The first atomic bomb was at White Sands, near Alamogordo.

Interesting Fact: Santa Fe is the oldest capital city in the United States.

New York

Nickname: Empire State

Capital: Albany

Major Cities: New York City, Buffalo, Rochester, Syracuse

Topography: Adirondack Mountains, Catskill Mountains, Long Island

Waterways: St. Lawrence River, Hudson River, Mohawk River, Delaware River, Lake Erie, Lake Ontario, Long Island Sound, Atlantic Ocean

National Parks: None

Key Products: Publishing, finance, machinery

History

1664: British seized New York from Dutch.

1788: Eleventh state to ratify Constitution.

1825: Erie Canal completed, turning New York City into a major port.

2001: World Trade Center towers destroyed in terrorist attack.

Interesting Facts

New York City was nation's capital from 1785 to 1790.

The U.S. Military Academy is located at West Point.

The headquarters of the United Nations is in New York City.

The Statue of Liberty is on Liberty Island in New York Harbor.

North Carolina

Nicknames: Tar Heel State, Old North State

Capital: Raleigh

Major Cities: Charlotte, Greensboro, Winston-Salem

Topography: Outer Banks along coast, Appalachian Mountains, Blue Ridge Mountains, Great Smokey Mountains

Waterways: Roanoke River, Atlantic Ocean

National Park: Great Smoky Mountains NP (shared with Tennessee)

Key Product: Tobacco

History

1585: First English colony established at Roanoke, though it did not last long.

1789: Twelfth state to ratify Constitution.

1861: Seceded from Union.

Interesting Facts

North Carolina leads the country in the production of cigarettes.

The Wright Brothers made the first powered flight at Kitty Hawk.

Raleigh, Durham, and Chapel Hill form the "Research Triangle," consisting of several universities and many research organizations.

North Dakota

Nicknames: Peace Garden State, Flickertail State

Capital: Bismarck

Major Cities: Fargo, Grand Forks

Topography: Great Plains

Waterways: Red River, Missouri River

National Park: Theodore Roosevelt NP

Key Products: Wheat, rye, barley

History:

1889: Admitted to Union as thirty-ninth state.

Interesting Fact: The town of Rugby is the geographic center of North America.

Ohio

Nickname: Buckeye State

Capital: Columbus

Major Cities: Cleveland, Cincinnati, Toledo, Akron, Dayton

Topography: Allegheny Plateau (east), Great Lakes Plains (north)

Waterways: Ohio River, Lake Erie

National Parks: None

Key Products: Soybeans, corn, rubber products

History

1787: Ohio made part of Northwest Territory.

1803: Admitted to Union as seventeenth state; the first state west of the Alleghenies.

Interesting Facts

Cleveland is home to the Rock & Roll Hall of Fame.

Water is one of state's most prevalent natural resources.

Oklahoma

Nickname: Sooner State

Capital: Oklahoma City

Major City: Tulsa

Topography: Ouachita Mountains, Wichita Mountains

Waterways: Red River, Arkansas River, Canadian River

National Parks: None

Key Products: Petroleum, wheat

History

1803: Acquired as part of Louisiana Purchase.

1834: Established as Indian Territory for resettlement.

1889: Opened to nonindigenous settlers.

1907: Admitted to Union as forty-sixth state.

1930s: Dust Bowl caused by drought; most "Okies" fled west.

1995: Federal building in Oklahoma City bombed in country's worst terrorist attack until 2001.

Interesting Facts

Oklahoma is known for its panhandle.

Westernmost Cimarron County touches four states in addition to Oklahoma.

Oregon

Nickname: Beaver State

Capital: Salem

Major Cities: Portland, Ashland, Medford, Eugene, Bend

Topography: Coast Range, Cascade Range, plateau in rest of state

Waterways: Columbia River, Snake River, Pacific Ocean, Crater Lake

National Park: Crater Lake NP

Key Products: Lumber, fishing, grass seed

History

1805: Lewis and Clark's corps built Fort Clatsop on the coast and spent the winter in Oregon.

1843: Many settlers began to arrive via the Oregon Trail.

1859: Admitted to Union as thirty-third state.

Interesting Facts

Crater Lake is the deepest in the United States.

Hells Canyon is the deepest canyon in the United States (extends into Idaho).

The D River is the shortest in the world at 120 feet long.

Pennsylvania

Nickname: Keystone State

Capital: Harrisburg

Major Cities: Philadelphia, Pittsburgh, Erie, Lancaster, Allentown

Topography: Appalachian Mountains, Piedmont, Allegheny Mountains, Allegheny Plateau, coastal plain

Waterways: Delaware River, Susquehanna River, Lake Erie, Allegheny River, Ohio River

National Parks: None

Key Products: Iron and steel, manufacturing

History

1681: Land granted to William Penn.

1774: Continental Congress met in Philadelphia.

1776: Declaration of Independence signed in Philadelphia.

1787: Second state in the Union.

1863: Battle of Gettysburg.

Interesting Facts

Hershey has the largest chocolate and cocoa processing plant in the world.

Philadelphia was the nation's capital from 1790 to 1800.

The first oil well in the world was drilled near Titusville in 1859.

Rhode Island

Nicknames: Little Rhody, Ocean State

Capital: Providence

Major City: Newport

Topography: Dozens of islands, including Aquidneck Island (also known as Rhode Island). Mostly coastal lowlands and gentle rolling hills.

Waterways: Narragansett Bay, Rhode Island Sound, Atlantic Ocean, Sakonnet River

National Parks: None

Key Products: Textiles, jewelry

History

1636: Roger Williams settled Providence.

1790: Thirteenth state to ratify Constitution, the last of the colonies.

Interesting Facts

The official name of state is "State of Rhode Island and Providence Plantations."

Rhode Island is the smallest state in area.

Touro Synagogue, in Newport, is the oldest in the nation.

South Carolina

Nickname: Palmetto State

Capital: Columbia

Major City: Charleston

Topography: Blue Ridge Mountains (northwest), Piedmont

Waterways: Broad River, Pee Dee River, Savannah River, Atlantic Ocean

National Parks: None

Key Products: Tobacco, cotton

History

1670: Settlement at Charles Towne, later moved and renamed Charleston.

1788: Eighth state to join Union.

1860: First state to secede from Union.

Interesting Facts

The Civil War began with the attack on Fort Sumter in Charleston Harbor.

Hilton Head and Myrtle Beach are popular golf resorts.

South Dakota

Nicknames: Mount Rushmore State, Coyote State

Capital: Pierre

Major Cities: Sioux Falls, Rapid City

Topography: Black Hills (west), Great Plains (east)

Waterways: Missouri River, Cheyenne River, White River

National Parks: Badlands NP, Wind Cave NP

Key Products: Corn, wheat, oats

History

1803: United States took control after Louisiana Purchase.

1889: Admitted to Union as fortieth state.

1890: Slaughter of two hundred Sioux at Wounded Knee.

Interesting Fact: Mount Rushmore contains the faces of four presidents (Washington, Jefferson, Theodore Roosevelt, Lincoln) sculpted into the side of the mountain.

Tennessee

Nickname: Volunteer State

Capital: Nashville

Major Cities: Memphis, Knoxville, Chattanooga

Topography: Appalachian Mountains (east), Great Smokey Mountains

Waterways: Mississippi River, Tennessee River, Cumberland River

National Parks: Great Smokey Mountains (shared with North Carolina)

Key Products: Tobacco, aluminum

History

1796: Admitted to Union as sixteenth state.

1861: Seceded from Union.

Interesting Facts

The Tennessee Valley Authority (TVA) built a number of dams and reservoirs to provide hydroelectric power to the state.

Nashville is the country music capital.

Graceland, in Memphis, was the home of Elvis Presley.

Texas

Nickname: Lone Star State

Capital: Austin

Major Cities: Houston, Dallas, San Antonio, El Paso, Fort Worth, Arlington, Corpus Christi, Galveston, Lubbock, Waco

Topography: Santiago Mountains, Davis Mountains, Guadalupe Mountains, Great Plains, Rolling Plains, Galveston Island, Edwards Plateau, Llano Estacado

Waterways: Rio Grande River, Red River, Colorado River, Brazos River, Pecos River, Gulf of Mexico

National Parks: Big Bend NP, Guadalupe Mountains NP

Key Products: Petroleum, cotton, chemicals

History

1821: Became a part of Mexico.

1836: Declared independence from Mexico, becoming the independent Republic of Texas.

1845: Admitted to Union as twenty-eighth state.

1861: Seceded from Union.

Interesting Facts

Number one producer of cotton in the nation.

The Alamo is in San Antonio.

Largest state in area in the forty-eight conterminous states.

Texas has 254 counties, more than any other state.

President George W. Bush hails from Texas.

Utah

Nickname: Beehive State

Capital: Salt Lake City

Major Cities: Provo, Ogden, Horem

Topography: Rocky Mountains, Wasatch Range, Great Salt Lake Desert, Bonneville Salt Flats

Waterways: Colorado River, Green River, Great Salt Lake

National Parks: Arches NP, Bryce Canyon NP, Canyonlands NP, Capitol Reef NP, Zion NP

Key Products: Mining, tourism

History

1847: Brigham Young and Mormon pioneers settled in the valley of the Great Salt Lake.

1869: Transcontinental railroad completed at Promontory Point.

1896: Admitted to Union as forty-fifth state.

Interesting Fact: The Great Salt Lake is the largest salt lake in North America.

Vermont

Nickname: Green Mountain State

Capital: Montpelier

Major City: Burlington

Topography: Green Mountains

Waterways: Connecticut River, Lake Champlain

National Parks: None

Key Products: Granite, maple syrup

History

1791: Admitted to Union as fourteenth state.

Interesting Fact: Montpelier is the smallest state capital (measured by population).

Virginia

Nickname: Old Dominion

Capital: Richmond

Major Cities: Virginia Beach, Norfolk, Arlington, Alexandria, Charlottesville

Topography: Tidewater, Piedmont, Blue Ridge Mountains, Appalachian Mountains

Waterways: Potomac River, James River, Shenandoah River, Chesapeake Bay, Atlantic Ocean

National Park: Shenandoah NP

Key Products: Dairy, tobacco, government

History

1607: Jamestown was first permanent British settlement in the Americas.

1788: Tenth state to ratify Constitution.

1861: Seceded from Union.

Interesting Facts

Richmond was the capital of the Confederacy.

Robert E. Lee surrendered to Ulysses S. Grant at Appomattox Courthouse, formally ending the Civil War.

Arlington National Cemetery is located in the state.

Washington

Nickname: Evergreen State

Capital: Olympia

Major Cities: Seattle, Spokane, Tacoma, Yakima

Topography: Coast Range, Olympic Mountains, Cascade Range, Mount St. Helens, Mount Rainier

Waterways: Puget Sound, Columbia River, Snake River, Pacific Ocean, Strait of Juan de Fuca

National Parks: Mount Rainier NP, North Cascades NP, Olympic NP

Key Products: Apples, cherries, peas, lumber, aircraft

History

1846: Treaty with Britain gave United States control over Washington.

1889: Admitted to Union as forty-second state.

1980: Mount St. Helens erupted.

Interesting Facts

National leader in both apples and hops (for brewing).

The Olympic Peninsula contains a rain forest.

West Virginia

Nickname: Mountain State

Capital: Charleston

Major City: Huntington

Topography: Blue Ridge Mountains, Allegheny Mountains

Waterways: Ohio River, Kanawha River, Potomac River

National Parks: None

Key Products: Natural gas, coal

History

1788: Part of the state of Virginia.

1861: West Virginia seceded from Virginia because Virginia seceded from Union.

1863: Admitted to Union as thirty-fifth state.

Wisconsin

Nickname: Badger State

Capital: Madison

Major Cities: Milwaukee, Green Bay

Topography: Lake Superior Lowlands, Northern Highlands, Great Plains

Waterways: Mississippi River, St. Croix River, Wisconsin River, Lake Winnebago, Lake Superior, Lake Michigan, Green Bay

National Parks: None

Key Products: Paper products

History

1783: Became part of United States.

1848: Admitted to Union as thirtieth state.

Interesting Fact: Green Bay is the smallest city with a professional football team.

Wyoming

Nicknames: Equality State, Cowboy State

Capital: Cheyenne

Major Cities: Casper, Laramie

Topography: Rocky Mountains, Great Plains, Continental Divide

Waterways: North Platte River, Bighorn River, Green River, Yellowstone River, Snake River, Yellowstone Lake

National Parks: Grand Teton NP, Yellowstone NP (also partly in Idaho and Montana)

Key Products: Coal, cattle, uranium

History

1869: Allowed women the right to vote (first state to do so).

1872: Yellowstone became first national park in the United States.

1890: Admitted to Union as forty-fourth state.

6

Level 3: We Are the World

A Guide to Studying the Countries of the World

If you study the world for a few weeks, several months, many years, or even your entire lifetime, you would not be able to unravel or understand everything there is to know about it. There are nearly two hundred countries, each made up of boundaries, places, people, and history. Think how complicated learning about U.S. history can be, and then think about all the other countries that often have longer and more complicated histories. How can we fit all of this knowledge into one chapter? We can't. We can only give you the very basics of each country, chosen because of the likelihood that this information will appear in the Geography Bee.

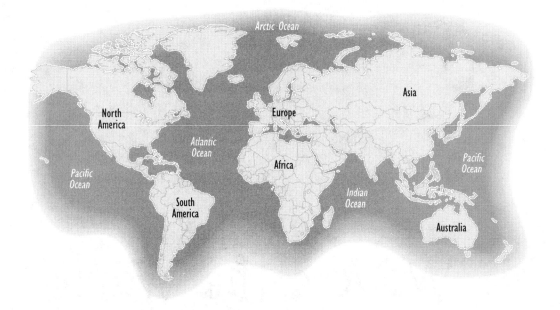

How to Study the Countries

To learn all of the information needed in a short period of time, you have to concentrate on the most important aspects of each country. Unfortunately, the important aspects of each country can change from one country to the next. For instance, for Bolivia, it is important to know that it has two capitals and that Bolivians speak Spanish. For the Vatican City, on the other hand, the most important aspects are that it is an autonomous country enclosed within the city of Rome and that its religion is Roman Catholic. The challenge is to know what makes a country different or unique from all the others.

There is no one right way to study the countries of the world. We recommend that you use the information in this chapter to make study cards.

If you have time, it would also be very helpful if you used blank maps (see chapter 4) and labeled each country's capital, major cities, and geographical features. If you don't have time for the blank maps, sneak a peak in your atlas and locate all of these places. For instance, knowing which countries share Mount Everest might be good to know for the Bee. You can use the appendix or an atlas to help you locate the places on your blank maps.

The Quick Guides

The information in this chapter should help you in Geography Bee rounds about cultural geography, economic geography, and political geography. However, these country quick guides only contain the very basics, so to do really well in these rounds, you will need to know more than is contained in these quick guides. Much of this information, especially the "Geographical Facts" and "History," comes directly from the *2001 CIA World Factbook*.

Each quick guide includes the following:

Capital: Often given as a hint in questions. Make sure you keep your eye out for the countries that have more than one capital.

Major Cities: Some questions can be answered simply by knowing in which country a city is located. Some countries, however, are so small, they have no major cities.

Religion: In the past, and sometimes in the present, countries have used religion as their identity. Knowing a country's religion could help you understand its culture, political system, wars, and history. Some nations have more than one religion.

Language: Knowing that South Africa has eleven official languages or that Greenlandic is spoken in Denmark may help you with a variety of cultural geography questions.

Geographical Facts: This section describes the important aspects of the country's geography, including its major mountain ranges, waterways, and other landforms.

History: Though major events may be asked about, this section will also give you a sense of the country—its history, problems, and people.

Afghanistan

Capital: Kabul

Major Cities: Kandahar, Herat, Mazar-i-Sharif

Religion: Sunni Muslim

Languages: Afghan Persian (Dari), Pashto

Geographical Facts: Landlocked; the Hindu Kush mountains that run northeast to southwest divide the northern provinces from the rest of the country; the highest peaks are in the northern Vakhan (Wakhan Corridor).

History: In 1979, the Soviet Union invaded and occupied Afghanistan. After ten years of occupying the land, the USSR was forced to withdraw by anti-communist mujahideen forces supplied and trained by the United States, Saudi Arabia, Pakistan, and others. Fighting continued among the various mujahideen factions, but the fundamentalist Islamic Taliban movement seized most of the country. In addition to the continuing civil strife, the country suffers from enormous poverty, a crumbling infrastructure, and widespread land mines. A U.S.-led coalition attacked Afghanistan following the 2001 terrorist attack on the United States. The coalition forces ended fundamental Islamic Taliban rule.

Albania

Capital: Tiranë

Religions: Muslim, Albanian Orthodox

Languages: Albanian (Tosk is the official dialect), Greek

Geographical Facts: Strategic location along Strait of Otranto (links Adriatic Sea to Ionian Sea and Mediterranean Sea).

History: In 1990, Albania ended forty-four years of xenophobic communist rule and established a multiparty democracy. The transition has proven difficult, as corrupt governments have tried to deal with high unemployment, a dilapidated infrastructure, widespread gangsterism, and disruptive political opponents.

Algeria

Capital: Algiers

Major Cities: Oran, Annaba, Constantine

Religion: Sunni Muslim

Languages: Arabic (official), French, Berber dialects

Geographical Fact: Second-largest country in Africa (after Sudan).

History: After a century of rule by France, Algeria became independent in 1962. The surprising first-round success of the fundamentalist FIS (Islamic Salvation Front) party in December 1991 balloting caused the army to intervene, crack down on the FIS, and postpone the subsequent elections. The FIS response has resulted in a continuous low-grade civil conflict with the secular state apparatus, which nonetheless has allowed elections featuring progovernment and moderate religious-based parties. FIS's armed wing, the Islamic Salvation Army, disbanded itself in January 2000, and many armed militants surrendered under an amnesty program designed to promote national reconciliation. Nevertheless, residual fighting continues. Other concerns include large-scale unemployment and the need to diversify the petroleum-based economy.

Andorra

Capital: Andorra la Vella

Religion: Roman Catholic

Languages: Catalan (official), French, Castilian

Geographical Facts: Landlocked; straddles a number of important crossroads in the Pyrenees.

History: Long isolated and impoverished, mountainous Andorra has achieved considerable prosperity since World War II through its tourist industry. Many immigrants (legal and illegal) are attracted to the thriving economy with its lack of income taxes.

Angola

Capital: Luanda

Major Cities: Huambo, Benguela

Religions: Indigenous beliefs, Roman Catholic

Languages: Portuguese (official), Bantu and other African languages

Geographical Fact: Cabinda is separated from rest of country by the Democratic Republic of the Congo.

History: Civil war has been the norm in Angola since independence from Portugal in 1975. A 1994 peace accord between the government and the National Union for the Total Independence of Angola (UNITA) provided for the integration of former UNITA insurgents into the government and armed forces. A national unity government was installed in April 1997, but serious fighting resumed in late 1998, rendering hundreds of thousands of people homeless. Up to 1.5 million lives may have been lost in fighting over the past quarter century.

Antigua and Barbuda

Capital: St. John's

Religion: Anglican

Languages: English (official), local dialects

Geographical Facts: Antigua has a deeply indented shoreline with many natural harbors and beaches; Barbuda has a very large western harbor.

History: The islands of Antigua and Barbuda became an independent state within the British Commonwealth of Nations in 1981. Since 1995, some 3,000 refugees fleeing a volcanic eruption on nearby Montserrat have settled in Antigua and Barbuda.

Argentina

Capital: Buenos Aires

Major Cities: Córdoba, Rosario, La Plata, Mar del Plata

Religion: Roman Catholic

Languages: Spanish (official), English, Italian, German, French

Geographical Facts: Second-largest country in South America (after Brazil); strategic location relative to sealanes between the South Atlantic and the South Pacific Oceans (Strait of Magellan, Beagle Channel, Drake Passage); Aconcagua is South America's tallest mountain, while the Valdes Peninsula is the lowest point on the continent; Ushuaia is the southernmost city in the world.

History: Following independence from Spain in 1816, Argentina experienced periods of internal political conflict between conservatives and liberals and between civilian and military factions. After World War II, a long period of Perónist dictatorship was followed by a military junta that took power in 1976. Democracy returned in 1983, and numerous elections since then have underscored Argentina's progress in democratic consolidation.

Armenia

Capital: Yerevan

Religion: Armenian Orthodox

Language: Armenian

Geographical Facts: Landlocked in the Lesser Caucasus Mountains; Lake Sevan is the largest lake in this mountain range.

History: An Orthodox Christian country, Armenia was incorporated into Russia in 1828 and the USSR in 1920. Since that time, Armenian leaders have been preoccupied by the long conflict with Azerbaijan over Nagorno-Karabakh, a primarily Armenian-populated exclave assigned to Soviet Azerbaijan in the 1920s by Moscow. Armenia and Azerbaijan began fighting over the exclave in 1988; the struggle escalated after both countries attained independence from the Soviet Union in 1991. By May 1994, when a cease-fire took hold, Armenian forces held not only Nagorno-Karabakh but also a significant portion of Azerbaijan proper. The economies of both sides have been hurt by their inability to make substantial progress toward a peaceful resolution.

Australia

Capital: Canberra

Major Cities: Sydney, Melbourne, Adelaide, Perth, Brisbane

Religions: Anglican, Roman Catholic, other Christian

Languages: English, native languages

Geographical Facts: World's smallest continent but sixth-largest country; population concentrated along the eastern and southeastern coasts; regular, tropical, invigorating, sea breeze known as "the Doctor" occurs along the west coast in the summer.

History: Australia became a commonwealth of the British Empire in 1901. It was able to take advantage of its natural resources to rapidly develop its agricultural and manufacturing industries and to make a major contribution to the British effort in World Wars I and II. Long-term concerns include pollution, particularly depletion of the ozone layer, and management and conservation of coastal areas, especially the Great Barrier Reef. A referendum to change Australia's status, from a commonwealth headed by the British monarch to an independent republic, was defeated in 1999.

Austria

Capital: Vienna

Major Cities: Salzburg, Innsbruck, Linz, Graz

Religion: Roman Catholic

Language: German

Geographical Facts: Landlocked; strategic location at the crossroads of central Europe with many easily traversable Alpine passes and valleys; major river is the Danube; population is concentrated on eastern lowlands because of steep slopes, poor soils, and low temperatures elsewhere.

History: Once the center of power for the large Austro-Hungarian Empire, Austria was reduced to a small republic after its defeat in World War I. Following annexation by Nazi Germany in 1938 and subsequent occupation by the victorious Allies, Austria's 1955 State Treaty declared the country "permanently neutral" as a condition of Soviet military withdrawal. Neutrality, once ingrained as part of the Austrian cultural identity, has been called into question since the Soviet collapse of 1991 and Austria's increasingly prominent role in European affairs. A prosperous country, Austria joined the European Union in 1995 and the euro monetary system in 1999.

Azerbaijan

Capital: Baku

Religion: Muslim

Language: Azerbaijani (Azeri)

Geographical Facts: Both the main area of the country and the Naxcivan exclave are landlocked.

History: Azerbaijan, a nation of Turkic Muslims, has been an independent republic since the collapse of the Soviet Union in 1991. Despite a cease-fire with Armenia, in place since 1994, Azerbaijan has yet to resolve its conflict with that country over the Azerbaijani Nagorno-Karabakh enclave (largely Armenian populated). Azerbaijan has lost almost 20 percent of its territory and must support some 750,000 refugees and internally displaced persons as a result of the conflict. Corruption is everywhere, and the promise of widespread wealth from Azerbaijan's undeveloped petroleum resources remains largely unfulfilled.

Bahamas

Capital: Nassau

Major City: Freeport

Religions: Baptist, Anglican, Roman Catholic

Languages: English, Creole

Geographical Facts: Strategic location adjacent to the United States and Cuba; extensive island chain.

History: Since attaining independence from the United Kingdom in 1973, the Bahamas have prospered through tourism, international banking, and investment management. Because of its geography, the country is a major transshipment point for illegal drugs, particularly shipments to the United States. Its territory is also used for smuggling illegal migrants into the United States.

Bahrain

Capital: Manama

Religions: Shiite Muslim, Sunni Muslim

Languages: Arabic, English, Farsi, Urdu

Geographical Facts: Close to primary Middle Eastern petroleum sources; strategic location in Persian Gulf, which much of Western world's petroleum must transit to reach open ocean.

History: Bahrain's small size and central location among Persian Gulf countries require it to play a delicate balancing act in foreign affairs among its larger neighbors. Possessing minimal oil reserves, Bahrain has turned to petroleum processing and refining and has transformed itself into an international banking center. The new emir is pushing economic and political reforms and has worked to improve relations with the Shiite community. In 2001, the International Court of Justice awarded the Hawar Islands, long disputed with Qatar, to Bahrain.

Bangladesh

Capital: Dhaka

Major Cities: Khulna, Chittagong

Religion: Muslim

Languages: Bangla (official, also known as Bengali), English

Geographical Facts: Most of the country is situated on deltas of large rivers flowing from the Himalayas; the Jamuna unites with part of the Ganges to form the Padma, which, after joining with a third large river, the Meghna, continues to the Bay of Bengal.

History: Bangladesh came into existence in 1971, when Bengali East Pakistan seceded from its union with West Pakistan. About a third of this extremely poor country floods annually during the monsoon rainy season, hampering economic development.

Barbados

Capital: Bridgetown

Religion: Protestant

Language: English

Geographical Fact: Easternmost Caribbean island.

History: The island of Barbados was uninhabited when first settled by the British in 1627. Its economy remained heavily dependent on sugar, rum, and molasses production through most of the twentieth century. In the 1990s, tourism and manufacturing surpassed the sugar industry in economic importance.

Belarus

Capital: Minsk

Major City: Homyel

Religion: Eastern Orthodox

Languages: Byelorussian, Russian

Geographical Facts: Landlocked; glacial scouring accounts for the flatness of Belarusian terrain and for its 11,000 lakes; the country is geologically well endowed with extensive deposits of granite, dolomitic limestone, marl, chalk, sand, gravel, and clay.

History: After seven decades as a constituent republic of the USSR, Belarus attained its independence in 1991. It has retained closer political and economic ties to Russia than any of the other former Soviet republics. Belarus and Russia signed a treaty on a two-state union on December 8, 1999, envisioning greater political and economic integration, but to date, neither side has actively sought to implement the accord.

Belgium

Capital: Brussels

Major Cities: Antwerp, Ghent

Religion: Roman Catholic

Languages: Dutch, French

Geographical Facts: Crossroads of western Europe; majority of western European capitals are within 600 miles of Brussels, which is the seat of both the European Union and NATO.

History: Belgium became independent from the Netherlands in 1830 and was occupied by Germany during World Wars I and II. It has prospered in the past half century as a modern, technologically advanced European state and member of NATO and the EU. Tensions between the Dutch-speaking Flemings of the north and the French-speaking Walloons of the south have led, in recent years, to constitutional amendments granting these regions formal recognition and autonomy.

Belize

Capital: Belmopan

Religions: Roman Catholic, Protestant

Languages: English (official), Spanish, Mayan, Garifuna (Carib), Creole

Geographical Fact: Only country in Central America without a coastline on the North Pacific Ocean.

History: Territorial disputes between the United Kingdom and Guatemala delayed the independence of Belize (formerly British Honduras) until 1981. Guatemala refused to recognize the new nation until 1992. Tourism has become the mainstay of the economy. The country remains plagued by high unemployment, growing involvement in the South American drug trade, and increased urban crime.

Benin

Capitals: Porto-Novo (official), Cotonou (de facto)

Religions: Indigenous beliefs, Christian, Muslim

Languages: French (official), Fon and Yoruba (tribal languages)

Geographical Fact: Sandbanks create difficult access to a coast with no natural harbors, river mouths, or islands.

History: Formerly known as Dahomey, Benin gained its independence from France in 1960. The name was changed to Benin in 1975. From 1974 to 1989, the country was a socialist state; free elections were reestablished in 1991.

Bhutan

Capital: Thimphu

Religions: Lamaistic Buddhist, Indian- and Nepalese-influenced Hindu

Languages: Dzongkha (official), Tibetan dialects

Geographical Facts: Landlocked; strategic location between China and India; controls several key Himalayan mountain passes.

History: Under British influence, a monarchy was set up in Bhutan in 1907. Three years later, a treaty was signed whereby the country became a British protectorate. Independence was attained in 1949, with India subsequently guiding foreign relations and supplying aid. A refugee issue of some 100,000 Bhutanese in Nepal remains unresolved; 90 percent of these displaced persons are housed in seven UN Office of the High Commissioner for Refugees (UNHCR) camps. Maoist Assamese separatists from India, who have established themselves in the southeast portion of Bhutan, have drawn Indian cross-border incursions.

Bolivia

Capitals: La Paz (administrative), Sucre (judicial)

Major City: Santa Cruz

Religion: Roman Catholic

Languages: Spanish (official), Quechua (official), Aymara (official)

Geographical Facts: Landlocked; shares control of Lake Titicaca, world's highest navigable lake, with Peru.

History: Bolivia, named after independence fighter Simón Bolívar, broke away from Spanish rule in 1825. Much of its subsequent history has consisted of a series of nearly 200 coups and counter-coups. Comparatively democratic civilian rule was established in the 1980s, but leaders have faced difficult problems of deep-seated poverty, social unrest, and drug production. Current goals include attracting foreign investment, strengthening the educational system, continuing the privatization program, and waging an anti-corruption campaign.

Bosnia and Herzegovina

Capital: Sarajevo

Major City: Banja Luka

Religions: Muslim, Orthodox

Languages: Croatian, Serbian, Bosnian

Geographical Facts: Within Bosnia and Herzegovina's recognized borders, the country is divided into a joint Bosniak/Croat Federation (about 51 percent of the territory) and the Bosnian Serb-led Republika Srpska, or RS (about 49 percent of the territory); the region called Herzegovina is contiguous to Croatia and traditionally has been settled by an ethnic Croat majority.

History: Bosnia and Herzegovina's declaration of sovereignty in October 1991 was followed, in February 1992, by a referendum for independence from the former Yugoslavia. The Bosnian Serbs—supported by neighboring Serbia—responded with armed resistance aimed at partitioning the republic along ethnic lines and joining Serb-held areas to form a "greater Serbia." In March 1994, Bosniaks and Croats reduced the number of warring factions from three to two by signing an agreement creating a joint Bosniak/Croat Federation of Bosnia and Herzegovina. On November 21, 1995, in Dayton, Ohio, the warring parties signed a peace agreement that brought to a halt three years of interethnic civil strife. (The final agreement was signed in Paris on December 14, 1995.) The Dayton Agreement retained Bosnia and Herzegovina's international boundaries and created a joint multiethnic and democratic government. This national government is charged with conducting foreign, economic, and fiscal policy. Also recognized was a second tier of government comprised of two entities roughly equal in size: the Bosniak/Croat Federation of Bosnia and Herzegovina and the Bosnian Serb-led Republika Srpska (RS). The Federation and RS governments are charged with overseeing internal functions. In 1995–1996, a NATO-led international peacekeeping force (IFOR) of 60,000 troops served in Bosnia to implement and monitor the military aspects of the agreement. IFOR was succeeded by a smaller, NATO-led Stabilization Force (SFOR), whose mission is to deter renewed hostilities. SFOR remains in place at a level of approximately 21,000 troops.

Botswana

Capital: Gaborone

Major City: Francistown

Religions: Indigenous beliefs, Christian

Languages: English (official), Setswana

Geographical Facts: Landlocked; population concentrated in eastern part of the country.

History: Formerly the British protectorate of Bechuanaland, Botswana adopted its new name upon independence in 1966. The economy, one of the most robust on the continent, is dominated by diamond mining.

Brazil

Capital: Brasilia

Major Cities: São Paulo, Rio de Janeiro, Belo Horizonte, Salvador, Manaus

Religion: Roman Catholic

Languages: Portuguese (official), Spanish, English, French

Geographical Facts: Largest country in South America; shares common boundaries with every South American country except Chile and Ecuador.

History: Following three centuries under Portuguese rule, Brazil became an independent nation in 1822. By far the largest and most populous country in South America, Brazil has overcome more than half a century of military intervention in the governance of the country to pursue industrial and agricultural growth and development of the interior. Exploiting vast natural resources and a large labor pool, Brazil became Latin America's leading economic power by the 1970s. Highly unequal income distribution remains a pressing problem.

Brunei

Capital: Bandar Seri Begawan

Religion: Muslim

Languages: Malay (official), English, Chinese

Geographical Facts: Close to vital sealanes through South China Sea linking Indian and Pacific Oceans; two parts physically separated by Malaysia; almost an enclave of Malaysia.

History: The Sultanate of Brunei's heyday occurred between the fifteenth and seventeenth centuries, when its control extended over coastal areas of northwest Borneo and the southern Philippines. Brunei subsequently entered a period of decline brought on by internal strife over royal succession, colonial expansion of European powers, and piracy. In 1888, Brunei became a British protectorate; independence was achieved in 1984. Brunei benefits from extensive petroleum and natural gas fields, which give the country one of the highest per capita GDPs in less-developed countries. The same family has now ruled in Brunei for more than six centuries.

Bulgaria

Capital: Sofiya

Major Cities: Burgas, Varna

Religion: Bulgarian Orthodox

Language: Bulgarian

Geographical Facts: Strategic location near Turkish Straits; controls key land routes from Europe to Middle East and Asia.

History: Bulgaria earned its independence from the Ottoman Empire in 1878, but having fought on the losing side in both world wars, it fell within the Soviet sphere of influence and became a People's Republic in 1946. Communist domination ended in 1990, when Bulgaria held its first multiparty election since World War II and began the contentious process of moving toward political democracy and a market economy while combating inflation, unemployment, corruption, and crime. Today, reforms and democratization keep Bulgaria on a path toward eventual integration into NATO and the EU, with which it began accession negotiations in 2000.

Burkina Faso

Capital: Ouagadougou

Major City: Bobo-Dioulasso

Religions: Muslim, indigenous beliefs

Languages: French (official), native African languages

Geographical Fact: Landlocked savanna cut by the three principal rivers of the Black, Red, and White Voltas.

History: Independence from France came to Burkina Faso (formerly Upper Volta) in 1960. Governmental instability during the 1970s and 1980s was followed by multiparty elections in the early 1990s. Several hundred thousand farmworkers migrate south every year to Côte d'Ivoire and Ghana.

Burundi

Capital: Bujumbura

Religions: Christian, indigenous beliefs

Languages: Kirundi (official), French (official), Swahili

Geographical Facts: Landlocked; straddles crest of the Nile–Congo watershed; the Kagera, which drains into Lake Victoria, is the most remote headstream of the White Nile.

History: Between 1993 and 2000, widespread, often intense ethnic violence between Hutu and Tutsi factions in Burundi created hundreds of thousands of refugees and left tens of thousands dead. Although some refugees have returned from neighboring countries, continued ethnic strife has forced many others to flee. Burundian troops, seeking to secure their borders, have intervened in the conflict in the Democratic Republic of the Congo.

Cambodia

Capital: Phnom Penh

Religion: Theravada Buddhist

Languages: Khmer (official), French, English

Geographical Fact: A land of paddies and forests dominated by the Mekong River and Tonle Sap.

History: In 1975, following a five-year struggle, communist Khmer Rouge forces captured Phnom Penh and ordered the evacuation of all cities and towns; more than one million displaced people died from execution or enforced hardships. A 1978 Vietnamese invasion drove the Khmer Rouge into the countryside and touched off thirteen years of fighting. UN-sponsored elections in 1993 helped restore some semblance of normalcy, as did the rapid diminishment of the Khmer Rouge in the mid-1990s. A coalition government, formed after national elections in 1998, brought renewed political stability and the surrender of remaining Khmer Rouge forces.

Cameroon

Capital: Yauundé

Major City: Douala

Religions: Indigenous beliefs, Christian, Muslim

Languages: English (official), French (official), 24 major African language groups

Geographical Facts: Sometimes referred to as the hinge of Africa; throughout the country there are areas of thermal springs and indications of current or prior volcanic activity; Mount Cameroon, the highest mountain in Sub-Saharan west Africa, is an active volcano.

History: In 1961, the former French Cameroon and part of the former British Cameroon merged to form the present country. In general, Cameroon has enjoyed stability, thus permitting the development of agriculture, roads, and railways, as well as a petroleum industry. Despite movement toward democratic reform, political power remains firmly in the hands of an ethnic oligarchy.

Canada

Capital: Ottawa

Major Cities: Montreal, Toronto, Calgary, Vancouver, Winnipeg, Edmonton

Religions: Roman Catholic, Protestant

Languages: English (official), French (official)

Geographical Facts: Second-largest country in the world (after Russia); strategic location between Russia and the United States via north polar route; approximately 85 percent of the population is concentrated within 200 miles of the U.S./Canada border.

History: A land of vast distances and rich natural resources, Canada became a self-governing dominion in 1867, while retaining ties to the British crown. Economically and technologically, the nation has developed in parallel with the United States, its neighbor to the south across an unfortified border. Its paramount political problem continues to be the relationship of the province of Quebec, with its French-speaking residents and unique culture, to the remainder of the country.

Cape Verde

Capital: Praia

Religions: Roman Catholic (infused with indigenous beliefs), Protestant (mostly Church of the Nazarene)

Languages: Portuguese, Crioulo (a blend of Portuguese and West African words)

Geographical Facts: Strategic location 310 miles from west coast of Africa near major north-south sea routes; important communications station; important sea and air refueling site.

History: The uninhabited islands were discovered and colonized by the Portuguese in the fifteenth century. They subsequently became a trading center for African slaves. Most Cape Verdeans descend from African slaves and Portuguese settlers. Independence was achieved in 1975.

Central African Republic

Capital: Bangui

Major City: Bossangoa

Religions: Indigenous beliefs, Protestant, Roman Catholic

Languages: French (official), Sangho (lingua franca and national language), Arabic, Hunsa, Swahili

Geographical Facts: Landlocked; almost the precise center of Africa.

History: The former French colony of Ubangi-Shari became the Central African Republic upon independence in 1960. After three tumultuous decades of misrule—mostly by military governments—a civilian government was installed in 1993.

Chad

Capital: N'Djamena

Major Cities: Moundou, Sarh

Religions: Muslim, Christian, indigenous beliefs

Languages: French (official), Arabic (official), Sara and Sango (in south)

Geographical Facts: Landlocked; Lake Chad is the most significant water body in the Sahel.

History: Chad, part of France's African holdings until 1960, endured three decades of ethnic warfare as well as invasions by Libya before a semblance of peace was finally restored in 1990. The government eventually suppressed or came to terms with most political-military groups, settled a territorial dispute with Libya on terms favorable to Chad, drafted a democratic constitution, and held multiparty presidential and National Assembly elections in 1996 and 1997, respectively. In 1998, a new rebellion broke out in northern Chad, which continued to escalate throughout 2000. Despite movement toward democratic reform, power remains in the hands of a northern ethnic oligarchy.

Chile

Capital: Santiago

Major Cities: Valparaiso, Concepción, Viña del Mar

Religion: Roman Catholic

Language: Spanish

Geographical Facts: Strategic location relative to sealanes between Atlantic and Pacific Oceans (Strait of Magellan, Beagle Channel, Drake Passage); Atacama Desert is one of world's driest regions.

History: A three-year-old Marxist government was overthrown in 1973 by a dictatorial military regime led by Augusto Pinochet. Pinochet's government ruled until a freely elected president was installed in 1990. Sound economic policies, first implemented by the Pinochet dictatorship, led to unprecedented growth in 1991–1997 and have helped secure the country's commitment to democratic and representative government. Growth slowed in 1998–1999, but recovered strongly in 2000.

China

Capital: Beijing

Major Cities: Guangzhou, Shanghai, Tianjin, Chongqing, Shenyang, Xi'an, Wuhan, Harbin, Hong Kong

Religions: Daoist, Buddhist

Languages: Standard Chinese or Mandarin, Yue (Cantonese), Wu (Shanghaiese), Minbei (Fuzhou), Minnan (Hokkien-Taiwanese)

Geographical Facts: World's fourth-largest country (after Russia, Canada, and United States); it's ranked as the second largest country if Taiwan is included; Mount Everest, on the border with Nepal, is the world's highest peak.

History: For centuries, China has stood as a leading civilization, outpacing the rest of the world in the arts and sciences. But in the first half of the twentieth century, China was beset by major famines, civil unrest, military defeats, and foreign occupation. After World War II, the Communists under Mao Tse-tung established a dictatorship that, while ensuring China's sovereignty, imposed strict controls over everyday life and cost the lives of tens of millions of people. After 1978, Mao's successor, Teng Hsiao-p'ing, gradually introduced market-oriented reforms and decentralized economic decision making. Output quadrupled in the next twenty years, and China now has the world's second largest GDP (following the United States). Political controls remain tight even while economic controls continue to weaken.

Colombia

Capital: Bogotá

Major Cities: Medellín, Cali, Barranquilla

Religion: Roman Catholic

Language: Spanish

Geographical Fact: Only South American country with coastlines on both North Pacific Ocean and Caribbean Sea.

History: Colombia was one of the three countries that emerged from the collapse of Gran Colombia in 1830 (the others being Ecuador and Venezuela). A forty-year insurgent campaign to overthrow the Colombian government escalated during the 1990s, supported in part by funds from the drug trade. Although the violence is deadly and large swaths of the country-side are under guerrilla influence, the movement lacks the military strength or popular support necessary to overthrow the government. Bogotá continues to try to negotiate a settlement, but other neighboring countries worry about the violence spilling over their borders.

Comoros

Capital: Moroni

Religion: Sunni Muslim

Languages: Arabic (official), French (official), Comoran (a blend of Swahili and Arabic)

Geographical Fact: Important location at northern end of Mozambique Channel.

History: Unstable Comoros has endured nineteen coups or attempted coups since gaining independence from France in 1975.

Congo, Democratic Republic of the

Capital: Kinshasa

Major City: Lubumbashi

Religions: Roman Catholic, Protestant

Languages: French (official), Lingala (a lingua franca trade language), Kingwana (a dialect of Kiswahili or Swahili), Kikongo, Tshiluba

Geographical Facts: Straddles equator; very narrow strip of land that controls the lower Congo River and is only outlet to South Atlantic Ocean; dense tropical rain forest in central river basin and eastern highlands.

History: Since 1994, the Democratic Republic of the Congo (DROC; formerly Zaire) has been rent by ethnic strife and civil war, touched off by a massive inflow of refugees from the fighting in neighboring Rwanda and Burundi. In May 1997, the government of former president Mobutu Sese Seko was toppled by a rebellion led by Laurent Kabila, whose regime was subsequently challenged by a Rwanda/Uganda-backed rebellion in August 1998. A cease-fire was signed on July 10, 1999, but sporadic fighting continued. Kabila was assassinated in January 2001, and his son Joseph Kabila was named head of state. The new president quickly began overtures to end the war.

Congo, Republic of the

Capital: Brazzaville

Major City: Pointe-Noire

Religions: Christian, animism

Languages: French (official), Lingala and Monokutuba (lingua franca trade languages), many local languages and dialects

Geographical Fact: About 70 percent of the population lives in Brazzaville, Pointe-Noire, or along the railroad between them.

History: Upon independence from France in 1960, the former French region of Middle Congo became the Republic of the Congo. A quarter century of experimentation with Marxism was abandoned in 1990, and a democratically elected government was installed in 1992. A brief civil war in 1997 restored the former Marxist president.

Costa Rica

Capital: San José

Religion: Roman Catholic

Languages: Spanish (official), English

Geographical Facts: Four volcanoes, two of them active, rise near the capital of San Jose in the center of the country; one of the volcanoes, Irazu, erupted destructively in 1963–1965.

History: Costa Rica is a Central American success story: Since the late nineteenth century, only two brief periods of violence have marred its democratic development. Although still a largely agricultural country, it has achieved a relatively high standard of living. Land ownership is widespread. Tourism is a rapidly expanding industry.

Côte d'Ivoire

Capitals: Yamoussoukro (official), Abidjan (de facto)

Religions: Christian, Muslim

Languages: French (official), 60 native dialects

Geographical Facts: Most of the inhabitants live along the sandy coastal region; apart from the capital area, the forested interior is sparsely populated; Côte d'Ivoire is French for "Ivory Coast."

History: Close ties to France since independence in 1960, the development of cocoa production for export, and foreign investment have made Côte d'Ivoire one of the most prosperous of the tropical African states. Falling cocoa prices and political turmoil, however, sparked an economic downturn in 1999 and 2000. On December 25, 1999, a military coup—the first ever in Côte d'Ivoire's history—overthrew the government led by President Henri Konan Bedie. Presidential and legislative elections held in October and December 2000 provoked violence due to the exclusion of opposition leader Alassane Ouattara. In October 2000, Laurent Gbagbo replaced junta leader Robert Guei as president, ending ten months of military rule.

Croatia

Capital: Zagreb

Major City: Split

Religion: Roman Catholic

Language: Croatian

Geographical Fact: Controls most land routes from western Europe to Aegean Sea and Turkish Straits.

History: In 1918, the Croats, Serbs, and Slovenes formed a kingdom known after 1929 as Yugoslavia. Following World War II, Yugoslavia became an independent communist state under the strong hand of Marshal Tito. Although Croatia declared its independence from Yugoslavia in 1991, it took four years of sporadic but often bitter fighting before occupying Serb armies were mostly cleared from Croatian lands. Under UN supervision, the last Serb-held enclave in eastern Slovenia was returned to Croatia in 1998.

Cuba

Capital: Havana

Major Cities: Holguín, Guantánamo

Religion: Roman Catholic

Language: Spanish

Geographical Fact: Largest country in Caribbean.

History: In 1959, Fidel Castro led a rebel army to victory; his iron rule has held the country together ever since. Cuba's communist revolution, with Soviet support, was exported throughout Latin America and Africa during the 1960s through the 1980s. The country is now slowly recovering from a severe economic recession in 1990, following the withdrawal of former Soviet subsidies, worth $4 billion to $6 billion annually. Havana portrays its difficulties as the result of the U.S. embargo, which has been in place since 1961. Illicit migration to the United States, using homemade rafts, alien smugglers, or falsified visas, is a continuing problem. In 2000, approximately 3,000 Cubans took to the Straits of Florida in attempts to get into the United States; the U.S. Coast Guard interdicted only about 35 percent of these.

Cyprus

Capital: Nicosia

Major Cities: Larnaca, Limassol

Religion: Greek Orthodox

Languages: Greek, Turkish, English

Geographical Fact: The third largest island in the Mediterranean Sea (after Sicily and Sardinia).

History: Independence from the United Kingdom was approved in 1960, with constitutional guarantees by the Greek Cypriot majority to the Turkish Cypriot minority. In 1974, a Greek-sponsored attempt to seize the government was met by military intervention from Turkey, which soon controlled almost 40 percent of the island. In 1983, the Turkish-held area declared itself the "Turkish Republic of Northern Cyprus," but it is recognized only by Turkey. UN-led talks on the status of Cyprus resumed in December 1999 to prepare the ground for meaningful negotiations leading to a comprehensive settlement.

Czech Republic

Capital: Prague

Major City: Brno

Religions: Atheist, Roman Catholic

Language: Czech

Geographical Facts: Landlocked; strategically located astride some of the oldest and most significant land routes in Europe; Moravian Gate is a traditional military corridor between the North European Plain and the Danube in central Europe.

History: After World War II, Czechoslovakia fell within the Soviet sphere of influence. In 1968, an invasion by Warsaw Pact troops ended the efforts of the country's leaders to liberalize party rule and create "socialism with a human face." Anti-Soviet demonstrations the following year ushered in a period of harsh repression. With the collapse of Soviet authority in 1989, Czechoslovakia regained its freedom through a peaceful "Velvet Revolution." On January 1, 1993, the country underwent a "velvet divorce" into its two national components, the Czech Republic and Slovakia. Now a member of NATO, the Czech Republic has moved toward integration in world markets, a development that poses both opportunities and risks.

Denmark

Capital: Copenhagen

Major Cities: Alborg, Odense

Religion: Evangelical Lutheran

Languages: Danish, Faroese, Greenlandic, German, English

Geographical Facts: Controls Danish Straits (Skagerrak and Kattegat) linking Baltic and North Seas; about one-quarter of the population lives in greater Copenhagen.

History: Once the seat of Viking raiders and later a major north European power, Denmark has evolved into a modern, prosperous nation that is participating in the political and economic integration of Europe. So far, however, the country has opted out of some aspects of the European Union's Maastricht Treaty, including the economic and monetary system (EMU) and issues concerning certain internal affairs.

Djibouti

Capital: Djibouti

Religion: Muslim

Languages: French (official), Arabic (official), Somali, Afar

Geographical Facts: Strategic location near world's busiest shipping lanes and close to Arabian oilfields; terminus of rail traffic into Ethiopia; mostly wasteland; Lac Assal (Lake Assal) is the lowest point in Africa.

History: In 1977, the French Territory of the Afars and the Issas became Djibouti. A peace accord in 1994 ended a three-year uprising by Afars rebels.

Dominica

Capital: Roseau

Religion: Roman Catholic

Languages: English (official), French patois

Geographical Facts: Known as "The Nature Island of the Caribbean" due to its spectacular, lush, and varied flora and fauna, which are protected by an extensive natural park system; the most mountainous of the Lesser Antilles, its volcanic peaks are cones of lava craters and include Boiling Lake, the second-largest, thermally active lake in the world.

History: Dominica was the last of the Caribbean islands to be colonized by Europeans, due chiefly to the fierce resistance of the native Caribs. France ceded possession to Great Britain in 1763, which made the island a colony in 1805. In 1980, two years after independence, Dominica's fortunes improved when a corrupt and tyrannical administration was replaced by that of Mary Eugenia Charles, the first female prime minister in the Caribbean, who remained in office for fifteen years.

Dominican Republic

Capital: Santo Domingo

Major City: Santiago de los Caballeros

Religion: Roman Catholic

Language: Spanish

Geographical Facts: Shares island of Hispaniola with Haiti (eastern two-thirds is the Dominican Republic; western one-third is Haiti).

History: A legacy of unsettled, mostly nonrepresentative, rule for much of the twentieth century was brought to an end in 1996, when free and open elections ushered in a new government.

Ecuador

Capital: Quito

Major City: Guayaquil

Religion: Roman Catholic

Languages: Spanish (official), Amerindian languages

Geographical Fact: Cotopaxi in Andes is highest active volcano in the world.

History: The "Republic of the Equator" was one of three countries that emerged from the collapse of Gran Colombia in 1830 (the others being Colombia and Venezuela). Between 1904 and 1942, Ecuador lost territories in a series of conflicts with its neighbors. A border war with Peru that flared in 1995 was resolved in 1999.

Egypt

Capital: Cairo

Major Cities: Aswan, Giza, Alexandria

Religion: Muslim

Language: Arabic (official)

Geographical Facts: Controls Sinai Peninsula, only land bridge between Africa and Eurasia; controls Suez Canal, shortest sea link between Indian Ocean and Mediterranean Sea; size and juxtaposition to Israel establish its major role in Middle Eastern geopolitics; dependence on upstream neighbors; dominance of Nile basin issues; prone to influxes of refugees.

History: Nominally independent from the United Kingdom in 1922, Egypt acquired full sovereignty following World War II. The completion of the Aswan High Dam in 1971 and the resultant Lake Nasser have altered the time-honored place of the Nile River in Egypt's agriculture and ecology. A rapidly growing population (the largest in the Arab world), limited arable land, and dependence on the Nile all continue to overtax resources and stress society. The government has struggled to ready the economy for the new millennium through economic reform and massive investment in communications and physical infrastructure.

El Salvador

Capital: San Salvador

Major City: Santa Ana

Religion: Roman Catholic

Languages: Spanish, Nahua

Geographical Facts: Smallest Central American country and only one without a coastline on Caribbean Sea.

History: El Salvador achieved independence from Spain in 1821 and from the Central American Federation in 1839. A twelve-year civil war, which cost the lives of approximately 75,000 people, was brought to a close in 1992, when the government and leftist rebels signed a treaty that provided for military and political reforms.

Equatorial Guinea

Capital: Malabo

Religion: Nominally Christian and predominantly Roman Catholic

Languages: Spanish (official), French (official), pidgin English, Fang, Bubi, Ibo

Geographical Facts: Composed of a mainland portion (Mbini), the island of Bioko (where the capital is located), the island of Pagulu, and several other small islands.

History: Composed of a mainland portion and five inhabited islands, Equatorial Guinea has been ruled by ruthless leaders, who have mismanaged the economy since independence from 190 years of Spanish rule in 1968. Although nominally a constitutional democracy since 1991, the 1996 presidential and 1999 legislative elections were widely seen as being flawed.

Eritrea

Capital: Asmara

Religions: Muslim, Coptic Christian, Roman Catholic, Protestant

Languages: Afar, Amharic, Arabic, Tigre and Kunama, Tigrinya, other Cushitic languages

Geographical Facts: Strategic geopolitical position along world's busiest shipping lanes; Eritrea retained the entire coastline of Ethiopia along the Red Sea upon de jure independence from Ethiopia in 1993.

History: Eritrea was awarded to Ethiopia in 1952 as part of a federation. Ethiopia's annexation of Eritrea as a province ten years later sparked a thirty-year struggle for independence that ended in 1991 with Eritrean rebels defeating governmental forces. Independence was overwhelmingly approved in a 1993 referendum. A two-and-a-half-year border war with Ethiopia that erupted in 1998 ended under UN auspices on December 12, 2000.

Estonia

Capital: Tallinn

Major Cities: Narva, Tartu

Religions: Evangelical Lutheran, Russian Orthodox

Languages: Estonian (official), Russian, Ukrainian, English, Finnish

Geographical Facts: The mainland terrain is flat, boggy, and partly wooded; offshore lay more than 1,500 islands.

History: After centuries of Swedish and Russian rule, Estonia attained independence in 1918. Forcibly incorporated into the USSR in 1940, it regained its freedom in 1991 with the collapse of the Soviet Union. Since the last Russian troops left in 1994, Estonia has been free to promote economic and political ties with Western Europe.

Ethiopia

Capital: Addis Ababa

Major City: Diredawa

Religions: Muslim, Ethiopian Orthodox

Languages: Amharic, Tigrinya, Oromigna, Guaragigna, Somali, Arabic

Geographical Facts: Landlocked—entire coastline along the Red Sea was lost with the de jure independence of Eritrea in 1993; the Blue Nile, the chief headstream of the Nile, rises in Lake Tana in northwest Ethiopia.

History: Unique among African countries, the ancient Ethiopian monarchy maintained its freedom from colonial rule, one exception being the Italian occupation of 1936–1941. In 1974, a military junta, the Derg, deposed Emperor Haile Selassie (who had ruled since 1930) and established a socialist state. Torn by bloody coups, uprisings, wide-scale drought, and massive refugee problems, the regime was finally toppled by a coalition of rebel forces, the Ethiopian People's Revolutionary Democratic Front (EPRDF), in 1991. A constitution was adopted in 1994, and Ethiopia's first multiparty elections were held in 1995. A two-and-a-half-year border war with Eritrea that ended with a peace treaty on December 12, 2000, has strengthened the ruling coalition, but has hurt the nation's economy.

Fiji

Capital: Suva

Religions: Christian, Hindu

Languages: English (official), Fijian, Hindustani

Geographical Facts: Includes 332 islands, of which approximately 110 are inhabited.

History: Fiji became independent in 1970, after nearly a century as a British colony. Democratic rule was interrupted in 1987 by two military coups caused by concern over a government perceived as dominated by the Indian community (descendants of contract laborers brought to the islands by the British in the nineteenth century). A 1990 constitution favored native Melanesian control of Fiji, but led to heavy Indian emigration; the population loss resulted in economic difficulties, but ensured that Melanesians became the majority. Amendments enacted in 1997 made the constitution more equitable. Free and peaceful elections in 1999 resulted in a government led by an Indo-Fijian, but a coup in May 2000 ushered in a prolonged period of political turmoil.

Finland

Capital: Helsinki

Major Cities: Turku, Tampere

Religion: Evangelical Lutheran

Language: Finnish (official)

Geographical Facts: Long boundary with Russia; Helsinki is northernmost national capital on European continent; population concentrated on small southwestern coastal plain.

History: Ruled by Sweden from the twelfth through the nineteenth centuries and by Russia from 1809, Finland finally won its independence in 1917. During World War II, it was able to successfully defend its freedom and fend off invasions by the Soviet Union and Germany. In the subsequent half century, the Finns have made a remarkable transformation from a farm/forest economy to a diversified modern industrial economy; per capita income is now on par with Western Europe. As a member of the European Union, Finland was the only Nordic state to join the euro system at its initiation in January 1999.

France

Capital: Paris

Major Cities: Marseille, Lyon, Toulouse

Religion: Roman Catholic

Language: French

Geographical Fact: Largest western European nation.

History: The French Revolution of 1789 established France as a republic. Although ultimately a victor in World Wars I and II, France suffered extensive losses in its empire, wealth, manpower, and rank as a dominant nation-state. Nevertheless, France today is one of the most modern countries in the world and is a leader among European nations. Since 1958, it has constructed a presidential democracy resistant to the instabilities experienced in earlier parliamentary democracies. In recent years, its reconciliation and cooperation with Germany have proved central to the economic integration of Europe, including the advent of the euro in January 1999. France is at the forefront of European states seeking to exploit the momentum of monetary union to advance the creation of a more unified and capable European defense and security apparatus.

Gabon

Capital: Libreville

Major City: Port-Gentil

Religion: Christian

Languages: French (official), Fang, Myene, Bateke, Bapounou/Eschira, Bandjabi

Geographical Facts: A small population and oil and mineral reserves have helped Gabon become one of Africa's wealthier countries; in general, these circumstances have allowed the country to maintain and conserve its pristine rain forest and rich biodiversity.

History: Ruled by autocratic presidents since independence from France in 1960, Gabon introduced a multiparty system and a new constitution in the early 1990s. The system allowed for a more transparent electoral process and for reforms of governmental institutions.

Gambia

Capital: Banjul

Major City: Serrekunda

Religion: Muslim

Languages: English (official), Mandinka, Wolof, Fula

Geographical Facts: Almost an enclave of Senegal; smallest country on the continent of Africa.

History: Gambia gained its independence from the United Kingdom in 1965. With Senegal, it formed a short-lived federation of Senegambia between 1982 and 1989. In 1991, the two nations signed a friendship and cooperation treaty. A military coup in 1994 overthrew the president and banned political activity, but a new 1996 constitution and presidential elections, followed by parliamentary balloting in 1997, have completed a nominal return to civilian rule.

Georgia

Capital: Tbilisi

Religion: Christian Orthodox

Language: Georgian

Geographical Facts: Strategically located east of the Black Sea; Georgia controls much of the Caucasus Mountains and the routes through them.

History: In the nineteenth century, Georgia was absorbed into the Russian Empire. Independent for three years (1918–1921) following the Russian revolution, it was forcibly incorporated into the USSR until the Soviet Union dissolved in 1991. Despite a badly degraded transportation network—brought on by ethnic conflict, criminal activities, and fuel shortages—the country continues to move toward a market economy and greater integration with Western institutions.

Germany

Capital: Berlin

Major Cities: Bonn, Frankfurt, Munich, Cologne, Hamburg, Essen

Religions: Protestant, Roman Catholic

Language: German

Geographical Facts: Strategic location on north European plain and along the entrance to the Baltic Sea.

History: As Western Europe's richest and most populous nation, Germany remains a key member of the continent's economic, political, and defense organizations. European power struggles immersed the country in two devastating world wars in the first half of the twentieth century and left the country occupied by the victorious Allied powers of the united States, United Kingdom, France, and the Soviet Union in 1945. With the advent of the Cold War, two German states were formed in 1949: the western Federal Republic of Germany (FRG) and the eastern German Democratic Republic (GDR). The democratic FRG embedded itself in key Western economic and security organizations, the EC and NATO, while the communist GDR was on the front line of the Soviet-led Warsaw Pact. The decline of the USSR and the end of the Cold War allowed for German unification in 1990. Since then Germany has expended considerable funds to bring eastern productivity and wages up to western standards. In January 1999, Germany and ten other EU countries formed a common European currency, the euro.

Ghana

Capital: Accra

Major Cities: Tamale, Kumasi

Religions: Indigenous beliefs, Muslim, Christian

Languages: English (official), African languages

Geographical Facts: Lake Volta is the world's largest artificial lake; northeasterly harmattan wind (January to March).

History: Formed from the merger of the British colony of the Gold Coast and the Togoland trust territory, Ghana, in 1957, became the first country in colonial Africa to gain its independence. A long series of coups resulted in the suspension of the constitution in 1981 and the banning of political parties. A new constitution, restoring multiparty politics, was approved in 1992.

Greece

Capital: Athens

Major City: Thessaloníki

Religion: Greek Orthodox

Language: Greek

Geographical Facts: Strategic location dominating the Aegean Sea and southern approach to Turkish Straits; a peninsular country, possessing an archipelago of about two thousand islands.

History: In 1829, Greece achieved its independence from the Ottoman Empire. During the second half of the nineteenth century and the first half of the twentieth century, it gradually added neighboring islands and territories with Greek-speaking populations. Following the defeat of communist rebels in 1949, Greece joined NATO in 1952. A military dictatorship, which in 1967 suspended many political liberties and forced the king to flee the country, lasted seven years. Democratic elections in 1974 and a referendum created a parliamentary republic and abolished the monarchy. Greece joined the European Community, or EC (which became the EU in 1992), in 1981.

Grenada

Capital: St. George's

Religion: Roman Catholic

Languages: English (official), French patois

Geographical Facts: The administration of the islands of the Grenadines group is divided between Saint Vincent and the Grenadines and Grenada; one of the smallest independent countries in the Western Hemisphere.

History: A Marxist military council seized Grenada on October 19, 1983. Six days later, U.S. forces, and those of six other Caribbean nations, invaded the island. These forces quickly captured the ringleaders and their hundreds of Cuban advisers. Free elections were reinstituted the following year.

Guatemala

Capital: Guatemala City

Religions: Roman Catholic, Protestant, traditional Mayan beliefs

Languages: Spanish, Amerindian languages

Geographical Fact: No natural harbors on west coast.

History: Guatemala was freed of Spanish colonial rule in 1821. During the second half of the twentieth century, it experienced a variety of military and civilian governments as well as a thirty-six-year guerrilla war. In 1996, the government signed a peace agreement formally ending the conflict, which had led to the death of more than 100,000 people and had created approximately one million refugees.

Guinea

Capital: Conakry

Major City: Kankan

Religion: Muslim

Language: French (official)

Geographical Fact: The Niger and its important tributary, the Milo, have their sources in the Guinean highlands.

History: Independent from France since 1958, Guinea did not hold democratic elections until 1993, when General Lansana Conte (head of the military government) was elected president of the civilian government. He was re-elected in 1998. Unrest in Sierra Leone has spilled over into Guinea, threatening stability and creating a humanitarian emergency.

Guinea-Bissau

Capital: Bissau

Religions: Indigenous beliefs, Muslim

Languages: Portuguese (official), Crioulo, African languages

Geographical Facts: This small country is swampy along its western coast and low-lying further inland.

History: In 1994, twenty years after independence from Portugal, the country's first multiparty legislative and presidential elections were held. An army uprising that triggered a bloody civil war in 1998 created hundreds of thousands of displaced persons. In May 1999, a military junta ousted the president. An interim government turned over power in February 2000, when opposition leader Koumba Yalla took office following two rounds of transparent presidential elections. Guinea-Bissau's transition back to democracy will be complicated by a crippled economy devastated by civil war and the military's predilection for governmental meddling.

Guyana

Capital: Georgetown

Religions: Christian, Hindu

Languages: English, Amerindian dialects, Creole, Hindi, Urdu

Geographical Facts: The third-smallest country in South America after Suriname and Uruguay; substantial portions of its western and eastern territories are claimed by Venezuela and Suriname, respectively.

History: Guyana achieved independence from the United Kingdom in 1966 and became a republic in 1970. In 1989, Guyana launched an economic recovery program, which marked a dramatic reversal from a state-controlled, socialist economy toward a more open, free-market system. Results through the first decade have proven encouraging.

Haiti

Capital: Port-au-Prince

Religion: Roman Catholic

Languages: French (official), Creole (official)

Geographical Facts: Shares island of Hispaniola with Dominican Republic (western one-third is Haiti; eastern two-thirds is the Dominican Republic).

History: One of the poorest countries in the Western Hemisphere, Haiti has been plagued by political violence for most of its history. More than three decades of dictatorship followed by military rule ended in 1990, when Jean-Bertrand Aristide was elected president. Most of his term was usurped by a military takeover, but he was able to return to office in 1994 and oversee the installation of a close associate to the presidency in 1996. Aristide won a second term as president in 2000 and took office early the following year.

Honduras

Capital: Tegucigalpa

Major City: San Pedro Sula

Religion: Roman Catholic

Languages: Spanish, Amerindian dialects

Geographical Facts: Has only a short Pacific coast but a long Caribbean shoreline, including the virtually uninhabited eastern Mosquito Coast.

History: Part of Spain's vast empire in the New World, Honduras became an independent nation in 1821. After two and a half decades of mostly military rule, a freely elected civilian government came to power in 1982. During the 1980s, Honduras proved a haven for anti-Sandinista contras fighting the Marxist Nicaraguan government and an ally to Salvadoran government forces fighting against leftist guerrillas.

Hungary

Capital: Budapest

Major Cities: Szeged, Debrecen

Religions: Roman Catholic, Calvinist

Language: Hungarian

Geographical Facts: Landlocked; strategic location astride mainland routes between western Europe and Balkan Peninsula as well as between Ukraine and Mediterranean basin.

History: Hungary was part of the polyglot Austro-Hungarian Empire, which collapsed during World War I. The country fell under communist rule following World War II. In 1956, a revolt and announced withdrawal from the Warsaw Pact were met with a massive military intervention by Moscow. In the more open Gorbachev years, Hungary led the movement to dissolve the Warsaw Pact and steadily shifted toward multiparty democracy and a market-oriented economy. Following the collapse of the USSR in 1991, Hungary developed close political and economic ties to Western Europe. It joined NATO in 1999 and is a frontrunner in a future expansion of the EU.

Iceland

Capital: Reykjavik

Religion: Evangelical Lutheran

Language: Icelandic

Geographical Facts: Strategic location between Greenland and Europe; westernmost European country; Reykjavik is the northernmost national capital in the world; more land covered by glaciers than in all of continental Europe.

History: Settled by Norwegian and Celtic (Scottish and Irish) immigrants during the late ninth and tenth centuries A.D., Iceland boasts the world's oldest functioning legislative assembly, the Althing, established in 930. Independent for more than three hundred years, Iceland was subsequently ruled by Norway and Denmark. Fallout from the Askja volcano of 1875 devastated the Icelandic economy and caused widespread famine. Over the next quarter century, 20 percent of the island's population emigrated, mostly to Canada and the United States. Limited home rule from Denmark was granted in 1874 and complete independence attained in 1944. Literacy, longevity, income, and social cohesion are first-rate by world standards.

India

Capital: New Delhi

Major Cities: Mumbai (Bombay), Kolkata (Calcutta), Delhi, Bangalore, Chennai (Madras), Hyderabad

Religion: Hindu

Languages: Hindi (the national language), Bengali (official), Telugu (official), Marathi (official), Tamil (official), Urdu (official), Gujarati (official), Malayalam (official), Kannada (official), Oriya (official), Punjabi (official), Assamese (official), Kashmiri (official), Sindhi (official), Sanskrit (official), English

Geographical Facts: Dominates South Asian subcontinent; near important Indian Ocean trade routes.

History: The Indus Valley civilization, one of the oldest in the world, goes back at least five thousand years. Aryan tribes from the northwest invaded in about 1500 B.C.; their merger with the earlier inhabitants created classical Indian culture. Arab incursions starting in the eighth century and Turkish in the twelfth were followed by European traders beginning in the late fifteenth century. By the nineteenth century, Britain had assumed political control of virtually all Indian lands. Nonviolent resistance to British colonialism under Mohandas Gandhi and Jawaharlal Nehru led to independence in 1947. The subcontinent was divided into the secular state of India and the smaller Muslim state of Pakistan. A third war between the two countries in 1971 resulted in East Pakistan becoming the separate nation of Bangladesh. Fundamental concerns in India include the ongoing dispute with Pakistan over Kashmir, massive overpopulation, environmental degradation, extensive poverty, and ethnic strife—all this despite impressive gains in economic investment and output.

Indonesia

Capital: Jakarta

Major Cities: Bandung, Medan, Surabaja, Palembang

Religion: Muslim

Languages: Bahasa Indonesia (official, modified form of Malay), English, Dutch

Geographical Facts: The world's largest archipelago, with seventeen thousand islands (six thousand inhabited); straddles equator; strategic location astride or along major sealanes from Indian Ocean to Pacific Ocean.

History: Indonesia achieved independence from the Netherlands in 1949. Current issues include implementing IMF-mandated reforms of the banking sector, effecting a transition to a popularly elected government after four decades of authoritarianism, addressing charges of cronyism and corruption, holding the military accountable for human rights violations, and resolving growing separatist pressures in Aceh and Irian Jaya (West Irian). On August 30, 1999, the people of Timor Timur overwhelmingly approved a provincial referendum for independence. Concurrence followed by Indonesia's national legislature, and the name East Timor was provisionally adopted. East Timor's official independence took place in mid-2002, making it the newest country on Earth.

Iran

Capital: Tehran

Major Cities: Esfahān, Shiraz, Mashhad, Tabriz

Religion: Shiite Muslim

Languages: Persian and Persian dialects, Turkic and Turkic dialects

Geographical Facts: Strategic location on the Persian Gulf and Strait of Hormuz, which are vital maritime pathways for crude oil transport.

History: Known as Persia until 1935, Iran became an Islamic republic in 1979 after the ruling shah was forced into exile. Conservative clerical forces subsequently crushed westernizing liberal elements. Militant Iranian students seized the U.S. Embassy in Tehran on November 4, 1979, and held it until January 20, 1981. During 1980–1988, Iran fought a bloody, indecisive war with Iraq over disputed territory. The key current issue is how rapidly the country should open up to the modernizing influences of the outside world.

Iraq

Capital: Baghdad

Major Cities: Basra, Mosul

Religions: Shiite Muslim, Sunni Muslim

Languages: Arabic, Kurdish (official in Kurdish regions), Assyrian, Armenian

Geographical Facts: Strategic location on Shatt al Arab waterway and at the head of the Persian Gulf.

History: Formerly part of the Ottoman Empire, Iraq became an independent kingdom in 1932. A "republic" was proclaimed in 1958, but in actuality a series of military strongmen have ruled the country since then, the latest being Saddam Hussein. Territorial disputes with Iran led to an inconclusive and costly eight-year war (1980–1988). In August 1990, Iraq seized Kuwait, but was expelled by U.S.-led UN-coalition forces during January–February 1991. The victors did not occupy Iraq, however, thus allowing the regime to stay in control. Following Kuwait's liberation, the UN Security Council (UNSC) required Iraq to scrap all weapons of mass destruction and long-range missiles and to allow UN verification inspections. UN trade sanctions remain in effect due to incomplete Iraqi compliance with relevant UNSC resolutions.

Ireland

Capital: Dublin

Major Cities: Cork, Limerick

Religion: Roman Catholic

Languages: English, Irish (Gaelic)

Geographical Facts: Strategic location on major air and sea routes between North America and northern Europe; over 40 percent of the population resides within 97 kilometers of Dublin.

History: A failed 1916 Easter Monday Rebellion touched off several years of guerrilla warfare, which in 1921 resulted in independence from the United Kingdom for the twenty-six southern counties; the six northern counties (Ulster) remained part of Great Britain. In 1948, Ireland withdrew from the British Commonwealth. It joined the European Community in 1973. Irish governments have sought the peaceful unification of Ireland and have cooperated with Britain against terrorist groups. A peace settlement for Northern Ireland, approved in 1998, was implemented the following year.

Israel

Capital: Jerusalem (most embassies are located in Tel Aviv)

Major Cities: Haifa, Tel Aviv-Jaffa

Religion: Jewish

Languages: Hebrew (official), Arabic

Geographical Fact: The Sea of Galilee is an important freshwater source.

History: Following World War II, the British withdrew from their mandate of Palestine, and the UN partitioned the area into Arab and Jewish states, an arrangement rejected by the Arabs. Subsequently, the Israelis defeated the Arabs in a series of wars without ending the deep tensions between the two sides. In keeping with the framework established at the Madrid Conference in October 1991, bilateral negotiations are being conducted between Israel and Palestinian representatives (from the Israeli-occupied West Bank and Gaza Strip) and Israel and Syria, to achieve a permanent settlement. On April 25, 1982, Israel withdrew from the Sinai pursuant to the 1979 Israel-Egypt Peace Treaty. Outstanding territorial and other disputes with Jordan were resolved in the October 26, 1994, Israel-Jordan Treaty of Peace. On May 25, 2000, Israel withdrew unilaterally from southern Lebanon, which it had occupied since 1982.

Italy

Capital: Rome

Major Cities: Milan, Naples, Genoa, Turin, Florence

Religion: Roman Catholic

Languages: Italian (official), German

Geographical Facts: Strategic location dominating central Mediterranean as well as southern sea and air approaches to western Europe; Vatican City and San Marino are independent countries located within Italy.

History: Italy became a belated nation-state in 1861, when the city-states of the peninsula, along with Sardinia and Sicily, were united under King Victor Emmanuel. An era of parliamentary government came to a close in the early 1920s, when Benito Mussolini established a Fascist dictatorship. His disastrous alliance with Nazi Germany led to Italy's defeat in World War II. A democratic republic replaced the monarchy in 1946, and economic revival followed. Italy was a charter member of NATO and the European Economic Community (EEC). It has been at the forefront of European economic and political unification, joining the European Monetary Union in 1999. Persistent problems include illegal immigration, the ravages of organized crime, corruption, high unemployment, and the low incomes and technical standards of southern Italy compared with the more prosperous north.

Jamaica

Capital: Kingston

Major City: Montego Bay

Religion: Protestant

Languages: English, Creole

Geographical Facts: Strategic location between Cayman Trench and Jamaica Channel, the main sealanes for Panama Canal.

History: In 1962, Jamaica gained full independence within the British Commonwealth. Deteriorating economic conditions during the 1970s led to recurrent violence and a drop-off in tourism. Elections in 1980 saw the democratic socialists voted out of office. Subsequent governments have been open-market oriented. Political violence marred elections during the 1990s.

Japan

Capital: Tokyo

Major Cities: Osaka, Kobe, Hiroshima, Yokohama, Sapporo, Kyoto, Nagoya

Religions: Shinto, Buddhist

Language: Japanese

Geographical Fact: Strategic location in northeast Asia.

History: While retaining its time-honored culture, Japan rapidly absorbed Western technology during the late nineteenth and early twentieth centuries. After its devastating defeat in World War II, Japan recovered to become the second most powerful economy in the world and a staunch ally of the United States. While the emperor retains his throne as a symbol of national unity, actual power rests in networks of powerful politicians, bureaucrats, and business executives. The economy experienced a major slowdown in the 1990s following three decades of unprecedented growth.

Jordan

Capital: Amman

Major City: Az Zarqa

Religion: Sunni Muslim

Language: Arabic (official)

Geographical Facts: Strategic location at the head of the Gulf of 'Aqaba and as the Arab country that shares the longest border with Israel and the occupied West Bank.

History: For most of its history since independence from British administration in 1946, Jordan was ruled by King Hussein. A pragmatic ruler, he successfully navigated competing pressures from the major powers (U.S., USSR, and U.K.), various Arab states, Israel, and a large internal Palestinian population through several wars and coup attempts. In 1989, he resumed parliamentary elections and gradually permitted political liberalization. In 1994, a formal peace treaty was signed with Israel. King Abdallah II, the eldest son of King Hussein and Princess Muna, assumed the throne following his father's death in February 1999. Since then, he has consolidated his power and established his domestic priorities.

Kazakhstan

Capital: Astana

Major City: Almaty

Religions: Muslim, Russian Orthodox

Languages: Russian (official), Kazakh (Qazaq, state language)

Geographical Facts: Landlocked; Russia leases the territory enclosing the Baykonur Cosmodrome.

History: Native Kazakhs, a mix of Turkic and Mongol nomadic tribes who migrated into the region in the thirteenth century, were rarely united as a single nation. The area was conquered by Russia in the eighteenth century, and Kazakhstan became a Soviet Republic in 1936. During the agricultural "Virgin Lands" program of the 1950s and 1960s, Soviet citizens were encouraged to help cultivate Kazakhstan's northern pastures. This influx of immigrants (mostly Russians, but also some other deported nationalities) skewed the ethnic mixture and enabled non-Kazakhs to outnumber natives. Independence has caused many of these newcomers to emigrate. Current issues include developing a cohesive national identity, expanding the development of the country's vast energy resources and exporting them to world markets, and continuing to strengthen relations with neighboring states and other foreign powers.

Kenya

Capital: Nairobi

Major Cities: Kisumu, Mombasa, Nakuru

Religions: Protestant, Roman Catholic, indigenous beliefs

Languages: English (official), Kiswahili (official)

Geographical Facts: The Kenyan Highlands comprise one of the most successful agricultural production regions in Africa; glaciers are found on Mount Kenya, Africa's second highest peak; unique physiography supports abundant and varied wildlife of scientific and economic value.

History: Revered president and liberation struggle icon Jomo Kenyatta led Kenya from its independence in 1963 until his death in 1978, when current President Daniel Toroitich arap Moi took power in a constitutional succession. The country was a de facto one-party state from 1969 until 1982, when the ruling Kenya African National Union (KANU) made itself the sole legal party in Kenya. In late 1991, Moi acceded to internal and external pressure for political liberalization. The ethnically fractured opposition failed to dislodge KANU from power in 1992 and 1997 elections, which were both marred by violence and fraud, but which are viewed as having reflected the general will of the Kenyan people. The country faces a period of political uncertainty because Moi is required constitutionally to step down at the next elections that must be held by early 2003.

Kiribati

Capital: Tarawa

Religions: Roman Catholic, Protestant

Languages: English (official), I-Kiribati

Geographical Facts: Twenty of the thirty-three islands are inhabited; Banaba (Ocean Island) in Kiribati is one of the three great phosphate rock islands in the Pacific Ocean; the others are Makatea in French Polynesia and Nauru.

History: In 1971, the Gilbert Islands were granted self-rule by the United Kingdom. Complete independence under the then new name of Kiribati was granted in 1979. The United States relinquished all claims to the sparsely inhabited Phoenix and Line Island groups in a 1979 treaty of friendship.

Korea, North

Capital: Pyongyang

Major City: Chongjin

Religions: Buddhist, Confucianist

Language: Korean

Geographical Facts: Strategic location bordering China, South Korea, and Russia; mountainous interior is isolated and sparsely populated.

History: Following World War II, Korea was split into a northern, communist half and a southern, Western-oriented half. Kim Chong-il has ruled North Korea since his father and the country's founder, president Kim Il-song, died in 1994. After decades of mismanagement, the North relies heavily on international food aid to feed its population, while continuing to expend resources to maintain an army of about one million. North Korea's long-range missile development and research into nuclear and chemical weapons are of major concern to the international community.

Korea, South

Capital: Seoul

Major Cities: Inchon, Pusan, Taegu

Religions: Christian, Buddhist

Language: Korean

Geographical Fact: Strategic location on Korea Strait.

History: After World War II, a republic was set up in the southern half of the Korean Peninsula, while a communist-style government was installed in the north. In the Korean War (1950–1953), U.S. and other UN forces intervened to defend South Korea from North Korean attacks supported by the Chinese. An armistice was signed in 1953 splitting the peninsula at the 38th parallel, known as the DMZ (demilitarized zone). Thereafter, South Korea achieved rapid economic growth, with per capita income rising to thirteen times the level of North Korea's. In 1997, the nation suffered a severe financial crisis from which it continues to make a solid recovery. South Korea has also maintained its commitment to democratize its political processes. In June 2000, a historic first South-North summit took place between the South's President Kim Dae-jung and the North's leader Kim Chong-il.

Kuwait

Capital: Kuwait City

Religions: Sunni Muslim, Shiite Muslim

Language: Arabic (official)

Geographical Fact: Strategic location at head of Persian Gulf.

History: Kuwait gained independence from the United Kingdom in 1961. On August 2, 1990, Kuwait was attacked and overrun by Iraq. Following several weeks of aerial bombardment, a U.S.-led UN coalition began a ground assault on February 23, 1991 that completely liberated Kuwait in four days. Kuwait has spent more than $5 billion to repair oil infrastructure damaged during 1990–1991.

Kyrgyzstan

Capital: Bishkek

Major City: Osh

Religions: Muslim, Russian Orthodox

Language: Arabic (official)

Geographical Facts: A central Asian country of incredible natural beauty and proud nomadic traditions; landlocked; entirely mountainous, dominated by the Tien Shan range; many tall peaks, glaciers, and high-altitude lakes.

History: Kyrgyzstan was annexed by Russia in 1864. It achieved independence from the Soviet Union in 1991. Current concerns include privatization of state-owned enterprises, expansion of democracy and political freedoms, interethnic relations, and terrorism.

Laos

Capital: Vientiane

Major City: Louangphrabang

Religions: Buddhist, animism

Languages: Lao (official), French, English

Geographical Facts: Landlocked; most of the country is mountainous and thickly forested; the Mekong River forms a large part of the western boundary with Thailand.

History: In 1975, the communist Pathet Lao took control of the government, ending a six-century-old monarchy. Initial closer ties to Vietnam and socialization were replaced with a gradual return to private enterprise, an easing of foreign investment laws, and the admission into the Association of Southeast Asia Nations (ASEAN) in 1997.

Latvia

Capital: Riga

Religions: Lutheran, Roman Catholic, Russian Orthodox

Languages: Lao (official), French, English

Geographical Facts: Most of the country is composed of fertile, low-lying plains, with some hills in the east.

History: After a brief period of independence between the two world wars, Latvia was annexed by the USSR in 1940. Latvia reestablished its independence in 1991, following the breakup of the Soviet Union. Although the last Russian troops left in 1994, the status of the Russian minority (some 30 percent of the population) remains of concern to Moscow. Latvia continues to revamp its economy for eventual integration into various Western European political and economic institutions.

Lebanon

Capital: Beirut

Major City: Tripoli

Religion: Muslim

Languages: Arabic (official), French, English, Armenian

Geographical Facts: Nahr al Litani is the only major river in Near East not crossing an international boundary; rugged terrain historically helped isolate, protect, and develop numerous factional groups based on religion, clan, and ethnicity.

History: Lebanon has made progress toward rebuilding its political institutions and regaining its national sovereignty since 1991 and the end of the devastating sixteen-year civil war. Under the Ta'if Accord—the blueprint for national reconciliation—the Lebanese have established a more equitable political system, particularly by giving Muslims a greater say in the political process while institutionalizing sectarian divisions in the government. Since the end of the war, the Lebanese have conducted several successful elections, most of the militias have been weakened or disbanded, and the Lebanese Armed Forces (LAF) have extended central government authority over about two-thirds of the country. Hizballah, the radical Shiite party, retains its weapons. Syria maintains about twenty-five thousand troops in Lebanon based mainly in Beirut, North Lebanon, and the Bekaa Valley. Syria's troop deployment was legitimized by the Arab League during Lebanon's civil war and in the Ta'if Accord. Damascus justifies its continued military presence in Lebanon by citing the continued weakness of the LAF, Beirut's requests, and the failure of the Lebanese government to implement all of the constitutional reforms in the Ta'if Accord. Israel's withdrawal from its security zone in southern Lebanon in May 2000, however, has emboldened some Lebanese Christians and Druze to demand that Syria withdraw its forces as well.

Lesotho

Capital: Maseru

Religions: Christian, indigenous beliefs

Languages: Sesotho (southern Sotho), English (official), Zulu, Xhosa

Geographical Facts: Landlocked, completely surrounded by South Africa; mountainous, more than 80 percent of the country is 5,900 feet above sea level.

History: Basutoland was renamed the Kingdom of Lesotho upon independence from the United Kingdom in 1966. Constitutional government was restored in 1993, after twenty-three years of military rule.

Liberia

Capital: Monrovia

Religions: Indigenous beliefs, Christian, Muslim

Languages: English (official), some twenty ethnic group languages

Geographical Facts: Facing the Atlantic Ocean, the coastline is characterized by lagoons, mangrove swamps, and river-deposited sandbars; the inland grassy plateau supports limited agriculture.

History: Seven years of civil strife were brought to a close in 1996, when free and open presidential and legislative elections were held. A still-unsettled domestic security situation has slowed the process of rebuilding the social and economic structure of this war-torn country.

Libya

Capital: Tripoli

Religion: Sunni Muslim

Languages: Arabic, Italian, English

Geographical Fact: More than 90 percent of the country is desert or semidesert.

History: Since he took power in a 1969 military coup, Colonel Mu'ammar Gadhafi has developed his own political system—a combination of socialism and Islam—which he calls the Third International Theory. Viewing himself as a revolutionary leader, he used oil funds during the 1970s and 1980s to promote his ideology outside Libya, even supporting subversives and terrorists abroad to hasten the end of Marxism and capitalism. Libyan military adventures failed; for example, the prolonged foray of Libyan troops into the Aozou Strip in northern Chad was finally repulsed in 1987. Libyan support for terrorism decreased after UN sanctions were imposed in 1992. Those sanctions were suspended in April 1999.

Liechtenstein

Capital: Vaduz

Religion: Roman Catholic

Languages: German (official), Alemannic dialect

Geographical Facts: Along with Uzbekistan, one of only two doubly landlocked countries in the world (surrounded by landlocked countries); variety of microclimatic variations based on elevation.

History: The Principality of Liechtenstein was established within the Holy Roman Empire in 1719; it became a sovereign state in 1806. Until the end of World War I, it was closely tied to Austria, but the economic devastation caused by that conflict forced Liechtenstein to conclude a customs and monetary union with Switzerland. Since World War II (in which Liechtenstein remained neutral), the country's low taxes have spurred outstanding economic growth. However, shortcomings in banking regulatory oversight have resulted in concerns about the use of the financial institutions for money laundering.

Lithuania

Capital: Vilnius

Major City: Kaunas

Religion: Roman Catholic

Languages: Lithuanian (official), Polish, Russian

Geographical Facts: Fertile central plains are separated by hilly uplands that are ancient glacial deposits.

History: Independent between the two world wars, Lithuania was annexed by the USSR in 1940. On March 11, 1990, Lithuania became the first of the Soviet republics to declare its independence, but this proclamation was not generally recognized until September 1991 (following the abortive coup in Moscow). The last Russian troops withdrew in 1993. Lithuania has subsequently restructured its economy for eventual integration into Western European institutions.

Luxembourg

Capital: Luxembourg

Religion: Roman Catholic

Languages: Luxembourgish (national language), German (administrative language), French (administrative language)

Geographical Facts: Landlocked; the only grand duchy in the world, it is the smallest of the European Union member states.

History: Founded in A.D. 963, Luxembourg became a grand duchy in 1815 and an independent state under the Netherlands. It lost more than half of its territory to Belgium in 1839, but gained a larger measure of autonomy. Full independence was attained in 1867. Overrun by Germany in both world wars, it ended its neutrality in 1948, when it entered into the Benelux Customs Union and then when it joined NATO the following year. In 1957, Luxembourg became one of the six founding countries of the European Economic Community (later the European Union), and in 1999, it joined the euro currency area.

Macedonia

Capital: Skopje

Religions: Macedonian Orthodox, Muslim

Languages: Macedonian, Albanian

Geographical Facts: Landlocked; major transportation corridor from western and central Europe to Aegean Sea and southern Europe to western Europe.

History: International recognition of the Former Yugoslav Republic of Macedonia's (FYROM) independence from Yugoslavia in 1991 was delayed by Greece's objection to the new state's use of what it considered a Greek name and symbols. Greece finally lifted its trade blockade in 1995, and the two countries agreed to normalize relations, despite continued disagreement over FYROM's use of "Macedonia." FYROM's large Albanian minority and the de facto independence of neighboring Kosovo continue to be sources of ethnic tension.

Madagascar

Capital: Antananarivo

Religions: Indigenous beliefs, Christian

Languages: French (official), Malagasy (official)

Geographical Facts: World's fourth-largest island; strategic location along Mozambique Channel.

History: Formerly an independent kingdom, Madagascar became a French colony in 1886, but regained its independence in 1960. During 1992–1993, free presidential and National Assembly elections were held, ending seventeen years of single-party rule. In 1997, in the second presidential race, Didier Ratsiraka, the leader during the 1970s and 1980s, was returned to the presidency.

Malawi

Capital: Lilongwe

Major City: Blantyre

Religions: Protestant, Roman Catholic, Muslim

Languages: English (official), Chichewa (official)

Geographical Facts: Landlocked; Lake Nyasa, some 360 miles long, is the country's most prominent physical feature.

History: Established in 1891, the British protectorate of Nyasaland became the independent nation of Malawi in 1964. After three decades of one-party rule, the country held multiparty elections in 1994, under a provisional constitution, which took full effect the following year. National multiparty elections were held again in 1999.

Malaysia

Capital: Kuala Lumpur

Religions: Muslim, Buddhist, Daoist, Hindu, Christian, Sikh

Languages: Bahasa Melayu (official), English, Chinese dialects

Geographical Facts: Strategic location along Strait of Malacca and southern South China Sea.

History: Malaysia was created in 1963 through the merging of Malaya (independent in 1957) and the former British Singapore, both of which formed West Malaysia, and Sabah and Sarawak in north Borneo, which composed East Malaysia. The first three years of independence were marred by hostilities with Indonesia. Singapore separated from the union in 1965.

Maldives

Capital: Male

Religion: Sunni Muslim

Language: Maldivian Dhivehi (dialect of Sinhala)

Geographical Facts: 1,190 coral islands grouped into 26 atolls (200 inhabited islands, plus 80 islands with tourist resorts); archipelago of strategic location astride and along major sealanes in Indian Ocean.

History: The Maldives were long a sultanate, first under Dutch and then under British protection. They became a republic in 1968, three years after independence. Tourism and fishing are being developed on the archipelago.

Mali

Capital: Bamako

Religion: Muslim

Languages: French (official), Bambara

Geographical Facts: Landlocked; divided into three natural zones: the southern, cultivated Sudanese; the central, semiarid Sahelian; and the northern, arid Saharan.

History: The Sudanese Republic and Senegal became independent of France in 1960 as the Mali Federation. When Senegal withdrew after only a few months, the Sudanese Republic was renamed Mali. Rule by dictatorship was brought to a close in 1991 with a transitional government. In 1992, Mali's first democratic presidential election was held.

Malta

Capital: Valletta

Religion: Roman Catholic

Languages: Maltese (official), English (official)

Geographical Facts: The country is composed of an archipelago, with only the three largest islands (Malta, Ghawdex or Gozo, and Kemmuna or Comino) being inhabited; numerous bays provide good harbors; Malta and Tunisia are discussing the commercial exploitation of the continental shelf between their countries, particularly for oil exploration.

History: Great Britain formally acquired possession of Malta in 1814. The island staunchly supported the United Kingdom through both world wars and remained in the Commonwealth when Malta became independent in 1964. A decade later, Malta became a republic. Over the past fifteen years, the island has become a major freight transshipment point, financial center, and tourist destination. It is an official candidate for EU membership.

Marshall Islands

Capital: Majuro

Religion: Protestant

Languages: English (official), two major Marshallese dialects, Japanese

Geographical Facts: Two archipelagic island chains of 30 atolls and 1,152 islands; Bikini and Eniwetok are former U.S. nuclear test sites; Kwajalein, the famous World War II battleground, is now used as a U.S. missile test range.

History: After almost four decades under U.S. administration as the easternmost part of the UN Trust Territory of the Pacific Islands, the Marshall Islands attained independence in 1986 under a Compact of Free Association. Compensation claims continue as a result of U.S. nuclear testing on some of the islands between 1947 and 1962.

Mauritania

Capital: Nouakchott

Religion: Muslim

Languages: Hasaniya Arabic (official), Pular, Soninke, Wolof (official), French

Geographical Facts: Most of the population concentrated in the cities of Nouakchott and Nouadhibou and along the Senegal River in the southern part of the country.

History: Independent from France in 1960, Mauritania annexed the southern third of the former Spanish Sahara (now Western Sahara) in 1976, but relinquished it after three years of raids by the Polisario guerrilla front seeking independence for the territory. Opposition parties were legalized and a new constitution approved in 1991. Two multiparty presidential elections since then were widely seen as being flawed; Mauritania remains, in reality, a one-party state. The country continues to experience ethnic tensions between its black minority population and the dominant Maur (Arab-Berber) populace.

Mauritius

Capital: Port Louis

Religions: Hindu, Roman Catholic

Languages: English (official), Creole, French, Hindi, Urdu, Hakka, Bojpoori

Geographical Facts: The main island, from which the country derives its name, is of volcanic origin and is almost entirely surrounded by coral reefs.

History: Discovered by the Portuguese in 1505, Mauritius was subsequently held by the Dutch, French, and British before independence was attained in 1968. A stable democracy with regular free elections and a positive human rights record, the country has attracted considerable foreign investment and has earned one of Africa's highest per capita incomes. Poor weather and declining sugar prices have slowed economic growth, leading to some protests over standards of living in the Creole community.

Mexico

Capital: Mexico City

Major Cities: Puebla, Guadalajara, Monterrey

Religion: Roman Catholic

Languages: Spanish, various Mayan, Nahuatl

Geographical Facts: Sierra Madre Mountains, Yucatán Peninsula, Grijalva River, Usumacinta River, Rio Bravo (Rio Grande in United States).

History: The site of advanced Amerindian civilizations, Mexico came under Spanish rule for three centuries before achieving independence early in the nineteenth century. A devaluation of the peso in late 1994 threw Mexico into economic turmoil, triggering the worst recession in over half a century. The nation continues to make an impressive recovery. Ongoing economic and social concerns include low real wages, underemployment for a large segment of the population, inequitable income distribution, and few advancement opportunities for the largely Amerindian population in the impoverished southern states.

Micronesia

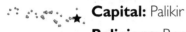

Capital: Palikir

Religions: Roman Catholic, Protestant

Languages: English (official), Trukese, Pohnpeian, Yapese, Kosrean

Geographical Facts: Four major island groups totaling 607 islands.

History: In 1979, the Federated States of Micronesia, a UN Trust Territory under U.S. administration, adopted a constitution. In 1986, independence was attained under a Compact of Free Association with the United States. Present concerns include large-scale unemployment, overfishing, and overdependence on U.S. aid.

Moldova

Capital: Chisinau

Religion: Eastern Orthodox

Languages: Moldovan (official), Russian, Gagauz (a Turkish dialect)

Geographical Facts: Landlocked; well endowed with various sedimentary rocks and minerals, including sand, gravel, gypsum, and limestone.

History: Formerly ruled by Romania, Moldova became part of the Soviet Union at the close of World War II. Although independent from the USSR since 1991, Russian forces have remained on Moldovan territory east of the Nistru (Dniester) River, supporting the Slavic majority population, mostly Ukrainians and Russians, who have proclaimed a "Transnistria" republic. One of the poorest nations in Europe and plagued by a moribund economy, in 2001 Moldova became the first former Soviet state to elect a communist as its president.

Monaco

Capital: Monaco

Religion: Roman Catholic

Languages: French (official), English, Italian, Monegasque

Geographical Facts: Second-smallest independent state in the world (after Vatican City); almost entirely urban.

History: Economic development was spurred in the late nineteenth century with a railroad linkup to France and the opening of a casino. Since then, the principality's mild climate, splendid scenery, and gambling facilities have made Monaco world famous as a tourist and recreation center.

Mongolia

Capital: Ulan Bator

Religion: Tibetan Buddhist Lamaism

Language: Khalkha Mongol

Geographical Facts: Landlocked; strategic location between China and Russia; the world's least densely populated country.

History: Long a province of China, Mongolia won its independence in 1921 with Soviet backing. A communist regime was installed in 1924. During the early 1990s, the ex-communist Mongolian People's Revolutionary Party (MPRP) gradually yielded its monopoly on power. In 1996, the Democratic Union Coalition (DUC) defeated the MPRP in a national election. During the next four years, the Coalition implemented a number of key reforms to modernize the economy and institutionalize democratic reforms. The former communists, however, were a strong opposition that stalled additional reforms and made implementation difficult. In 2000, the MPRP won seventy-two of the seventy-six seats in Parliament and completely reshuffled the government. Although it continues many of the reform policies, the MPRP is focusing on social welfare and public order priorities.

Morocco

Capital: Rabat

Major Cities: Casablanca, Fez, Marrakech

Religion: Muslim

Languages: Arabic (official), Berber dialects

Geographical Fact: Strategic location along Strait of Gibraltar.

History: Morocco's long struggle for independence from France ended in 1956. The internationalized city of Tangier was turned over to the new country that same year. Morocco virtually annexed Western Sahara during the late 1970s, but final resolution on the status of the territory remains unresolved. Gradual political reforms in the 1990s resulted in the establishment of a bicameral legislature in 1997.

Mozambique

Capital: Maputo

Religions: Indigenous beliefs, Christian, Muslim

Languages: Portuguese (official), indigenous dialects

Geographical Facts: The mighty Zambezi flows through the north-central and most fertile part of the country.

History: Almost five centuries as a Portuguese colony came to a close with independence in 1975. Large-scale emigration by whites, economic dependence on South Africa, a severe drought, and a prolonged civil war hindered the country's development. The ruling party formally abandoned Marxism in 1989, and a new constitution the following year provided for multiparty elections and a free-market economy. A UN-negotiated peace agreement with rebel forces ended the fighting in 1992.

Myanmar (Burma)

Capital: Yangon (Rangoon)

Major City: Mandalay

Religion: Buddhist

Language: Burmese

Geographical Fact: Strategic location near major Indian Ocean shipping lanes.

History: Despite multiparty elections in 1990 that resulted in the main opposition party winning a decisive victory, the military junta ruling the country refused to hand over power. Key opposition leader and Nobel Peace Prize recipient Aung San Suu Kyi, under house arrest from 1989 to 1995, was again placed under house detention in September 2000; her supporters are routinely harassed or jailed.

Namibia

Capital: Windhoek

Religion: Christian

Languages: English (official), Afrikaans, German, indigenous languages, Oshivambo, Herero, Nama

Geographical Facts: First country in the world to incorporate the protection of the environment into its constitution; some 14 percent of the land is protected, including virtually the entire Namib Desert coastal strip.

History: South Africa occupied the German colony of Sud-West Afrika during World War I and administered it as a mandate until after World War II, when it annexed the territory. In 1966, the Marxist South-West Africa People's Organization (SWAPO) guerrilla group launched a war of independence for the area that was soon named Namibia; but it was not until 1988 that South Africa agreed to end its administration in accordance with a UN peace plan for the entire region. Independence came in 1990.

Nauru

Capital: Yaren

Religions: Protestant, Roman Catholic

Language: Nauruan (official)

Geographical Facts: Nauru is one of the three great phosphate rock islands in the Pacific Ocean; the others are Banaba (Ocean Island) in Kiribati and Makatea in French Polynesia; only 33 miles south of the equator.

History: Nauru's phosphate deposits began to be mined early in the twentieth century by a German-British consortium; the island was occupied by Australian forces in World War I. Upon achieving independence in 1968, Nauru became the smallest independent republic in the world; it joined the United Nations in 1999.

Nepal

Capital: Kathmandu

Major City: Darjeeling

Religion: Hindu

Language: Nepali (official)

Geographical Facts: Landlocked; strategic location between China and India; contains eight of world's ten highest peaks, including Mount Everest on the border with China, which is the world's tallest.

History: In 1951, the Nepalese monarch ended the century-old system of rule by hereditary premiers and instituted a cabinet system of government. Reforms in 1990 established a multiparty democracy within the framework of a constitutional monarchy. The refugee issue of some 100,000 Bhutanese in Nepal remains unresolved; 90 percent of these displaced persons are housed in seven UN Offices of the High Commissioner for Refugees (UNHCR) camps.

Netherlands

Capitals: Amsterdam (de jure), The Hague (de facto)

Major Cities: Utrecht, Rotterdam

Religions: Roman Catholic, Protestant

Language: Dutch

Geographical Facts: Located at mouths of three major European rivers (Rhine, Maas or Meuse, and Schelde).

History: The Kingdom of the Netherlands was formed in 1815. In 1830, Belgium seceded and formed a separate kingdom. The Netherlands remained neutral in World War I but suffered a brutal invasion and occupation by Germany in World War II. A modern, industrialized nation, the Netherlands is also a large exporter of agricultural products. The country was a founding member of NATO and the EC and participated in the introduction of the euro in 1999.

New Zealand

Capital: Wellington

Major Cities: Auckland, Christchurch

Religions: Anglican, Presbyterian, Roman Catholic

Languages: English (official), Maori (official)

Geographical Facts: About 80 percent of the population lives in cities; Wellington is the southernmost national capital in the world.

History: The British colony of New Zealand became an independent dominion in 1907 and supported the United Kingdom militarily in both world wars. New Zealand withdrew from a number of defense alliances during the 1970s and 1980s. In recent years, the government has sought to address longstanding native Maori grievances. (The Maori are indigenous New Zealanders.)

Nicaragua

Capital: Managua

Major City: Leon

Religion: Roman Catholic

Language: Spanish (official)

Geographical Facts: Largest country in Central America; contains the largest freshwater body in Central America, Lago de Nicaragua.

History: Settled as a Spanish colony in the 1520s, Nicaragua gained its independence in 1821. Violent opposition to governmental manipulation and corruption spread to all classes by 1978 and resulted in a short-lived civil war that brought the Marxist Sandinista guerrillas to power in 1979. Nicaraguan aid to leftist rebels in El Salvador caused the United States to sponsor anti-Sandinista contra guerrillas through much of the 1980s. Free elections in 1990 and again in 1996 saw the Sandinistas defeated. The country has slowly rebuilt its economy during the 1990s, but was hard hit by Hurricane Mitch in 1998.

Niger

Capital: Niamey

Religion: Muslim

Languages: French (official), Hausa, Djerma

Geographical Facts: Landlocked; one of the hottest countries in the world: northern four-fifths is desert, southern one-fifth is savanna, suitable for livestock and limited agriculture.

History: Not until 1993, thirty-three years after independence from France, did Niger hold its first free and open elections. A 1995 peace accord ended a five-year Tuareg insurgency in the north. Coups in 1996 and 1999 were followed by the creation of a National Reconciliation Council that effected a transition to civilian rule in December 1999.

Nigeria

Capital: Abuja

Major Cities: Ibadan, Lagos

Religions: Muslim, Christian

Languages: English (official), Hausa, Yoruba, Igbo (Ibo), Fulani

Geographical Facts: The Niger enters the country in the northwest and flows southward through tropical rain forests and swamps to its delta in the Gulf of Guinea.

History: Following nearly sixteen years of military rule, a new constitution was adopted in 1999 and a peaceful transition to civilian government completed. The new president faces the daunting task of rebuilding a petroleum-based economy, whose revenues have been squandered through corruption and mismanagement, and institutionalizing democracy. In addition, the Obasanjo administration must defuse long-standing ethnic and religious tensions if it is to build a sound foundation for economic growth and political stability.

Norway

Capital: Oslo

Major Cities: Bergen, Trondheim

Religion: Evangelical Lutheran

Language: Norwegian (official)

Geographical Facts: About two-thirds mountains; some fifty thousand islands off its much-indented coastline; strategic location adjacent to sealanes and air routes in North Atlantic; one of most rugged and longest coastlines in the world; Norway is the only NATO member having a land boundary with Russia.

History: Despite its neutrality, Norway was not able to avoid occupation by Germany in World War II. In 1949, neutrality was abandoned, and Norway became a member of NATO. Discovery of oil and gas in adjacent waters in the late 1960s boosted Norway's economic fortunes. The current focus is on containing spending on the extensive welfare system and planning for the time when petroleum reserves are depleted. In referenda held in 1972 and 1994, Norway rejected joining the EU.

Oman

Capital: Muscat

Religion: Ibadhi Muslim

Languages: Arabic (official), English, Baluchi, Urdu, Indian dialects

Geographical Facts: Strategic location on Musandam Peninsula adjacent to Strait of Hormuz, a vital transit point for world crude oil.

History: In 1970, Qaboos bin Said Al Said ousted his father and has ruled as sultan ever since. His extensive modernization program has opened the country to the outside world and has preserved a long-standing political and military relationship with the United Kingdom. Oman's moderate, independent foreign policy has sought to maintain good relations with all Middle Eastern countries.

Pakistan

Capital: Islamabad

Major Cities: Hyderabad, Karachi, Lahore

Religions: Sunni Muslim, Shiite Muslim

Languages: Punjabi, Sindhi

Geographical Facts: Controls Khyber Pass and Bolan Pass, traditional invasion routes between central Asia and the Indian subcontinent.

History: The separation in 1947 of British India into the Muslim state of Pakistan (with two sections West and East) and largely Hindu India was never satisfactorily resolved. A third war between these countries in 1971 resulted in East Pakistan seceding and becoming the separate nation of Bangladesh. A dispute over the state of Kashmir is ongoing. In response to Indian nuclear weapons testing, Pakistan conducted its own tests in 1998.

Palau

Capital: Koror

Religions: Christian, Modekngei (indigenous)

Languages: English, Palauan

Geographical Facts: Westernmost archipelago in the Caroline chain, consists of six island groups totaling over two hundred islands; includes World War II battleground of Beliliou (Peleliu) and world-famous rock islands.

History: After three decades as part of the UN Trust Territory of the Pacific under U.S. administration, this westernmost cluster of the Caroline Islands opted for independent status in 1978 rather than join the Federated States of Micronesia. A Compact of Free Association with the United States was approved in 1986, but not ratified until 1993. It went into force the following year when the islands gained their independence.

Panama

Capital: Panama City

Major City: Colon

Religion: Roman Catholic

Language: Spanish (official)

Geographical Facts: Strategic location on eastern end of isthmus forming land bridge connecting North and South America; controls Panama Canal that links North Atlantic Ocean via Caribbean Sea with North Pacific Ocean.

History: With U.S. backing, Panama seceded from Colombia in 1903 and promptly signed a treaty with the United States allowing for the construction of a canal and U.S. sovereignty over a strip of land on either side of the structure (the Panama Canal Zone). The U.S. Army Corps of Engineers built the Panama Canal between 1904 and 1914. On September 7, 1977, an agreement was signed for the complete transfer of the Canal from the United States to Panama by the end of 1999. Certain portions of the zone and increasing responsibility over the Canal were turned over in the intervening years. With U.S. military help, dictator Manuel Noriega was ousted in 1989. The entire Panama Canal, the area supporting the Canal, and remaining U.S. military bases were turned over to Panama by or on December 31, 1999.

Papua New Guinea

Capital: Port Moresby

Religions: Roman Catholic, Lutheran

Languages: Pidgin English widespread, 715 indigenous languages

Geographical Facts: Shares island of New Guinea with Indonesia; one of the world's largest swamps along southwest coast.

History: The eastern half of the island of New Guinea—second largest island in the world—was divided between Germany (north) and the United Kingdom (south) in 1885. The southern area was transferred in 1902 to Australia, which occupied the northern portion during World War I and continued to administer the combined areas until independence in 1975. A nine-year secessionist revolt on the island of Bougainville ended in 1997, after claiming some twenty thousand lives.

Paraguay

Capital: Asunción

Religion: Roman Catholic

Languages: Spanish (official), Guarani (official)

Geographical Facts: Landlocked; lies between Argentina, Bolivia, and Brazil; population concentrated in southern part of country.

History: In the disastrous War of the Triple Alliance (1865–1870), Paraguay lost two-thirds of all adult males and much of its territory. It stagnated economically for the next half century. In the Chaco War of 1932–1935, large, economically important areas were won from Bolivia. The thirty-five-year military dictatorship of Alfredo Stroessner was overthrown in 1989, and, despite a marked increase in political infighting in recent years, relatively free and regular presidential elections have been held since then.

Peru

Capital: Lima

Religion: Roman Catholic

Languages: Spanish (official), Quechua (official), Aymara

Geographical Facts: Shares control of Lake Titicaca, world's highest navigable lake, with Bolivia; remote Lake McIntyre is the ultimate source of the Amazon River.

History: After a dozen years of military rule, Peru returned to democratic leadership in 1980. In recent years, bold reform programs and significant progress in curtailing guerrilla activity and drug trafficking have resulted in solid economic growth.

Philippines

Capital: Manila

Major Cities: Cebu, Davao, Quezon City

Religion: Roman Catholic

Languages: Filipino (based on Tagalog), English

Geographical Facts: Favorably located in relation to many of Southeast Asia's main water bodies: the South China Sea, Philippine Sea, Sulu Sea, Celebes Sea, and Luzon Strait.

History: The Philippines were ceded by Spain to the United States in 1898, following the Spanish-American War. They attained their independence in 1946 after being occupied by the Japanese in World War II. The twenty-one-year rule of Ferdinand Marcos ended in 1986 when a widespread popular rebellion forced him into exile. In 1992, the United States closed down its last military bases on the islands. The government continues to struggle with ongoing Muslim insurgencies in the south.

Poland

Capital: Warsaw

Major Cities: Lodz, Kraków

Religion: Roman Catholic

Language: Polish

Geographical Facts: Historically, an area of conflict because of flat terrain and the lack of natural barriers on the north European plain.

History: Poland gained its independence in 1918, only to be overrun by Germany and the Soviet Union in World War II. It became a Soviet satellite country following the war, but one that was comparatively tolerant and progressive. Labor turmoil in 1980 led to the formation of the independent trade union "Solidarity," which over time became a political force and by 1990 had swept parliamentary elections and the presidency. A "shock therapy" program during the early 1990s enabled the country to transform its economy into one of the most robust in Central Europe, boosting hopes for acceptance to the EU. Poland joined the NATO alliance in 1999.

Portugal

Capital: Lisbon

Major City: Porto

Religion: Roman Catholic

Language: Portuguese

Geographical Facts: Azores and Madeira Islands, controlled by Portugal, occupy strategic locations along western sea approaches to Strait of Gibraltar.

History: Following its heyday as a world power during the fifteenth and sixteenth centuries, Portugal lost much of its wealth and status with the destruction of Lisbon in a 1755 earthquake, occupation during the Napoleonic Wars, and the independence in 1822 of Brazil as a colony. A 1910 revolution deposed the monarchy; for most of the next six decades, repressive governments ran the country. In 1974, a left-wing military coup installed broad democratic reforms. The following year, Portugal granted independence to all of its African colonies. Portugal entered the EC in 1985.

Qatar

Capital: Doha

Religion: Muslim

Languages: Arabic (official), English

Geographical Fact: Strategic location in central Persian Gulf near major petroleum deposits.

History: Ruled by the Al Thani family since the mid-1800s, Qatar transformed itself from a poor British protectorate noted mainly for pearling into an independent state with significant oil and natural gas revenues. During the late 1980s and early 1990s, the Qatari economy was crippled by a continuous siphoning off of petroleum revenues by the emir, who had ruled the country since 1972. He was overthrown by his son in a bloodless coup in 1995. In 2001, Qatar resolved its longstanding border disputes with both Bahrain and Saudi Arabia. Oil and natural gas revenues enable Qatar to have a per capita income not far below the leading industrial countries of Western Europe.

Romania

Capital: Bucharest

Religion: Romanian Orthodox

Languages: Romanian, Hungarian, German

Geographical Fact: Controls most easily traversable land route between the Balkans, Moldova, and Ukraine.

History: Soviet occupation following World War II led to the formation of a communist "peoples republic" in 1947 and the abdication of the king. The decades-long rule of President Nicolae Ceaușescu became increasingly draconian through the 1980s. He was overthrown and executed in late 1989. Former communists dominated the government until 1996, when they were swept from power. Much economic restructuring remains to be carried out before Romania can achieve its hope of joining the EU.

Russia

Capital: Moscow

Major Cities: St. Petersburg, Vladivostok, Nizhni Novgorod, Novosibirsk

Religion: Russian Orthodox

Language: Russian

Geographical Facts: Largest country in the world in terms of area but unfavorably located in relation to major sealanes of the world; despite its size, much of the country lacks proper soils and climates (either too cold or too dry) for agriculture; Mount Elbrus is Europe's tallest peak.

History: The defeat of the Russian Empire in World War I led to the seizure of power by the communists (the Bolshevik Revolution, in which the czar and his family were murdered) and the formation of the USSR. The brutal rule of Josef Stalin (1924–1953), which included forced labor camps and severe crackdowns on government opposition, strengthened Russian dominance of the Soviet Union at a cost of tens of millions of lives. The Soviet economy and society stagnated in the following decades until General Secretary Mikhail Gorbachev (1985–1991) introduced glasnost ("openness") and perestroika ("restructuring") in an attempt to modernize communism. But his initiatives inadvertently released forces that, by December 1991, splintered the USSR into fifteen independent republics. Since then, Russia has struggled in its efforts to build a democratic political system and market economy to replace the strict social, political, and economic controls of the communist period.

Rwanda

Capital: Kigali

Religions: Roman Catholic, Protestant

Languages: Kinyarwanda (official), French (official), English (official), Kiswahili (Swahili)

Geographical Facts: Landlocked; most of the country is savanna grassland, with the population predominantly rural.

History: In 1959, three years before independence, the majority ethnic group, the Hutus, overthrew the ruling Tutsi king. Over the next several years, thousands of Tutsis were killed, and some 150,000 were driven into exile in neighboring countries. The children of these exiles later formed a rebel group, the Rwandan Patriotic Front (RPF), and began a civil war in 1990. The war, along with several political and economic upheavals, exacerbated ethnic tensions, culminating, in April 1994, in the genocide of roughly 800,000 Tutsis and moderate Hutus. The Tutsi rebels defeated the Hutu regime and ended the killing in July 1994, but approximately 2 million Hutu refugees—many fearing Tutsi retribution—fled to neighboring Burundi, Tanzania, Uganda, and Zaire, now called the Democratic Republic of the Congo (DROC). Since then, most of the refugees have returned to Rwanda. Despite substantial international assistance and political reforms, including Rwanda's first local elections in March 1999, the country continues to struggle to boost investment and agricultural output and to foster reconciliation. A series of massive population displacements, a nagging Hutu extremist insurgency, and Rwandan involvement in two wars over the past four years in the neighboring DROC continue to hinder Rwanda's efforts.

Samoa

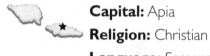

Capital: Apia

Religion: Christian

Language: Samoan (Polynesian), English

Geographical Fact: Occupies an almost central position within Polynesia.

History: New Zealand occupied the German protectorate of Western Samoa at the outbreak of World War I. It continued to administer the islands as a mandate and then as a trust territory until 1962, when the islands became the first Polynesian nation to reestablish independence in the twentieth century. The country dropped the "Western" from its name in 1997.

San Marino

Capital: San Marino

Religion: Roman Catholic

Language: Italian

Geographical Facts: Landlocked; smallest independent state in Europe after Vatican City and Monaco; dominated by the Apennines.

History: The third smallest state in Europe (after Vatican City and Monaco) also claims to be the world's oldest republic. According to tradition, it was founded by a Christian stonemason named Marinus in A.D. 301. San Marino's foreign policy is aligned with that of Italy. Social and political trends in the republic also track closely with those of its larger neighbor.

São Tomé and Principe

Capital: São Tomé

Religions: Roman Catholic, Protestant

Language: Portuguese (official)

Geographical Facts: The smallest country in Africa; the two main islands form part of a chain of extinct volcanoes, and both are fairly mountainous.

History: Discovered and claimed by Portugal in the late fifteenth century, the islands' sugar-based economy gave way to coffee and cocoa in the nineteenth century—all grown with plantation slave labor, a form of which lingered into the twentieth century. Although independence was achieved in 1975, democratic reforms were not instituted until the late 1980s. The first free elections were held in 1991.

Saudi Arabia

Capital: Riyadh

Major Cities: Jeddah, Mecca, Medina

Religion: Muslim

Language: Arabic

Geographical Facts: Extensive coastlines on Persian Gulf and Red Sea provide great leverage on shipping (especially crude oil) through Persian Gulf and Suez Canal.

History: In 1902, Abdul al-Aziz Ibn Sa'ūd captured Riyadh and set out on a thirty-year campaign to unify the Arabian Peninsula. In the 1930s, the discovery of oil transformed the country. Following Iraq's invasion of Kuwait in 1990, Saudi Arabia accepted the Kuwaiti royal family and four hundred thousand refugees while allowing Western and Arab troops to deploy on its soil for the liberation of Kuwait the following year. A burgeoning population, aquifer depletion, and an economy largely dependent on petroleum output and prices are all major governmental concerns.

Senegal

Capital: Dakar

Major Cities: St. Louis, Kaolack

Religion: Muslim

Languages: French (official), Wolof, Pulaar, Jola, Mandinka

Geographical Facts: Westernmost country on the African continent; Gambia is almost an enclave of Senegal.

History: Independent from France in 1960, Senegal joined with Gambia to form the nominal confederation of Senegambia in 1982. However, the envisaged integration of the two countries was never carried out, and the union was dissolved in 1989. Despite peace talks, a southern separatist group sporadically has clashed with government forces since 1982. Senegal has a long history of participating in international peacekeeping.

Seychelles

Capital: Victoria

Religion: Roman Catholic

Languages: English (official), French (official), Creole

Geographical Facts: Forty granitic and about fifty coralline islands.

History: A lengthy struggle between France and Great Britain for the islands ended in 1814, when they were ceded to the latter. Independence came in 1976. Socialist rule was brought to a close with a new constitution and free elections in 1993.

Sierra Leone

Capital: Freetown

Religions: Muslim, indigenous beliefs

Languages: English (official), Mende, Temne, Krio (English-based Creole, spoken by the descendants of freed Jamaican slaves who were settled in the Freetown area, a lingua franca)

Geographical Facts: Rainfall along the coast can reach 195 inches a year, making it one of the wettest places along coastal, western Africa.

History: Since 1991, an ongoing civil war between the government and the Revolutionary United Front (RUF) has resulted in tens of thousands of deaths and the displacement of more than two million people (well over one-third of the population), many of whom are now refugees in neighboring countries. A peace agreement, signed in July 1999, collapsed in May 2000 after the RUF took more than five hundred UN peacekeepers hostage.

Singapore

Capital: Singapore

Religions: Buddhist, Muslim

Languages: Chinese (official), Malay (official and national), Tamil (official), English (official)

Geographical Fact: Focal point for Southeast Asian sea routes.

History: Founded as a British trading colony in 1819, Singapore joined Malaysia in 1963, but withdrew two years later and became independent. It subsequently became one of the world's most prosperous countries, with strong international trading links (its port is one of the world's busiest) and with per capita GDP above that of the leading nations of Western Europe.

Slovakia

Capital: Bratislava

Major City: Kosice

Religion: Roman Catholic

Languages: Slovak (official), Hungarian

Geographical Facts: Landlocked; most of the country is rugged and mountainous; the Tatra Mountains in the north are interspersed with many scenic lakes and valleys.

History: In 1918, the Slovaks joined the closely related Czechs to form Czechoslovakia. Following the chaos of World War II, Czechoslovakia became a communist nation within Soviet-ruled Eastern Europe. Soviet influence collapsed in 1989, and Czechoslovakia once more became free. The Slovaks and the Czechs agreed to separate peacefully on January 1, 1993, in their "velvet divorce." Historic, political, and geographic factors have caused Slovakia to experience more difficulty in developing a modern market economy than some of its Central European neighbors.

Slovenia

Capital: Ljubljana

Religion: Roman Catholic

Language: Slovenian

Geographical Facts: Despite its small size, this eastern Alpine country controls some of Europe's major transit routes.

History: In 1918, the Slovenes joined the Serbs and Croats in forming a new nation, the kingdom of Serbs, Croats, and Slovenes. The union was renamed Yugoslavia in 1929. After World War II, Slovenia became a communist nation that distanced itself from Moscow's rule. Dissatisfied with the majority Serbs' exercise of power, the Slovenes succeeded in establishing their independence in 1991. Historical ties to Western Europe, a strong economy, and a stable democracy make Slovenia a leading candidate for future membership in the EU and NATO.

Solomon Islands

Capital: Honiara

Religions: Anglican, Roman Catholic

Languages: Melanesian pidgin (lingua franca), 120 indigenous languages

Geographical Facts: Strategic location on sea routes between the South Pacific Ocean, the Solomon Sea, and the Coral Sea.

History: The United Kingdom established a protectorate over the Solomon Islands in the 1890s. Some of the bitterest fighting of World War II occurred on these islands. Self-government was achieved in 1976 and independence two years later. Current issues include government deficits, deforestation, and malaria control.

Somalia

Capital: Mogadishu

Major City: Kismayu

Religion: Sunni Muslim

Languages: Somali (official), Arabic, Italian, English

Geographical Facts: Strategic location on Horn of Africa along southern approaches to Bab el Mandeb and route through Red Sea and Suez Canal.

History: A Siad Barre regime was ousted in January 1991; turmoil, factional fighting, and anarchy followed for nine years. In May of 1991, northern clans declared an independent Republic of Somaliland, which now includes the administrative regions of Awdal, Woqooyi Galbeed, Togdheer, Sanaag, and Sool. Although not recognized by any government, this entity has maintained a stable existence, aided by the overwhelming dominance of the ruling clan and economic infrastructure left behind by British, Russian, and American military assistance programs. The regions of Bari and Nugaal comprise a neighboring self-declared Republic of Puntland, which has also made strides toward reconstructing legitimate, representative government. Beginning in 1993, a two-year UN humanitarian effort (primarily in the south) was able to alleviate famine conditions. The United Nations multinational force withdrew in 1995, having suffered significant casualties (including U.S. soldiers); however, order still had not been restored. A transitional national government (TNG) was created in October 2000 in Arta, Djibouti, which was attended by a broad representation of Somali clans. The TNG has a three-year mandate to create a permanent national Somali government. The TNG does not recognize Somaliland or Puntland as independent republics but so far has been unable to reunite them with the unstable regions in the south; numerous warlords and factions are still fighting for control of Mogadishu and the other southern regions.

South Africa

Capitals: Pretoria (administrative), Cape Town (legislative), Bloemfontein (judicial)

Major Cities: Durban, Johannesburg

Religion: Christian

Languages: Eleven official languages, including Afrikaans, English, Ndebele, Pedi, Sotho, Swazi, Tsonga, Tswana, Venda, Xhosa, Zulu

Geographical Facts: South Africa completely surrounds Lesotho and almost completely surrounds Swaziland.

History: After the British seized the Cape of Good Hope area in 1806, many of the Dutch settlers (the Boers) trekked north to found their own republics. The discovery of diamonds (1867) and gold (1886) spurred wealth and immigration and intensified the subjugation of the native inhabitants. The Boers resisted British encroachments, but were defeated in the Boer War (1899–1902). The resulting Union of South Africa operated under a policy of apartheid, or the separate development of the races. The 1990s brought an end to apartheid politically and ushered in black majority rule.

Spain

Capital: Madrid

Major Cities: Barcelona, Seville, Valencia

Religion: Roman Catholic

Language: Castilian Spanish (official)

Geographical Fact: Strategic location along approaches to Strait of Gibraltar.

History: Spain's powerful world empire of the sixteenth and seventeenth centuries ultimately yielded command of the seas to England. Subsequent failure to embrace the mercantile and industrial revolutions caused the country to fall behind Britain, France, and Germany in economic and political power. Spain remained neutral in World Wars I and II but suffered through a devastating civil war (1936–1939). Since then, it has played a catch-up role in the Western international community. Continuing concerns are large-scale unemployment and the Basque separatist movement.

Sri Lanka

Capital: Colombo

Religion: Buddhist

Language: Sinhala (official and national language)

Geographical Fact: Strategic location near major Indian Ocean sealanes.

History: After having been occupied by the Portuguese in the sixteenth century and the Dutch in the seventeenth century, the island was ceded to the British in 1802. As Ceylon, it became independent in 1948; its name was changed in 1972. Tensions between the Sinhalese majority and Tamil separatists erupted in violence in the mid-1980s. Tens of thousands have died in an ethnic war that continues to fester.

St. Kitts and Nevis

Capital: Basseterre

Religions: Anglican, Roman Catholic

Language: English

Geographical Facts: With coastlines in the shape of a baseball bat and ball, the two volcanic islands are separated by a 3-kilometer-wide channel called The Narrows; on the southern tip of the long, bat-shaped St. Kitts lies the Great Salt Pond; Mount Nevis sits in the center of its almost circular namesake island, and its ball shape complements that of its sister island.

History: First settled by the British in 1623, the islands became an associated state with full internal autonomy in 1967. The island of Anguilla rebelled and was allowed to secede in 1971. St. Kitts and Nevis achieved independence in 1983. In 1998, a vote in Nevis on a referendum to separate from St. Kitts fell short of the two-thirds majority needed.

St. Lucia

Capital: Castries

Religion: Roman Catholic

Languages: English (official), French patois

Geographical Facts: The twin Pitons (Gros Piton and Petit Piton), striking cone-shaped peaks south of Soufrière, are one of the scenic natural highlights of the Caribbean.

History: The island, with its fine natural harbor at Castries, was contested between England and France throughout the seventeenth and early eighteenth centuries (changing possession fourteen times). It was finally ceded to the United Kingdom in 1814. Self-government was granted in 1967 and independence in 1979.

St. Vincent and the Grenadines

Capital: Kingstown

Religions: Anglican, Methodist

Languages: English, French patois

Geographical Fact: The administration of the islands of the Grenadines group is divided between St. Vincent and the Grenadines and Grenada.

History: Disputed between France and Great Britain in the eighteenth century, St. Vincent was ceded to the latter in 1783. Autonomy was granted in 1969, and independence in 1979.

Sudan

Capital: Khartoum

Religions: Sunni Muslim, indigenous beliefs

Languages: Arabic (official), Nubian, Ta Bedawie

Geographical Facts: Largest country in Africa; dominated by the Nile and its tributaries.

History: Military dictatorships promulgating an Islamic government have mostly run the country since independence from the United Kingdom in 1956. Over the past two decades, a civil war pitting black Christians and animists in the south against the Arab-Muslims of the north has cost at least 1.5 million lives in war- and famine-related deaths, as well as the displacement of millions of others.

Suriname

Capital: Paramaribo

Religions: Hindu, Protestant, Roman Catholic, Muslim

Languages: Dutch (official), English, Sranang Tongo (Surinamese)

Geographical Facts: Smallest independent country on South American continent; mostly tropical rain forest; great diversity of flora and fauna that, for the most part, is increasingly threatened by new development; relatively small population, most of which lives along the coast.

History: Independence from the Netherlands was granted in 1975. Five years later, the civilian government was replaced by a military regime that soon declared a socialist republic. It continued to rule through a succession of nominally civilian administrations until 1987, when international pressure finally brought about a democratic election. In 1989, the military overthrew the civilian government, but a democratically elected government returned to power in 1991.

Swaziland

Capital: Mbabane

Religion: Protestant

Languages: English (official), siSwati (official)

Geographical Facts: Landlocked; almost completely surrounded by South Africa.

History: Autonomy for the Swazis of southern Africa was guaranteed by the British in the late nineteenth century; independence was granted in 1968. Student and labor unrest during the 1990s pressured the monarchy (one of the oldest on the continent) to grudgingly allow political reform and greater democracy.

Sweden

Capital: Stockholm

Major City: Malmö

Religion: Lutheran

Language: Swedish

Geographical Facts: Strategic location along Danish Straits linking Baltic and North Seas.

History: A military power during the seventeenth century, Sweden has not participated in any war in almost two centuries. An armed neutrality was preserved in both world wars. Sweden's long-successful economic formula of a capitalist system combined with substantial welfare elements has recently been undermined by high unemployment, rising maintenance costs, and a declining position in world markets. Indecision over the country's role in the political and economic integration of Europe caused Sweden not to join the EU until 1995 and to forgo the introduction of the euro in 1999.

Switzerland

Capital: Bern

Major Cities: Zurich, Geneva

Religions: Roman Catholic, Protestant

Languages: German (official), French (official), Italian (official)

Geographical Facts: Landlocked; crossroads of northern and southern Europe; along with southeastern France and northern Italy, contains the highest elevations in Europe.

History: Switzerland's independence and neutrality have long been honored by the major European powers, and Switzerland was not involved in either of the two world wars. The political and economic integration of Europe over the past half-century, as well as Switzerland's role in many UN and international organizations, may be rendering obsolete the country's concern for neutrality.

Syria

Capital: Damascus

Religion: Sunni Muslim

Language: Arabic (official)

Geographical Facts: Much of the country is desert, although Syria includes approximately 80 miles of Mediterranean coastline.

History: Following the breakup of the Ottoman Empire during World War I, Syria was administered by the French until independence in 1946. In the 1967 Arab-Israeli War, Syria lost the Golan Heights to Israel. Since 1976, Syrian troops have been stationed in Lebanon, ostensibly in a peacekeeping capacity. In recent years, Syria and Israel have held occasional peace talks over the return of the Golan Heights.

Tajikistan

Capital: Dushanbe

Religion: Sunni Muslim

Language: Tajik (official)

Geographical Facts: Landlocked; mountainous region dominated by the Trans Alai Range in the north and the Pamirs in the southeast; highest point, Pik Imeni Ismail Samani (formerly Communism Peak), was the tallest mountain in the former USSR.

History: Tajikistan has experienced three changes in government and a five-year civil war since it gained independence in 1991 from the USSR. A peace agreement among rival factions was signed in 1997 and implementation reportedly completed by late 1999. Part of the agreement required the legalization of opposition political parties prior to the 1999 elections, which occurred, but such parties have made little progress in successful government participation. Random criminal and political violence in the country remains a complication, impairing Tajikistan's ability to engage internationally.

Tanzania

Capital: Dar es Salaam

Major City: Dodoma

Religions: Christian, Muslim, indigenous beliefs

Languages: Kiswahili or Swahili (official), Kiunguju (name for Swahili in Zanzibar), English (official)

Geographical Facts: Kilimanjaro is highest point in Africa; bordered by three of the largest lakes on the continent: Lake Victoria (the world's second-largest freshwater lake) in the north, Lake Tanganyika (the world's second deepest) in the west, and Lake Nyasa in the southwest.

History: Shortly after independence from the United Kingdom, Tanganyika and Zanzibar merged to form the nation of Tanzania in 1964. One-party rule came to an end in 1995, with the first democratic elections held in the country since the 1970s. Zanzibar's semi-autonomous status and popular opposition have led to two contentious elections since 1995, which the ruling party won despite international observers' claims of voting irregularities.

Thailand

Capital: Bangkok

Religion: Buddhist

Languages: Thai, English

Geographical Fact: Controls only land route from Asia to Malaysia and Singapore.

History: A unified Thai kingdom was established in the mid-fourteenth century; it was known as Siam until 1939. Thailand is the only Southeast Asian country never to have been taken over by a European power. A bloodless revolution in 1932 led to a constitutional monarchy. In alliance with Japan during World War II, Thailand became a U.S. ally following the conflict.

Togo

Capital: Lomé

Religions: Indigenous beliefs, Christian

Languages: French (official), Ewe and Mina (in the south), Kabye and Dagomba (in the north)

Geographical Facts: The country's length allows it to stretch through six distinct geographic regions; climate varies from tropical to savanna.

History: French Togoland became Togo in 1960. General Gnassingbe Eyadema, installed as military ruler in 1967, is Africa's longest-serving head of state. Despite the facade of multiparty elections that resulted in Eyadema's victory in 1993, the government continues to be dominated by the military. In addition, Togo has come under fire from international organizations for human rights abuses and is plagued by political unrest. Most bilateral and multilateral aid to Togo remains frozen.

Tonga

Capital: Nuku'alofa

Religion: Christian

Languages: Tongan, English

Geographical Facts: Archipelago of 170 islands (36 inhabited).

History: The archipelago of "The Friendly Islands" was united into a Poly-nesian kingdom in 1845. It became a constitutional monarchy in 1875 and a

British protectorate in 1900. Tonga acquired its independence in 1970 and became a member of the Commonwealth of Nations. It remains the only monarchy in the Pacific.

Trinidad and Tobago

Capital: Port of Spain

Religions: Roman Catholic, Hindu

Languages: English (official), Hindi, French, Spanish, Chinese

Geographical Facts: Pitch Lake, on Trinidad's southwestern coast, is the world's largest natural reservoir of asphalt.

History: The islands came under British control in the nineteenth century; independence was granted in 1962. The country is one of the most prosperous in the Caribbean, thanks largely to petroleum and natural gas production and processing. Tourism, mostly in Tobago, is targeted for expansion and is growing.

Tunisia

Capital: Tunis

Religion: Muslim

Languages: Arabic (official), French

Geographical Facts: Strategic location in central Mediterranean; Malta and Tunisia are discussing the commercial exploitation of the continental shelf between their countries, particularly for oil exploration.

History: Following independence from France in 1956, President Habib Bourguiba established a strict one-party state. He dominated the country for thirty-one years, repressing Islamic fundamentalism and establishing rights for women unmatched by any other Arab nation. In recent years, Tunisia has taken a moderate, nonaligned stance in its foreign relations. Domestically, it has sought to diffuse rising pressure for a more open political society.

Turkey

Capital: Ankara

Major Cities: Istanbul, Izmir

Religion: Muslim

Languages: Turkish (official), Kurdish, Arabic, Armenian, Greek

Geographical Facts: Strategic location controlling the Turkish Straits (Bosporus, Sea of Marmara, Dardanelles) that link Black and Aegean Seas; Mount Ararat, the legendary landing place of Noah's Ark, is in the far eastern portion of the country.

History: Turkey was created in 1923 from the Turkish remnants of the Ottoman Empire. Soon thereafter, the country instituted secular laws to replace traditional religious fiats. In 1945, Turkey joined the United Nations, and in 1952, it became a member of NATO. To prevent a Greek takeover of the island, Turkey occupied the northern portion of Cyprus in 1974; relations between the two countries remain strained. Periodic military offensives against Kurdish separatists have dislocated part of the population in southeast Turkey and have drawn international condemnation.

Turkmenistan

Capital: Ashgabat

Religion: Muslim

Language: Turkmen

Geographical Facts: Landlocked; the western and central low-lying, desolate portions of the country make up the great Garagum (Kara-Kum) desert, which occupies over 80 percent of the country; eastern part is plateau.

History: Annexed by Russia between 1865 and 1885, Turkmenistan became a Soviet republic in 1925. It achieved its independence upon the dissolution of the USSR in 1991. Extensive hydrocarbon/natural gas reserves could prove a boon to this underdeveloped country if extraction and delivery projects can be worked out.

Tuvalu

Capital: Funafuti

Religion: Church of Tuvalu

Languages: Tuvaluan, English

Geographical Facts: One of the smallest and most remote countries on Earth; five of the coral atolls enclose sizable lagoons, but the other four are just pinnacles.

History: In 1974, ethnic differences within the British colony of the Gilbert and Ellice Islands caused the Polynesians of the Ellice Islands to vote for separation from the Micronesians of the Gilbert Islands. The following year, the Ellice Islands became the separate British colony of Tuvalu. Independence was granted in 1978. In 2000, Tuvalu negotiated a contract leasing its Internet domain name ".tv" for $50 million in royalties over the next dozen years.

Uganda

Capital: Kampala

Religions: Roman Catholic, Protestant

Languages: English (official national language), Ganda or Luganda

Geographical Facts: Landlocked; fertile, well-watered country with many lakes and rivers.

History: Uganda achieved independence from the United Kingdom in 1962. The dictatorial regime of Idi Amin (1971–1979) was responsible for the deaths of some three hundred thousand opponents; guerrilla war and human rights abuses under Milton Obote (1980–1985) claimed another one hundred thousand lives. During the 1990s, the government promulgated non-party presidential and legislative elections.

Ukraine

Capital: Kiev

Major City: Odessa

Religion: Ukrainian Orthodox

Languages: Ukrainian, Russian, Romanian, Polish, Hungarian

Geographical Facts: Strategic position at the crossroads between Europe and Asia; second-largest country in Europe.

History: Richly endowed in natural resources, Ukraine has been fought over and subjugated for centuries; its twentieth-century struggle for liberty is not yet complete. A short-lived independence from Russia (1917–1920) was followed by brutal Soviet rule that engineered two artificial famines (1921–1922 and 1932–1933), in which more than eight million died, and World War II, in which German and Soviet armies were responsible for some seven million more deaths. Although independence was attained in 1991 with the dissolution of the USSR, true freedom remains elusive, as many of the former Soviet elite remain entrenched, stalling efforts at economic reform, privatization, and civic liberties.

United Arab Emirates

Capital: Abu Dhabi

Religion: Muslim

Languages: Arabic (official), Persian, English, Hindi, Urdu

Geographical Facts: Strategic location along southern approaches to Strait of Hormuz, a vital transit point for world crude oil.

History: The Trucial States of the Persian Gulf coast granted the United Kingdom control of their defense and foreign affairs in nineteenth century treaties. In 1971, six of these states—Abu Dhabi, Ajman, Fujaira, Sharja, Dubai, and Umm al Qaiwain—merged to form the UAE. They were joined in 1972 by Ras al Khaimah. The UAE's per capita GDP is not far below those of the leading Western European nations. Its generosity with oil revenues and its moderate foreign policy stance have allowed it to play a vital role in the affairs of the region.

United Kingdom

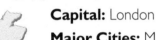

Capital: London

Major Cities: Manchester, Birmingham, Glasgow, Edinburgh, Belfast, Leeds, Liverpool

Religions: Anglican, Roman Catholic

Languages: English, Welsh, Scottish form of Gaelic

Geographical Facts: Lies near vital North Atlantic sealanes; only 22 miles from France and now linked by tunnel under the English Channel; because of heavily indented coastline, no location is more than 78 miles from tidal waters.

History: Great Britain, the dominant industrial and maritime power of the nineteenth century, played a leading role in developing parliamentary democracy and advancing literature and science. At its zenith, the British Empire stretched over one-fourth of the Earth. The first half of the twentieth century saw the United Kingdom's strength seriously depleted in two world wars. The second half witnessed the dismantling of the empire and the United Kingdom rebuilding itself into a modern and prosperous European nation. As one of five permanent members of the UN Security Council and a founding member of NATO and of the Commonwealth, the nation pursues a global approach to foreign policy; it currently is weighing the degree of its integration with continental Europe. A member of the EU, it chose to remain outside the European Monetary Union for the time being. Constitutional reform is also a significant issue in the United Kingdom. Regional assemblies with varying degrees of power opened in Scotland, Wales, and Northern Ireland in 1999.

United States

Capital: Washington, D.C.

Major Cities: New York, Los Angeles, San Francisco, Chicago, Houston, Philadelphia

Religions: Protestant, Roman Catholic, Jewish, Muslim, others

Languages: English, Spanish

Geographical Facts: World's third-largest country by size (after Russia and Canada) and by population (after China and India); Mount McKinley is the highest point and Death Valley the lowest point on the continent.

History: The United States became the world's first modern democracy after its break with Great Britain (1776) and the adoption of a constitution (1789). During the nineteenth century, many new states were added to the original thirteen as the nation expanded across the North American continent and acquired a number of overseas possessions. The two most traumatic experiences in the nation's history were the Civil War (1861–1865) and the Great Depression of the 1930s. Buoyed by victories in World Wars I and II and the end of the Cold War in 1991, the United States remains the world's most powerful nation-state. The economy is marked by steady growth, low unemployment and inflation, and rapid advances in technology.

Uruguay

Capital: Montevideo

Religion: Roman Catholic

Languages: Spanish, Portunol, or Brazilero

Geographical Facts: Second-smallest South American country (after Suriname); most of the low-lying landscape (three-quarters of the country) is grassland, ideal for cattle and sheep raising.

History: In 1973, a violent Marxist urban guerrilla movement, the Tupamaros, which was launched in the late 1960s, led Uruguay's president to agree to military control of his administration. By the end of the year, the rebels had been crushed, but the military continued to expand its hold throughout the government. Civilian rule was not restored until 1985. Uruguay's political and labor conditions are among the freest on the continent.

Uzbekistan

Capital: Tashkent

Major City: Samarkand

Religion: Sunni Muslim

Language: Uzbek

Geographical Facts: Along with Liechtenstein, one of the only two doubly landlocked countries in the world.

History: Russia conquered Uzbekistan in the late nineteenth century. Stiff resistance to the Red Army after World War I was eventually suppressed and a socialist republic set up in 1925. During the Soviet era, intensive production of "white gold" (cotton) and grain led to overuse of agrochemicals and the depletion of water supplies, which have left the land poisoned and the Aral Sea and certain rivers half dry. Independent since 1991, the country seeks to gradually lessen its dependence on agriculture while developing its mineral and petroleum reserves. Current concerns include insurgency by Islamic militants based in Tajikistan and Afghanistan, a nonconvertible currency, and the curtailment of human rights and democratization.

Vanuatu

Capital: Port-Vila

Religion: Presbyterian

Languages: English (official), French (official), pidgin (known as Bislama or Bichelama)

Geographical Facts: A Y-shaped chain of some eighty islands, seventy of which are inhabited; several of the islands have active volcanoes.

History: The British and French, who settled the New Hebrides in the nineteenth century, agreed in 1906 to an Anglo-French Condominium, which administered the islands until independence in 1980.

Vatican City (The Holy See)

Religion: Roman Catholic

Languages: Italian, Latin, French

Geographical Facts: Urban; landlocked; enclave of Rome, Italy; world's smallest state; outside the Vatican City, thirteen buildings in Rome and Castel Gandolfo (the pope's summer residence) enjoy extraterritorial rights.

History: Popes in their secular role ruled much of the Italian peninsula for more than a thousand years until the mid–nineteenth century, when many of the Papal States were seized by the newly united Kingdom of Italy. In 1870, the pope's holdings were further circumscribed when Rome itself was annexed. Disputes between a series of "prisoner" popes and Italy were resolved in 1929 by three Lateran Treaties, which established the independent state of Vatican City and granted Roman Catholicism special status in Italy. In 1984, a concordat between the Vatican and Italy modified certain of the earlier treaty provisions, including the primacy of Roman Catholicism as the Italian state religion. Present concerns of the Holy See include the failing health of Pope John Paul II, interreligious dialogue and reconciliation, and the adjustment of church doctrine in an era of rapid change and globalization. About one billion people worldwide profess the Catholic faith.

Venezuela

Capital: Caracas

Major City: Maracaibo

Religion: Roman Catholic

Languages: Spanish (official), numerous indigenous dialects

Geographical Facts: On major sea and air routes linking North and South America; Angel Falls in the Guiana Highlands is the world's highest waterfall.

History: Venezuela was one of the three countries that emerged from the collapse of Gran Colombia in 1830 (the others being Colombia and Ecuador). For most of the first half of the twentieth century, Venezuela was ruled by generally benevolent military strongmen, who promoted the oil industry and allowed for some social reforms. Democratically elected governments have held sway since 1959. Current concerns include drug-related conflicts along the Colombian border, increased internal drug consumption, overdependence on the petroleum industry with its price fluctuations, and irresponsible mining operations that are endangering the rain forest and indigenous peoples.

Vietnam

Capital: Hanoi

Major City: Ho Chi Minh City

Religion: Buddhist

Languages: Vietnamese (official), English

Geographical Facts: Extending 1,650 kilometers north to south, the country is only about 30 miles across at its narrowest point.

History: By 1884, France occupied all of Vietnam. Independence was declared after World War II, but the French continued to rule until 1954, when they were defeated by communist forces under Ho Chi Minh, who took control of the north. U.S. economic and military aid to South Vietnam grew through the 1960s in an attempt to bolster the government. U.S. military forces grew to a half-million in 1969 and resulted in significant protests across the United States against U.S. involvement in Vietnam. Finally, U.S. armed forces were withdrawn following a cease-fire agreement in 1973. Two years later, North Vietnamese forces overran the south. Economic reconstruction of the reunited country has proven difficult, as aging Communist Party leaders have only grudgingly initiated reforms necessary for a free market.

Yemen

Capital: San'a

Major City: Aden

Religions: Shiite Muslim, Sunni Muslim

Language: Arabic

Geographical Facts: Strategic location on Bab el Mandeb, the strait linking the Red Sea and the Gulf of Aden, one of world's most active shipping lanes.

History: North Yemen became independent of the Ottoman Empire in 1918. The British, who had set up a protectorate area around the southern port of Aden in the nineteenth century, withdrew in 1967 from what became South Yemen. Three years later, the southern government adopted a Marxist orientation. The massive exodus of hundreds of thousands of Yemenis from the south to the north contributed to two decades of hostility between the states. The two countries were formally unified as the Republic of Yemen in 1990. A southern secessionist movement in 1994 was quickly subdued. In 2000, Saudi Arabia and Yemen agreed to a delimitation of their border.

Yugoslavia (Serbia and Montenegro)

Capital: Belgrade

Major Cities: Novi Sad, Pristina

Religion: Orthodox

Language: Serbian

Geographical Facts: Controls one of the major land routes from western Europe to Turkey and the Near East; strategic location along the Adriatic coast.

History: The Kingdom of Serbs, Croats, and Slovenes was formed in 1918; its name was changed to Yugoslavia in 1929. In 1941, occupation by Nazi Germany was resisted by various partisan bands that fought themselves as well as the invaders. The group headed by Marshal Josip Tito took full control upon German expulsion in 1945. Although communist in name, Tito's new government successfully steered its own path between the Warsaw Pact nations and the West for the next four and a half decades. In the early 1990s, post-Tito Yugoslavia began to unravel along ethnic lines: Slovenia, Croatia, and the Former Yugoslav Republic of Macedonia all declared their independence in 1991; Bosnia and Herzegovina did the same in 1992. The remaining republics of Serbia and Montenegro declared a new Federal Republic of Yugoslavia in 1992 and, under President Slobodan Milosevic, Serbia led various military intervention efforts to unite Serbs in neighboring republics into a Greater Serbia. All of these efforts were ultimately unsuccessful. In 1999, massive expulsions by Serbs of ethnic Albanians living in the autonomous republic of Kosovo provoked an international response, including the NATO bombing of Serbia and the stationing of NATO and Russian peacekeepers in Kosovo. Blatant attempts to manipulate presidential balloting in October 2000 were followed by massive nationwide demonstrations and strikes that saw the election winner, Vojislav Kostunica, replace Milosevic. In 2002, Yugoslavia officially changed its name to Serbia and Montenegro.

Zambia

Capital: Lusaka

Religions: Christian, Muslim, Hindu

Language: English (official)

Geographical Facts: Landlocked; the Zambezi forms a natural riverine boundary with Zimbabwe.

History: The territory of Northern Rhodesia was administered by the South Africa Company from 1891 until takeover by the United Kingdom in 1923. During the 1920s and 1930s, advances in mining spurred development and immigration. The name was changed to Zambia upon independence in 1964. In the 1980s and 1990s, declining copper prices and a prolonged drought hurt the economy. Elections in 1991 brought an end to one-party rule, but the subsequent vote in 1996 saw blatant harassment of opposition parties.

Zimbabwe

Capital: Harare

Religions: Syneretic (part Christian, part indigenous beliefs), Christian, indigenous beliefs

Languages: English (official), Shona, Sindebele

Geographical Facts: Landlocked; the Zambezi forms a natural riverine boundary with Zambia; in full flood (February–April) the massive Victoria Falls on the river forms the world's largest curtain of falling water.

History: The United Kingdom annexed Southern Rhodesia from the South Africa Company in 1923. A 1961 constitution was formulated to keep whites in power. In 1965, the government unilaterally declared its independence, but Great Britain did not recognize the act and demanded voting rights for the black African majority in the country (then called Rhodesia). UN sanctions and a guerrilla uprising finally led to free elections in 1979 and independence (as Zimbabwe) in 1980. Robert Mugabe, the nation's first prime minister, has been the country's only ruler (as president since 1987) and has dominated the country's political system since independence.

7

Level 4: I've Got a Little List

uman geography can include any topic relating to humans—
a huge topic! But have no fear; human geography can be
broken down into four key areas: political geography, economic geography, cultural geography, and historical geography. Any one or
several of these topics may appear as an entire round in a Bee. The
questions are challenging because they require a broad knowledge of
world history, historical events, key products, major religions, languages, boundary disputes, political conflicts, and much, much more.
Whew! That's a lot to know!

Fortunately, some of this information you already know because
you studied it in the previous chapter. Now it's time to learn more.

In this chapter, we have organized information into thirty important lists. Many Geography Bee questions will ask you to name the
highest, lowest, biggest, smallest, most populous, or least populous.

Therefore we have included many lists of superlatives. The lists provide items such as the largest countries, major languages, and the deepest ocean trenches.

Notice that we don't include the numbers associated with the lists. If you are curious, you can look them up for such lists as population of the largest U.S. states or the elevations of the highest peaks. Also, we couldn't include every superlative; instead, we chose what you will most likely need to know for the Bee. If you have time, feel free to research additional data and create your own lists.

We'd love to tell you that simply putting this book under your pillow will help you absorb all the information you need. But it's just not true. The only way to learn this information is to study it. Use an atlas or your filled-in blank maps from Level 1 to look at each country as you read about them. Often, a country's location or size can help you remember the information on these lists. For instance, take a quick peek at the most populous countries of the world. Perhaps it would make sense that the larger the country, the more people it could contain. With that reasoning, Russia, China, Canada, the United States, and Brazil should be the top five in population. Although Russia is the largest country by size, why is it not even in the top five most populous? The answer lies in Siberia. Much of Russia—and Canada, too—is too cold to be hospitable to humans. Thus, from your atlas, you can understand why some countries may be large but may not hold as many people as other countries.

You've gained some knowledge about each country's culture from Level 3, but there is so much more that you should learn about each country. If you have time, use your additional reference books and the following online resources to build your cultural knowledge.

World Online Resources

Geography at About Atlas of the World (maps and information about each country, from your author):
geography.about.com/library/maps/blindex.htm

CIA World Factbook (the latest information from the CIA):
www.odci.gov/cia/publications/factbook/index.html

U.S. Department of State Background Notes (in-depth reports about the political situation in each country):
www.state.gov/r/pa/bgn/

Hillman Wonders of the World (100 important places around the world): www.hillmanwonders.com

Infoplease Countries of the World (data and a brief narrative about each country): www.infoplease.com/countries.html

Lonely Planet Destinations (in-depth information about each country): www.lonelyplanet.com/destinations/

Library of Congress Country Studies (full-length books about many countries): lcweb2.loc.gov/frd/cs/cshome.html

Cultural Profiles Project (learn about the culture of many countries): cwr.utoronto.ca/cultural/english/index.html

U.S. Online Resources

Geography at About Atlas of the U.S.A. (maps and information about each country, from your author):
geography.about.com/library/maps/blusx.htm

50 States (great data and facts about every state): www.50states.com

Stately Knowledge (essential information about each state):
www.ipl.org/youth/stateknow/skhome.html

And now, on with the lists!

Most Populous States

1. California
2. Texas
3. New York
4. Florida
5. Illinois

Least Populous States

1. Wyoming
2. Vermont
3. Alaska
4. North Dakota
5. South Dakota

Most Populous Countries (all above 100 million)

1. China
2. India
3. United States
4. Indonesia
5. Brazil
6. Russia
7. Pakistan
8. Bangladesh
9. Japan
10. Nigeria
11. Mexico

Least Populous Countries

1. Vatican City
2. Tuvalu
3. Nauru
4. Palau
5. San Marino

Continents in Order of Population

1. Asia
2. Africa
3. Europe

4. North America
5. South America
6. Australia/Oceania
7. Antarctica

Largest Countries in Area

1. Russia
2. Canada
3. United States
4. China
5. Brazil
6. Australia
7. India
8. Argentina
9. Kazakhstan
10. Sudan

Smallest Countries in Area

1. Vatican City
2. Monaco
3. Nauru
4. Tuvalu
5. San Marino
6. Liechtenstein

Largest States in Area

1. Alaska
2. Texas
3. California
4. Montana
5. New Mexico

Smallest States in Area

1. Rhode Island
2. Delaware
3. Connecticut
4. Hawaii
5. New Jersey

Highest Mountains in the World

1. Mount Everest, China-Nepal (29,035 feet)
2. K2, Pakistan-China
3. Kanchenjunga, India-Nepal

Highest Mountains on Each Continent

Africa: Mount Kilimanjaro, Tanzania

Antarctica: Vinson Massif

Asia: Mount Everest, China-Nepal

Australia: Kosciusko

Europe: Elbrus, Russia-Georgia

North America: Mount McKinley (Denali), Alaska, United States

South America: Mount Aconcagua, Argentina

Lowest Points on Each Continent

Africa: Lake Assal, Djibouti

Antarctica: Bentley Subglacial Trench

Asia: Dead Sea, Israel-Jordan

Australia: Lake Eyre

Europe: Caspian Sea, Russia-Kazakhstan

North America: Death Valley, California, United States

South America: Valdes Peninsula, Argentina

Deepest Point in Each Ocean

Pacific Ocean: Mariana Trench (deepest in the world)
Atlantic Ocean: Puerto Rico Trench
Indian Ocean: Sunda Trench

Most Populous Urban Areas in the World

1. Tokyo, Japan
2. New York City, United States
3. Seoul, South Korea
4. Mexico City, Mexico
5. Mumbai (Bombay), India

Most Populous Metropolitan Areas in the United States

1. New York City
2. Los Angeles
3. Chicago
4. Washington, D.C.
5. San Francisco

Most Populous Incorporated Cities in the United States

1. New York City
2. Los Angeles
3. Chicago
4. Houston
5. Philadelphia

Longest Rivers

1. Nile
2. Amazon

3. Yangtze
4. Mississippi-Missouri

Largest Oceans

1. Pacific Ocean
2. Atlantic Ocean
3. Indian Ocean
4. Southern Ocean
5. Arctic Ocean

Largest Lakes

1. Caspian Sea, Europe-Asia
2. Lake Superior, North America
3. Lake Victoria, Africa
4. Lake Huron, North America
5. Lake Michigan, North America

Continents in Order of Area

1. Asia
2. Africa
3. North America
4. South America
5. Antarctica
6. Australia/Oceania
7. Europe

Largest Islands

1. Greenland
2. New Guinea
3. Borneo
4. Madagascar
5. Baffin

Tallest Buildings

1. & 2. Petronas Towers in Kuala Lumpur, Malaysia
3. Sears Tower in Chicago, United States
4. Jin Mao Building in Shanghai, China

Major Religions

1. Christianity
2. Islam
3. Hinduism
4. Buddhism

Source Locations of Major Religions

Buddhism: Northern India

Christianity/Roman Catholicism: Middle East and Roman Empire

Church of Jesus Christ of Latter-day Saints (Mormons): New York, USA (but followers settled in Utah)

Confucianism: China

Eastern Orthodox: Constantinople, Turkey

Hinduism: India

Islam: Medina and Mecca, Saudi Arabia

Judaism: Israel/Palestine

Protestantism: Europe

Shinto: Japan

Sikhism: India

Taoism: China

Major Languages

1. Chinese/Mandarin
2. Spanish (Spain and most of Latin America)
3. English (most widely spoken—often as a second language)

4. Bengali (India, Bangladesh)
5. Hindi (India)
6. Portuguese (Portugal, Brazil)

Busiest Airports (by passengers)

1. Hartsfield Atlanta International
2. Chicago O'Hare
3. Los Angeles International
4. London Heathrow
5. Dallas–Fort Worth

Where Are They Now?

Countries that no longer exist and the locations of important civilizations throughout history:

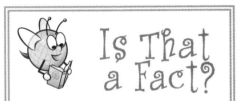

Is That a Fact?

English is spoken by more people around the world than any other language. But the largest native language is Mandarin Chinese.

Abyssinia: Ethiopia
Asia Minor: Turkey
Austro-Hungarian Empire: Austria, Hungary, and Czech Republic
Babylonia: Iraq
Basutoland: Lesotho
Berber States: Northern Africa
Carthage: Tunisia
Celtic: Great Britain
Ceylon: Sri Lanka
Czechoslovakia: Czech Republic and Slovakia
East Pakistan: Bangladesh
Etruscan: Italy

Formosa: Taiwan
Gaul: France
Gran Colombia: Colombia, Panama, Venezuela, and Ecuador
Han Empire: China

Iberia: Spain and Portugal

Incan: Andes and South America

Kampuchea: Cambodia

Knoisan: South Africa

Mayan: Mexico

Mesopotamia: Iraq/Middle East

Mughal Empire: India and Pakistan

Nubian: Sudan

Olmec: Mexico

Ottoman Empire: Middle East, Turkey, and North Africa

Persia: Iran

Phoenicia: Lebanon

Prussia: Poland and Germany

Rhodesia: Zimbabwe

Roman Empire: Rome and Mediterranean Sea area

Siam: Thailand

Sumer: Iraq

Tanganyika and Zanzibar: Tanzania

Tibet: China

Union of Soviet Socialist Republics (USSR): Russia and Armenia, Azerbaijan, Belarus, Estonia, Georgia, Kazakhstan, Kyrgyzstan, Latvia, Lithuania, Moldova, Tajikistan, Turkmenistan, Ukraine, and Uzbekistan

United Arab Republic: Egypt and Syria

Upper Volta: Burkina Faso

Western Sahara: Controlled by Morocco

Zaire: Democratic Republic of the Congo

Key International Organizations

United Nations: As of early 2003, there are 191 countries that are members of the United Nations. One country, the Vatican City, is not a member. A second quasicountry, Taiwan, was a member until 1971.

OPEC (Organization of Petroleum Exporting Countries): Sets oil prices. Members include Algeria, Indonesia, Iran, Iraq, Kuwait, Libya, Nigeria (only member south of the Sahara Desert in Africa), Qatar, Saudi Arabia, United Arab Emirates, and Venezuela (only South American member).

Organization of American States (OAS): Includes almost all North and South American countries.

Organization of African Unity: Includes almost all African countries.

Commonwealth of Independent States: Twelve of the fifteen countries that made up the former USSR (excludes Estonia, Latvia, and Lithuania)

The Commonwealth: Fifty-three former colonies of the British Empire and the United Kingdom itself

European Union (EU): Austria, Belgium, Denmark, Finland, France, Germany, Greece, Ireland, Italy, Luxembourg, Netherlands, Portugal, Spain, Sweden, and United Kingdom

G-8 (Group of Eight): Eight major industrial nations: Canada, France, Germany, Italy, Japan, Russia, United Kingdom, and United States

Interpol (International Criminal Police Organization): 178 members

The Euro: A common currency utilized by twelve EU countries: Austria, Belgium, Finland, France, Germany, Greece, Ireland, Italy, Luxembourg, Netherlands, Portugal, and Spain

NATO (North Atlantic Treaty Organization): A military treaty with seventeen members in Europe plus Canada and the United States

NAFTA (North American Free Trade Agreement): Treaty between Canada, United States, and Mexico

Dependencies/Territories

Australia: Ashmore and Cartier Islands, Christmas Island, Cocos (Keeling) Islands, Coral Sea Islands, Heard and McDonald Islands, and Norfolk Islands

Denmark: Faroe Islands and Greenland

France: French Guiana, French Polynesia, Guadeloupe, Martinique, Mayotte, New Caledonia, Reunion, St.-Pierre and Miquelon, and Wallis and Futuna Islands

Morocco: Western Sahara

Netherlands: Aruba and Netherlands Antilles

New Zealand: Cook Islands, Niue, and Tokelau Islands

Norway: Jan Mayen and Svalbard

Spain: Ceuta and Melilla

United Kingdom: Anguilla, Bermuda, British Indian Ocean Territory, British Virgin Islands, Cayman Islands, Channel Islands, Falkland Islands, Gibraltar, Isle of Man, Montserrat, Pitcairn Islands, South Georgia and the South Sandwich Islands, and Turks and Caicos Islands

United States: American Samoa, Baker Island, Guam, Howland Island, Jarvis Island, Johnson Atoll, Kingman Reef, Midway Islands, Northern Mariana Islands, Palmyra Atoll, Puerto Rico, U.S. Virgin Islands, and Wake Island

Taiwan: Also known as the Republic of China, Taiwan is unrecognized as a country by most of the world and claimed by China.

West Bank and Gaza Strip: Israeli territory under Palestinian control

Other Important Facts

Tallest Tower: Canadian National Tower (CN Tower) in Toronto, Ontario, Canada

Wettest Point: Mount Waialeale in Hawaii

Windiest Point: Mount Washington in New Hampshire

Highest Temperature: 136° Fahrenheit in Libya

Most Bordered: China is bordered by fourteen countries, more than any other.

Doubly Landlocked: Two countries are doubly landlocked and thus surrounded by landlocked countries—Uzbekistan and Liechtenstein.

Great Lakes: Remember "HOMES": Huron, Ontario, Michigan, Erie, and Superior.

8

Level 5: Earthworms to Earthquakes

A Guide to Studying Physical Geography

The previous Bee Prepared chapters have helped you build a foundation of knowledge that will help you in most of the Geography Bee rounds. The topic of physical geography is distinctly different, however, and your knowledge from the previous chapters will not help you. This chapter's subject is unusual because physical geography has very little to do with countries. Instead, physical geography is the description and study of physical features on the Earth. This includes the structure of the planet and its movement, weather and climate, rocks, tectonic processes, landforms, soils, and more.

Of all the topics in the Bee, physical geography is usually the most difficult and challenging because it requires a vast knowledge of geographic vocabulary. Though this means studying the subject from scratch, the good news is that physical geography will typically occupy only one round of a Geography Bee competition, which is why we have placed it as Level 5 rather than higher on the list.

Memorize the Terms

To excel in the physical geography round, you would need the knowledge gained from a semester-long, college-level, physical geography course. That's not often practical for students studying for the Bee, so in this chapter we try to describe the basics. Since most National Geographic Bee questions about physical geography provide a definition and ask for the term being defined, we've compiled the definitions of almost three hundred physical geography terms for you to read and learn.

We recommend memorizing these terms and their definitions by creating flash cards. On one side of an index card, write the term; on the other side, write the definition. Start studying by quizzing yourself. Then, when you think you have the terms mastered, ask someone else to shuffle the cards and then quiz you.

Worldly Tip

Although you may think you know the meaning of *sun*, *spring*, or *spit*, you need to know the importance of the term in relation to physical geography. So be sure to read all the definitions contained in this chapter.

Additional Sources

Although we highly recommend memorizing the terms in this chapter, we realize that not all of the definitions may make sense to you. For that reason, and if you have time to learn more, we suggest you obtain a copy of an introductory physical geography textbook to aid you in your studying. Large libraries and college bookstores are good sources for such a textbook. Several useful books to help you learn more about physical geography and the concepts behind these terms are Tom McKnight's *Physical Geography* or Robert Christopherson's *Geosystems* or *Elemental Geosystems*. Also, the *National Geographic Desk Reference* contains approximately two hundred pages of information about physical geography.

The Terms

aa A Hawaiian term for sharp and pointy basaltic lava flow. You can remember this flow is rough, versus *pahoehoe,* which is smooth, because if you were to walk on aa lava you would shout out "Aaaa, aaaa!" (which is how it is pronounced).

abrasion The erosion of rock by being either carried along a stream or sandblasted by wind. This process wears down the rock.

abyssal plain A large, flat area of the deep-ocean floor.

acid rain Rain that contains acid, which can cause serious environmental damage, including killing plant and animal life as well as deteriorating buildings. The acid is caused by pollution, especially from the burning of coal, car exhaust, and smoke from factories.

aeolian Any wind-related process. Refers to things carried, deposited, or eroded by the wind. Named after Aeolus, the Greek god of wind. It is often spelled *eolian.*

aftershock A *shock* (i.e., earthquake) that occurs *after* a large earthquake. After extremely large earthquakes, aftershocks may occur for several years.

air mass A body of air that has similar characteristics such as temperature, pressure, and moisture content.

air pressure The weight of the air above any point. Air pressure decreases as altitude increases. For example, the cabins of airplanes must be pressurized while flying because air pressure at that elevation is much lower than at ground level.

albedo The percentage of the sun's radiation that is reflected off a surface. For example, the albedo of snow is very high because its white color is very reflective; thus, remember to wear your sunglasses when skiing.

alluvial fan Fan-shaped deposits of sediment found at the foot of a mountain range brought there by mountain streams on their way from the mountains to the valley below.

alpine glacier A glacier that forms in the mountains.

anemometer An instrument that measures the speed of wind.

anticyclone An area of high pressure with winds that rotate clockwise in the Northern Hemisphere and counterclockwise in the Southern Hemisphere. Opposite of *cyclone*.

antipode Two points or regions on opposite sides of the planet from each other. For example, if you were able to dig a hole through the Earth from the United States, you would reach the Indian Ocean—not China—because the antipode of the United States is a region in the Indian Ocean.

aphelion The point in the Earth's orbit when the Earth is farthest from the sun. Opposite of *perihelion*.

apogee The point in the moon's orbit where the moon is farthest from the Earth. Opposite of *perigee*.

aquaclude An underground rock layer that groundwater cannot enter or pass through.

aquifer A rock layer that holds groundwater.

Arctic Circle and Antarctic Circle The Arctic Circle lies at 66° 30' North, and the Antarctic Circle lies at 66° 30' South. The entire area north of the Arctic Circle is light for a full twenty-four hours on June 21, and the entire area south of the Antarctic Circle is dark for a full twenty-four hours on June 21. On December 22 it is the opposite.

arid Dry. Often used in the term "arid land," which is an area that is dry due to limited precipitation.

arroyo A Spanish term meaning a dry streambed that fills with water following heavy rains. Similar to a wadi and a wash.

artesian well A well from which water rises due to underground pressure.

ash Volcanic ash are tiny particles ejected from a volcano during an eruption.

atmosphere One of the four spheres of the Earth. The layer of gas that surrounds the Earth, where weather and climate take place. Often referred to as air. The other three spheres are the biosphere, hydrosphere, and lithosphere.

atoll A ring of coral reef that encloses a lagoon.

aurora Colorful lights in the night sky. Also known in the Northern Hemisphere as the Northern Lights.

avalanche The rapid fall of snow, ice, or rocks from a mountainside.

axis An imaginary line that runs from the North Pole to the South Pole, around which the Earth turns. The axis is angled at 23.5°, which causes the seasons.

barometer An instrument that measures atmospheric pressure.

barrier island An island parallel to the shoreline, typically formed by sand deposited by waves.

bay A body of water formed by a curved indentation of a coastal shoreline, larger than a cove and smaller than a gulf.

Beaufort scale A scale developed by British admiral Francis Beaufort to measure wind speed using visual clues. The scale runs from 0 to 12, with 0 being calm and 12 being hurricane-force winds.

biodiversity The variety of living things in a given area. Hint: The prefix *bio-* means "life"; thus, *biodiversity* means the "diversity of life."

biosphere One of the four spheres of the Earth. The areas of the Earth that are home to all living things. The other three spheres are the lithosphere, hydrosphere, and atmosphere.

butte A flat-topped hill with steep sides. Larger than a pinnacle and smaller than a mesa.

caldera A large, circular cavity that remains after the explosion and collapse of a volcano.

calving The breaking off of large chunks of ice from a glacier or an ice sheet, sometimes forming icebergs.

canyon A deep valley with steep sides carved by a river.

cascade Rapids or a waterfall that flows down multiple steps.

cataract A series of rapids, especially those along the Nile River, or a large waterfall with a single drop.

Celsius A system for the measurement of temperature, with 0° Celsius as the temperature at which water freezes and 100° Celsius as the temperature at which water boils.

chinook winds A warm and dry wind that blows down the east slope of the Rocky Mountains.

TYPES OF CLOUDS

High clouds
6,000 meters

Middle clouds

Low clouds
2,000 meters

Cirrus

Cirrocumulus

Cirrostratus

Altostratus

Altocumulus

Cumulonimbus

Cumulus

Cumulus
(fair weather)

Stratocumulus

Nimbostratus

Stratus

Earth's surface

chlorofluorocarbons (CFCs) Chemicals that destroy ozone in the atmosphere.

cirque A circular basin in the high mountains carved by a glacier.

cirrus Very high, feathery-looking clouds made up of ice crystals.

climate The average weather for a place over a long period of time. Typically determined by thirty years of daily records.

cloud A collection of water moisture and ice crystals in the atmosphere.

cold front The boundary between a mass of cold air and a mass of warm air where the cold air is pushing the warm air upward, creating a storm.

condensation The transformation of water from gas (vapor) to liquid.

confluence The place where two rivers or streams meet.

continental divide The division on a continent between two watersheds. In North America, the Continental Divide lies in the Rocky Mountains, and water to the east of the Continental Divide flows toward the Atlantic Ocean, while water to the west of the Continental Divide flows toward the Pacific Ocean.

continental drift The theory that the continents have drifted from a single supercontinent called Pangaea to their present location by riding on plates that cover the Earth's crust.

continental glacier A large ice sheet that covers a continent.

continental shelf The outer edges of a continent that are submerged under oceans.

continental slope The edge between the continental shelf and the abyssal plain.

contour line Lines used to display elevation on a flat map, with each line representing a different elevation.

contrail A visible line of condensation in the sky following an airplane and consisting of water droplets and ice particles. Also known as a *condensation trail.*

convection The movement of warm air upward. (Hot air rises because it is less dense than cold air.)

Coordinated Universal Time (UTC) The official time reference for the entire world based on the time at Greenwich, England. The UTC abbreviation comes from the French translation of the term.

coral reef A ridge or barrier formed from the external skeleton of the marine animal coral. The Great Barrier Reef, off the east coast of Australia, is the world's largest coral reef.

core The center of the Earth, composed mostly of iron. Divided into two parts: a solid inner core and a liquid outer core.

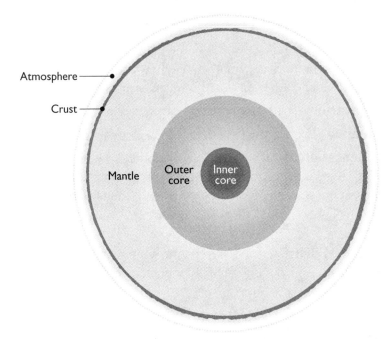

Coriolis effect The movement of objects like the wind and ocean currents to the right in the Northern Hemisphere and to the left in the Southern Hemisphere as a result of the Earth's rotation.

corrosion The erosion of rock by chemicals and water.

crater A cavity at the top or the side of a volcano created by an explosive eruption. Also can be a hole in the ground caused by a meteorite.

crest The top of a wave.

crust The outermost layer of the Earth's surface. Crust comes in two types: continental crust and oceanic crust. Continental crust is much thicker than oceanic crust.

cumulonimbus A large and tall thunderstorm cloud that produces lightning and thunder in addition to precipitation.

cumulus A type of cloud that looks white and puffy.

cyclone An area of low pressure with winds that rotate counterclockwise in the Northern Hemisphere and clockwise in the Southern Hemisphere. Opposite of *anticyclone*.

daylight saving time The changing of clocks to one hour ahead during the spring to take advantage of daylight.

delta A flat plain at the mouth of a river created by sediments deposited from the river. Named from the shape of the Nile's delta, which is shaped like the Greek letter delta, a triangle.

deposition The act of laying down sediments, often from air, water, or ice.

desert A dry region with little vegetation.

desertification The changing of non-desert land into desert due to drought.

dew point The temperature at which air cools causing water vapor to condense into water droplets, called *dew*. When you walk out of your house in the morning and find water droplets on your grass, that is the dew that was caused when the temperature reached the dew point sometime that night.

dike An outshoot of magma heading toward the surface that fills a crack within other layers of rock.

doldrums The calm surface winds near the equator.

drought A long period of time with minimal precipitation.

dune A hill of sand formed by the wind typically found in deserts.

earthquake A sudden release of energy causing the Earth's crust to move. Typically occurs along fault lines between tectonic plates.

ebb tide The receding of water after a high tide.

Is That a Fact?

Many people believe that when you flush a toilet, the water spins in one direction in the Northern Hemisphere and the other direction in the Southern Hemisphere because of the Coriolis effect. This is not true both because the Coriolis effect is not strong enough to influence such a small body of water and because the shape of the toilet bowl has a much greater effect.

ecology The study of the relationship between living things and their environment.

ecosystem The relationship of living things with each other and with their environment in a given area.

El Niño The periodic movement of a warm body of water from the South Pacific Ocean off the coast of Peru to the Western Pacific Ocean east of Australia. Affects global climate.

epicenter The point on the ground directly above the focus of an earthquake.

equator An imaginary line on the Earth's surface that is equal distance from the North and South Poles. It represents the 0° line of latitude and is the longest line of circumference around the Earth.

equinox The time when the sun is directly above the equator, causing day and night to be an equal length all over the planet. This occurs on March 21 and September 22. Equinox is the first day of spring and fall.

erg A sandy desert.

erosion The wearing away of rock.

estuary An area of a sea entering a river causing seawater and fresh water to be mixed.

evaporation The conversion of liquid water into water vapor (gas).

eye The calm and still, low-pressure center of a hurricane.

Fahrenheit A system for the measurement of temperature, with 32° Fahrenheit as the temperature at which water freezes and 212° Fahrenheit as the temperature at which water boils.

fault A fracture in the Earth's surface where opposing sides of the fracture move in relation to one another. A rapid movement along the fault can cause an earthquake.

fauna Animals.

fjord An inlet of a sea, with steep cliffs formed by glaciers. Most commonly associated with Norway.

flash flood A sudden rush of water typically caused by heavy rains in a normally arid area.

flood A large mass of water that takes over usually dry land.

floodplain The flat land surrounding a river that naturally floods when a river overflows its banks.

flood tide The rising of water to high tide.

TYPES OF FAULTS

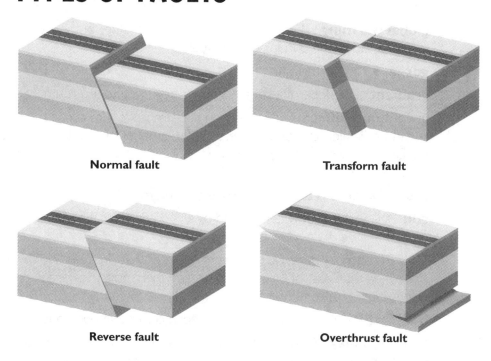

Normal fault

Transform fault

Reverse fault

Overthrust fault

flora Plants.

focus The point where the energy of an earthquake is released. Also called *hypocenter*.

fog A cloud on the ground's surface.

fossil fuels Coal, oil, or natural gas fuels that come from fossilized remains of plants and animals.

front The boundary between two different types of air masses.

Fujita scale A scale used to measure the intensity of a tornado, ranging from F0 as the weakest to F5 as the fastest and most destructive.

fumarole A volcanic crack in the ground from which steam and gases escape.

funnel cloud Swirling air beneath a cloud that becomes a tornado if it touches the ground.

geyser A hot spring that intermittently shoots up a jet of hot water or steam into the air.

glacier   A mass of ice that moves very slowly downhill, carving terrain along the way into cirques, U-shaped valleys, fjords, hanging valleys, and more.

global warming   The increase in overall temperature of the Earth believed to be caused by the burning of fossil fuels.

gorge   A narrow canyon.

gradient   The slope of a stream from its beginning to its mouth.

greenhouse effect   The increase in the atmosphere of certain gases, such as carbon dioxide, causes an increase in the amount of heat trapped near the Earth surface. As in a greenhouse for plants, the temperature rises in this closed system.

groundwater   Water that is trapped underground.

gulf   A large body of water formed by a curved indentation of a coastal shoreline, larger than a bay.

Gulf Stream   A large, warm current of water that circulates northward along the East Coast of North America and then moves toward Europe, where it moderates temperatures.

hail   Frozen balls of precipitation formed in cumulonimbus clouds.

hanging valley   When a tributary glacier meets a larger glacier with a deeper trough, the two merge and follow along the path of the larger glacier. When the glaciers recede, the tributary glacier leaves behind a hanging valley, a valley high above the larger glacier valley.

hemisphere   Half of the Earth. The Earth is commonly divided into north and south or east and west. The Northern Hemisphere lies north of the equator; the Southern Hemisphere lies south of the equator. The Western Hemisphere includes North and South America; the Eastern Hemisphere contains the remaining populated continents.

horse latitudes   Regions of calm winds around 30° to 35° north or south of the equator.

hot spot   A point in the Earth's surface where magma from the mantle escapes. The escaped magma sometimes builds up to create an island. Since the hot spot stays in the same location while tectonic plates above them move, the escaped magma sometimes builds multiple islands, creating island chains. Most notably the Hawaiian Island chain.

hot spring   A spring of warm water that has a temperature above 98.6° Fahrenheit (i.e., above human body temperature).

humidity   The amount of water vapor in the air.

humus Decomposed plant and animal material in the soil.

hurricane A tropical cyclone with wind speeds above 74 miles per hour. Also called a *typhoon* in the Western Pacific Ocean.

hydrologic cycle The natural process of Earth's water. Water vapor collects into clouds, then falls to the ground as precipitation, which collects in rivers and oceans, then evaporates to form water vapor once again.

hydrosphere One of the four spheres of the Earth. This layer includes all the Earth's water. The other three spheres are the atmosphere, biosphere, and lithosphere.

Ice Age A cold period in the Earth's past where vast ice sheets covered parts of several continents.

iceberg A large piece of ice that has broken off from a glacier or ice sheet and is floating in an ocean.

ice cap A very large glacier that is smaller than an ice sheet.

ice sheet A huge blanket of ice that can cover a continent. Ice sheets currently cover both Antarctica and Greenland.

igneous rock One of the three main types of rock. Rock formed by the cooling and hardening of magma or lava.

insolation The solar radiation received by the Earth.

internal drainage When rivers do not end by flowing into an ocean but rather end by evaporation or continue underground.

International Date Line An imaginary line near 180° longitude, agreed on internationally, where each day on the Earth's surface begins.

ionosphere A layer of the atmosphere, above the stratosphere, approximately 50 to 250 miles above the Earth's surface. AM radio waves bounce off this layer.

isobar Lines used to display atmospheric pressure on a flat map, with each line representing a different amount of pressure.

Is That a Fact?

The International Date Line can cause confusion for travelers who fly across it. For example, if you were to fly from Tokyo to Los Angeles, you might arrive before you left because as you cross the International Date Line, you turn the date back one day.

isotherm Lines used to display temperature on a flat map, with each line representing a different temperature.

isthmus A narrow strip of land with water on both sides that connects two larger landmasses.

ITCZ (intertropical convergence zone) A region of low pressure near the equator where air masses meet. Also known as the *doldrums*.

jet stream An upper-level current of westerly wind that can move at speeds greater than 200 miles per hour.

Worldly Tip

Do you have a hard time remembering which direction the lines of latitude and longitude run? Here's a trick to help you remember. The lines of latitude, which sounds like "ladder" (think "laddertude"), lie like the rungs of a ladder, and longitude lines are long and all run from the North Pole to the South Pole (i.e., there are no short ones).

karst A type of landscape characterized by subterranean limestone caverns carved by groundwater.

Koppen system A system used to divide the various regions of the Earth into different climate classifications, including polar, tropical, temperate, and more.

lagoon A shallow area of seawater located between the mainland and a barrier island. Also, water surrounded by an atoll.

lahar A volcanic mudflow caused by lava that mixes with rain or snow.

lake A body of water surrounded by land.

land breeze A cool wind that blows at night from the land to the sea. Opposite of *sea breeze*.

landslide A large section of a mountain that crumbles and quickly falls downhill as a mass of rock and debris.

latitude Imaginary lines on the Earth that run parallel to the equator, from 0° at the equator to 90° at the North and South Poles. The lines are the angular distance measured north and south of the equator.

lava Magma that has reached the surface of the Earth, commonly from volcanoes.

lightning A rapid electric discharge in the air during a thunderstorm, causing thunder.

limestone A sedimentary rock composed primarily of calcium carbonate.

liquefaction The process whereby water-saturated soil loses its ability to bear weight due to the vibrations of an earthquake.

lithification The compacting and cementing of sediments into sedimentary rock.

lithosphere One of the four spheres of the Earth. This layer includes the Earth's crust and the uppermost portion of the mantle. The other three spheres are the atmosphere, biosphere, and hydrosphere.

loam Soil with an equal mixture of sand, silt, and clay.

loess Sediments of silt and clay deposited by the wind, usually a yellowish color.

longitude Imaginary lines on the Earth that run perpendicular to the equator, from 0° at the prime meridian to 180° at the International Date Line. The lines are degrees of a circle that add up to 360.

magma Molten rock lying below the surface of the Earth.

magnetic north The point on the Earth's surface where a magnetic compass points. Not the geographic North Pole, but located in northern Canada.

mantle The area within the Earth between the outer core and the crust.

meander The S-shaped bend of a river.

Mercalli scale A scale used to measure the intensity of an earthquake based on damage and noticed effects, ranging from I to XII.

meridian A line of longitude.

mesa A flat-topped hill with steep sides. Larger than a butte. Hint: *Mesa* is Spanish for "table."

Is That a Fact?

Diamonds are a metamorphic rock. Underground, coal subjected to intense pressure for long periods of time can turn into diamonds.

metamorphic rock One of the three main types of rock. Rock formed from other rock that has undergone intense underground pressure and heat.

meteorology The scientific study of the atmosphere and the weather.

microclimate A climate of a small area, such as a farm or even a cave.

midocean ridge Mountain ranges that are under the ocean.

mineral A substance made up entirely of one element or one chemical compound. For example, a block of salt is a mineral because it is made up entirely of sodium chloride.

Moho Short for *Mohorovicic discontinuity*. The boundary between the mantle and the crust. Located approximately 25 miles beneath the continents and approximately 5 miles beneath the ocean crust.

monsoon Any wind that changes direction with the seasons, but most commonly used to refer to the annual wind cycle of the Indian Ocean and southern Asia. Known for bringing in storms from the southwest during the summer in southern Asia.

moraine A ridge composed of rocks of various sizes deposited by a glacier.

mountain breeze A wind that blows downhill during the night, from mountain to valley. Opposite of *valley breeze*.

natural levees Formed by sediments deposited by a river, a ridge that borders both sides of the river and keeps the river within its banks. Only in very heavy rain does the river rise to a level where it will overflow the levee and flood its floodplain.

Nuée ardente A superheated cloud of gas and lava that explodes from a volcano.

oasis An area of desert that has enough water to support plants.

oblate ellipsoid The shape of the Earth, slightly bulging at the equator. Although the Earth is almost a perfect sphere, the circumference of the Earth at the equator is approximately 41 miles longer than the circumference of the Earth through the poles.

ocean The body of water that covers 71 percent of the Earth. Although the five main oceans of the world are connected, they are typically referred to individually as the Arctic, Atlantic, Indian, Pacific, and Southern.

orogeny Mountain building.

orographic precipitation Precipitation that is caused by the uplift of air when it reaches a mountain barrier.

oxbow lake A crescent-shaped lake formed when a meander of a stream has been bypassed.

ozone Three molecules of oxygen, O_3. Near the Earth's surface, ozone is a pollutant, but between 20 and 50 miles above the Earth's surface, it forms the ozone layer that absorbs harmful ultraviolet radiation.

pahoehoe A Hawaiian term for smooth and pillowlike basaltic lava flow.

Pangaea The supercontinent that existed two hundred million years ago, consisting of all the modern continents combined into one.

parallel A line of latitude.

perigee The point in the moon's orbit where the moon is closest to the Earth. Opposite of *apogee*.

perihelion The point in the Earth's orbit when the Earth is closest to the sun. Opposite of *aphelion*.

permafrost Permanently or almost permanently frozen soil.

piedmont The area at the foot of a mountain.

plateau A flat-topped, elevated surface, larger than a mesa.

plate tectonics The theory that the crust of the Earth is broken up into several large plates that float like rafts on the asthenosphere, carrying the continents.

playa A dry lake bed in a desert.

pluton Magma that cools beneath the Earth's surface to form a large mass of igneous rock.

polar front A boundary between a cold air mass that originates at the poles and a warm air mass that originates in the tropics.

PLATE BOUNDARIES

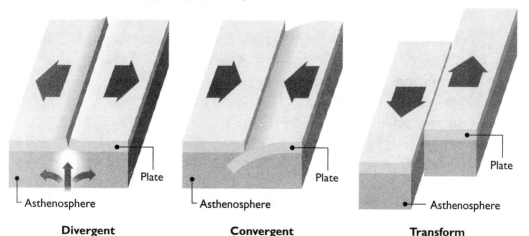

Divergent

Convergent
(subduction zone)

Transform

poles The northernmost and southernmost points of the planet. The North Pole lies at 90° North, and the South Pole lies at 90° South. The Earth's axis is the line between these two points.

pond A small lake.

precipitation Water falling from clouds in the form of rain, snow, sleet, or hail.

pressure gradient The difference in air pressure between two points. Pressure gradient is what causes wind because air will move from areas of higher pressure to areas of lower pressure.

prime meridian The 0° line of longitude from which all lines of longitude, and thus on which time zones, are based. It runs through Greenwich, England.

radiation Energy transmitted from an object.

rain Precipitation in the form of drops of water.

rain forest A moist area with dense vegetation, typically located in the tropics.

rain gauge A device that measures precipitation.

rain shadow The side of a mountain range that does not have orographic precipitation and is thus dry.

reg A rocky desert.

relative humidity A percentage that represents the amount of water vapor in the air compared to the amount of water vapor that the air can hold at its current temperature.

relief The difference in elevation between the highest and lowest points in a local area.

reservoir An artificial lake designed to store water for farming, energy, flood control, or even recreation. Often created by a dam on a river.

revolution The movement of the Earth around the sun, which takes precisely 365.242199 days.

Richter scale A scale used to measure the release of energy from an earthquake using whole numbers and decimals. For example, one of the strongest earthquakes to strike the United States was the 1964 Alaskan earthquake that had a magnitude of 9.2 on the Richter scale.

rift valley A valley formed when land between two faults sinks. The Great Rift Valley is a large rift valley found in Africa and the Middle East.

Ring of Fire An active earthquake and volcano zone that surrounds the Pacific Ocean.

rotation The movement of the Earth turning on its own axis, which takes twenty-three hours, fifty-six minutes, and four seconds (i.e., approximately twenty-four hours).

salinity The proportion of salt in seawater.

Santa Ana winds A hot and dry wind that blows down the Sierra Nevadas into southern California.

saturation When air can contain no more water vapor, thus causing some of the water to condense into dew.

savanna A tropical grassland.

scarp A clifflike slope, bordering a butte, a mesa, or a plateau. Also known as an *escarpment.*

sea breeze A cool wind that blows during the day from the sea to the land. Opposite of *land breeze.*

seamount A volcano under the ocean.

season One of the four divisions of the year (spring, summer, fall, and winter) based on the location of the Earth in its rotation around the sun and by hemisphere. They begin and end on either a solstice or an equinox.

sedimentary rock One of the three main types of rock. Rock formed by the collecting and hardening of small pieces of rock (sediments) together.

seismograph A device that measures the energy released by an earthquake.

seismology The study of earthquakes.

sensible heat Heat that can be felt and measured by a thermometer.

sinkhole A depression in the ground caused by the collapse of a karst cave.

sleet Precipitation consisting of rain that has partially frozen or snow that has partially thawed.

smog Although the term is formed from the words "smoke" and "fog," it is typically used to refer to any type of air pollution.

snow A form of precipitation made up of individual ice crystals.

soil Portion of the Earth's surface occupied by the roots of plants and composed of minerals, rock, humus, organisms, water, and gas.

soil texture The proportions of silt, clay, and sand in soil.

solstice The time when the sun is directly above the Tropic of Cancer or the Tropic of Capricorn, marking the beginning of summer or winter. The sun is directly over the Tropic of Cancer on June 21, marking the beginning of summer in the Northern Hemisphere and simultaneously marking the beginning of winter in the Southern Hemisphere. The sun is directly over the Tropic of Capricorn on December 21, marking the beginning of winter in the Northern Hemisphere and simultaneously marking the beginning of summer in the Southern Hemisphere.

spit A deposit of sand at the mouth of a bay. They are often straight or hook shaped. A very large and famous spit is Cape Cod in Massachusetts.

spring Water that naturally emerges from the ground.

stalactite An icicle-shaped mass of calcite that hangs from the roof of a cave.

stalagmite An icicle-shaped mass of calcite that protrudes from the floor of a cave.

stationary front A boundary between two air masses that does not move.

steppe A plain covered with short grasses.

storm surge The flood of water caused when the elevated dome of water created in the center of a tropical storm or hurricane by low pressure and wind is pushed ashore, often causing flooding.

strait A thin waterway between two larger bodies of water.

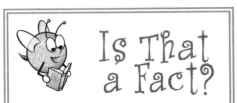

Is That a Fact?

To remember which limestone deposits are stalactites and stalagmites, just remember that stalac*tites* need to hold on *tight* to be able to hang from the roof of a cave.

stratosphere The layer of the atmosphere above the troposphere.

stratus A flat, low, gray sheet of clouds.

stream A small flowing body of water.

subduction The process of one tectonic plate sliding under another.

sublimation When ice converts directly to gas, bypassing the liquid state. For example, pieces of ice left in your freezer for a long period of time will shrink due to sublimation.

subsidence The sinking of land. For example, when too much groundwater has been pumped, the ground might sink, as in California's San Joaquin Valley. Also often found in a rift valley.

sun The star at the center of our solar system. Responsible for the energy that allows plants and animals to live.

thunder The sound produced by the violent expansion of air heated by a lightning bolt.

thunderstorm A storm that includes thunder and lightning, heavy rain, wind, and possibly hail from a cumulonimbus cloud.

tidal bore A wall of sea water that moves up a river during a flood tide.

tide The daily rise and fall of the level of the ocean caused by the gravitational pull of the moon.

till The mixture of sediments deposited by a glacier.

time zone One of the twenty-four divisions of the Earth that are based on the daylight hours for that 15° arc of longitude.

topography A description or depiction of surface features of an area.

tornado A violent, swirling column of air, created in a low-pressure zone, with winds exceeding 200 miles per hour. A funnel cloud that has touched the ground.

trade winds Winds that blow from tropical high-pressure zones toward the ITCZ.

tree line The elevation on a mountain where trees can no longer grow due to cold temperatures and limited water.

trench A deep valley underneath the ocean.

tributary A smaller river that flows into a larger river, thus contributing water to the larger river.

tropical depression A cyclone with sustained winds less than 37 miles per hour that usually forms within the tropics.

tropical storm A cyclone with sustained winds between 37 and 74 miles per hour, which usually forms within the tropics. Above 74 miles per hour, a tropical storm turns into a hurricane.

tropics The zone of the Earth between the Tropic of Cancer in the north at 23.5° North and the Tropic of Capricorn in the south at 23.5° South.

troposphere The layer of the atmosphere closest to the Earth's surface. It has a maximum height of 6 to 12 miles and is where almost all weather occurs.

trough A U-shaped valley carved by a glacier, or the point between two crests in a wave.

tsunami   A gigantic wave created by an earthquake or a volcanic eruption.

tundra   A cold region with only low-growing plants.

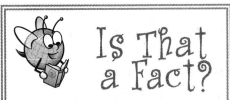

Is That a Fact?

In the morning of April 1, 1946, a large earthquake off the Aleutian Islands of Alaska spawned a tsunami. Traveling at hundreds of miles per hour, the tsunami went undetected as it traveled across the Pacific Ocean. Five hours later, it struck Hawaii, killing over 150 people and causing millions of dollars worth of damage.

ultraviolet (UV) radiation   Short-wave radiation from the sun, most of which is absorbed by the ozone layer. A large quantity can be harmful to living things.

upwelling   Where cold water from the deep ocean rises toward the surface.

U-shaped valley   A valley shaped like the letter *U* and formed by a glacier.

valley   A low-lying area surround by high terrain such as mountains or hills.

valley breeze   A wind that blows uphill during the day, from valley to mountain. Opposite of *mountain breeze*.

V-shaped valley   A valley shaped like the letter *V* and formed by water.

wadi   An Arabic term meaning a dry streambed that fills with water following heavy rains. Similar to an arroyo and a wash.

wash   A dry streambed that fills with water following heavy rains. Similar to an arroyo and a wadi.

watershed   An area defined by where its water drains. Specifically, a watershed is an area whose water drains into one stream or river.

water spout   A funnel cloud that touches down on water.

water table   A level underground at which the soil and rocks below are saturated with water.

water vapor   Water in its gas state.

weather   The condition of the atmosphere for one area for a short period of time, which takes into account wind, precipitation, temperature, humidity, pressure, and other factors.

wetland   An area of land covered in shallow water.

wind Moving air that flows from areas of higher pressure to areas of lower pressure.

wind chill The perceived drop in temperature caused by the presence of wind.

yazoo A tributary stream that flows parallel to a larger river until it finds a natural break. Named for the Yazoo River in Mississippi.

zone of accumulation An area of a glacier where ice accumulates, causing it to grow.

9

Level 6:
Extra! Extra!
Read All About It!

This chapter is the final lesson in preparing for the Geography Bee. Why are current events and map reading last, even though they appear in almost every Bee? The reason is because most questions found in these rounds give you enough clues to answer them without knowing current events or a particular map. What you really need to know is your world and U.S. geography—which you already do from Levels 1, 2, and 3. This chapter is designed simply to give you tips on how to become even more prepared for rounds that will focus on current events and maps.

Current Events

Almost every Geography Bee includes a round of questions about current events. Within the current events questions, you can nearly always find clues that allow you to use your geographic knowledge, rather than having to know the specific current event, to answer the question. Try this fictional current event question: "In January 2100, friendly aliens from the planet of Zolgar landed near the city of Sydney in which Southern Hemisphere country?" To answer this question, you don't even need to know about the event of aliens landing on Earth—you just need to know that Sydney is in Australia. Most of the current event questions in the Bee offer you a geographic clue, although they might not all be as easy as this sample question.

You should use your atlas like a dictionary, looking up unfamiliar places whenever you encounter them, not just when monitoring the news.

Nonetheless, if you have time, it is a good idea to learn about the major events of the year before your Bee. If you are to compete in the 2003 Geography Bee, you need to know the events of 2002. Remember, there are only twenty or so questions in each round, and you will only need to answer *one* question about a current event in any competition.

If It's Not in a Book, How Do I Find It?

You can be sure that many of the major events of each year will be asked about. The questions in the Bee tend to focus on global events rather than on events that occur in the United States. Thus, pay attention to world news. A good way to study current events is to read a newspaper or weekly newsmagazine or to watch the world news (not the local news) on television. Anytime you read or hear about an unfamiliar place while reading or listening, be sure to look it up in your atlas. By reading a newspaper or newsmagazine, you can learn more about the cultural and economic geography of the world.

It Is in a Book!

If you don't have much time to prepare for the Bee, a new almanac will list the most important events of the previous year. Also, you can often find lists of the most important events of a year online. If you have time, keep a journal of the major events as you find them, making sure to record both the event and the country or place where the event occurred.

When studying for current event questions, be on the lookout for major meetings of international organizations, treaties, major disasters, major political turmoil (such as coups) in countries, the election of new presidents and prime ministers, and geographic discoveries. Questions tend to focus on the latter half of the year before the Bee (for example, June through December 2002 for the 2003 Geography Bee).

Map Reading

Typically, map reading is a final round at the school, state, or national Geography Bee. Contestants are given a map to examine and are asked questions about the map. The map can be a weather map, a map of national parks, a map of major cities, or a map of just about anything. Each student is asked a different question about the map, and, as with all Geography Bee questions, the questions can vary widely in their level of difficulty. Thus, the student before you may get a really easy question, and you may get a really tough one; it's just the luck of the draw.

Maps

From the experience you have gained from the previous Bee Prepared levels, you should be a pro at using your atlas. This skill will come in handy if you are given a map question, because these questions are testing your ability to read maps. To do well, you should know the different components of maps and know how to use them.

Since you are often only allowed to see the map for a limited period of time, the first thing you should look at is the legend or key. The legend will tell you what the symbols on the map represent. Many of the map questions will be testing your ability to use the legend. As long as you pay attention to the map and legend, you should do fine. Prepare for map rounds by looking at maps everywhere— weather maps in the newspaper, subway maps in the city, road maps in the car, and especially maps in atlases.

Pictures

Sometimes, students will be shown an image and asked questions about it. For instance, in one state-level competition, the images projected onto a screen were the backs of state quarters issued by the U.S. Mint. The names of the states were removed from the quarters, and students were asked to identify the state from the image displayed on the quarter. Photographs of cities or other major features may be used as well. Most often, the moderator will provide a clue in a question about what is being viewed in a photograph. Knowing your geography will help you succeed in any type of image question.

Part Three

Parental Guidance Suggested

10

A Parent's Guide to the Bee

Although it is the student who stands up alone, facing the difficult questions during the Geography Bee competitions, parents play a very important role behind the scenes. This chapter is written for parents so they can help their child or children do well in the Geography Bee.

How Best to Support Your Child

One of the main ways to help a child is to give him or her plenty of support. The path to the National Geographic Bee is long and hard. It takes a lot of work and dedication from the student—far more than is required by school and society at that age. To do this, your child will need you there for support.

Worldly Tip

It is very important to attend your child's competitions. Find out when each competition is being held so you can make arrangements to be there. Even though competitions are held during the workday, just being there can be a great support for your child and help provide additional confidence during the competition.

Provide Encouragement

As a parent, you are your child's number one cheerleader. It is easy to become discouraged by all of the work and studying required to succeed in the Geography Bee. One of your jobs will be to cheer your kid on. Studying all fifty states and nearly two hundred countries can seem extremely daunting, especially to a fourth grader. Help your child to focus on just one state or country at a time.

Offer Rewards

Rewards can be a great motivator. Unfortunately, a $25,000 college scholarship does not mean a lot to students who haven't yet thought about junior high or high school, let alone college. Therefore, you may have to provide some shorter-term incentives. The key is to keep children focused on the Geography Bee and not on earning rewards. This requires a fine balance.

If possible, keep the rewards related to geography. For example, a reward for completing the research of all fifty states could be a globe to help research the countries of the world. Or it could just be going out for ice cream and spending time together. Avoid rewards such as toys or computer games that will divert the student's attention away from study. You do not want your child to just go through the motions so Mom or Dad will buy something.

What Can You Do?

In addition to offering support, you can actively do a number of things to help your child learn about geography and prepare for competition.

Provide Supplies

Preparing for the Geography Bee does not have to cost a lot of money, but some supplies are worth purchasing. An atlas is a good place to start. Remember to get a current and up-to-date atlas so your child can study the world as it is today and not as it was ten or twenty years ago. Many other reference books can be helpful; we've recommended several throughout this book.

Ask your child what other supplies would help him or her study. We recommend photocopies of outline maps found in this book, colored pencils, index cards to make flash cards, and a globe.

Discuss Current Events

Many students studying current events for the Geography Bee find the subject difficult because it is constantly changing and can rarely be found in one source. You can help your child study current events by watching the news with your child or circling articles in the newspaper or newsmagazines for your child to read. Choose major international events rather than U.S.-based news. Stay away from murders and mayhem, and focus on international conflicts, boundary disputes, large disasters, meeting of international organizations, and scientific achieve-

Worldly Tip

Reward your child's efforts to study for the Geography Bee. Rewards could include books on the subject, renting geography-themed educational programs, playing geography games, or going on trips to museums or parks.

ments. Be sure to take time to discuss these events with your child. Your child should know the location of the event, what happened, who was involved, and why the event is important. To reinforce the importance of location, you should always get out an atlas or a globe and ask your child to point out the location of the event.

Teach Map Reading

If you are going on a trip, get maps of your route and let your child help you plan it. Teach him or her how to read a map. It is important to give your child exposure to maps as representations of the real world. Then while traveling, let your child do the navigating along the way, including calculating how far it is to your destination, identifying the cities you pass through, and informing you when to make turns or get on different highways.

Another idea is to go on a hike. Try to find a topographic map of the area. Again, let your child plan the route. Along the way, you can discuss subjects such as natural landforms, erosion, types of rocks, and so forth.

Worldly Tip

Along with world news, encourage your child to watch the weather report. Since weather is a topic of physical geography, this could help your child learn more about this topic as well as how to read a weather map. National and world weather programs, such as those on the Weather Channel, can be great for observing weather patterns around the world and in different climates.

Visit Museums and Parks

A great way to make geography come to life is to visit places where your child can see firsthand what he or she has been studying. Natural history museums often contain exhibits on geology, cultures, and even plants and animals from around the world. Some larger museums may have exhibits illustrating earthquakes, volcanoes, weather, and wind.

National and state parks often have preserved natural landscapes from development. In parks, you can observe such geographical features as the ocean, rivers, the effects of erosion, geysers, gorges, waterfalls, and mountains. Try to tie in visits to both museums and parks to subjects included in the Geography Bee.

A Trip Around the World

A great way to cover a variety of geographical subjects is to plan an imaginary trip. This can be just cross-country or all the way around the world. As your child plans the route, you can discuss the areas you pass through. This can include interesting things to see or visit, the culture of the people, political information, and much more. Once the trip is planned, you can go one step further and pretend to be traveling. Each day have a theme based on a place along the route. You may have a traditional meal of the people of that place, watch a video about the area, or take a virtual tour of sites through pictures in a book or from a Web site.

Practice with Sample Questions

On a regular basis, you should offer your child practice question sessions. Use the sample Geography Bee–style questions we have provided in this book to test your child. Since all the questions at the Bee will be read aloud, read the sample questions out loud to your child for realistic practice. How often you give these quizzes is up to you. However, it is a good idea to do at least one a week. You don't have to spend a lot of time and ask lots of questions. Just twenty questions per practice session are usually plenty.

Worldly Tip

Keep track of your child's research and study schedule, and read ahead on the subjects by a day or two. Then, if you are asked questions, you are already familiar with the subject and can provide better guidance.

Worldly Tip

One family we know puts a question of the day on the refrigerator. It is usually a tough question. However, the children have all day to look up the answer if they need it. The mother says the children really learn a lot, and when they have to look up the answer, they remember it later.

Play Games

Several types of games that can be fun to play are also great practice for competition. Most stores selling educational toys carry geography games. Many have questions of various levels of difficulty so the entire family can play and learn together. Geography games can help teach your child to pay attention, listen carefully to a question, and analyze the question without looking at it. One good game is Trivial Pursuit, especially if you use only the blue geography questions.

Host Family Geography Bees

As the competitions near, put together a family Geography Bee. Invite friends and classmates to participate as well. Assemble lots of questions divided by topic. The bee should consist of a number of different rounds with a different topic for each round. The more you can make your bee resemble the real thing, the better prepared your child will be.

11

A Teacher's Guide to the Bee

As a teacher, you have many things to cover during the course of the school year. Depending on whether you teach a single subject or multiple subjects, the amount of preparation you can provide your students for the Geography Bee varies. The fact that you are reading this book in the first place probably means that you teach a subject somehow related to geography. Since most schools do not offer a separate course in geography, at least in grades 4 through 8, your class will cover only a portion of the material in the Bee. That is fine. You can still do a lot to help your students excel.

Geography As Part of Your Curriculum

The first step in helping students prepare for the Geography Bee is to look at the subject or subjects you are teaching and see where geography fits in. Review the topics covered by the Geography Bee and find

Note to Administrators and Department Heads

Having a student from your school win at the state level and go on to the national Geography Bee is an honor. If the student wins the national competition, it is even better. However, rather than just hoping one of your students does well, you can implement a program throughout the school to help students prepare. This should involve the social studies department as well as the science department. Within each class's normal curriculum, emphasize those areas covered by the Geography Bee. Make the classroom-level and schoolwide competitions exciting. Build up the competitions by putting posters around campus and inviting professionals in the geography field to speak. Be sure to invite the local media to attend. You may also consider finding local businesses to sponsor the event and donate prizes to the winners at different levels. The Geography Bee, as well as other academic competitions, should be given attention similar to that shown to athletic events.

similar areas in your current curriculum. For example, if you are teaching a multiple-subject class and the focus of your social studies for the year is South America, then concentrate on this continent. Teach about each country, including politics, economics, and culture. Don't worry that you are not covering the entire world. The same goes for physical geography. If you can fit weather, volcanoes, glaciers, and mountains into your science curriculum, do so. Whatever you can cover will help your students.

When Should You Start?

The classroom- and school-level competitions usually take place in December or January. So when should you get started? As soon as possible! While it would seem natural to cram as much information into your students' minds by December, you should also have a long-term strategy. It is important to concentrate on geography during the first few months leading up to the school competition. However, you should continue to cover Geography Bee topics throughout the year, since your students will be able to compete again next year (unless, of course, they are eighth graders).

Teaching Geography

Many different books and resources about teaching geography are available, and they vary from grade to grade. Details on teaching geography do not fit within the scope of this book. However, we would like to offer some suggestions and tips that teachers have shared with us.

Visualize the World

It is important for students to be able to visualize the world in their minds. If you mention Bangladesh, students should be able to picture where this country is located as well as point it out on a map or globe. It is amazing how many Americans, adults as well as students, have very little knowledge about the world.

One of the best ways to teach visualization is through the use of blank maps. It is usually best to use a separate map for each continent. The map contains national boundaries and possibly major rivers and mountain ranges. Give the students copies of the maps and assign them to write in names of countries and any other information you want, including capital cities. After filling out their maps, students should use them to study. Then test the students by giving them another blank map and ask them to fill in all of the information from memory.

Both teachers and students have told us this method works well. During the Geography Bee, students may be asked questions such as which country is directly north of another. Therefore, they must be able to visualize the map to find the correct answer.

Explore Different Cultures

One teacher shared with us her method of teaching students about different cultures around the world. On a regular basis, she invites guest speakers to come in and share their cultures with the class. This may include traditional dress, customs, food, games, and even a brief lesson in language. The cultures are chosen to coincide with countries or parts of the world that the class is studying at the time. Experiences like these will be remembered by students for a long time, and they put a personal face and voice to a culture that normally would only be read about in a textbook.

Focus on Current Events

Current events is an easy subject to add to a social studies curriculum. Not only does it encourage students to learn about what is going on in the world around them, but it also is necessary as preparation for the Geography Bee. Several teachers we spoke with asked students to keep a scrapbook of articles from newspapers and newsmagazines. They could also write a paragraph about a story they saw on a local news broadcast. Depending on the grade level, students might be required to write one article per week or even one per day. You can ask them to focus on national and world news rather than local news for the purpose of the Geography Bee or your curriculum. The key of this exercise is to encourage students to read and listen to world events.

Practice Geography Bees

Unfortunately for some students, the first time they hear of the Geography Bee is the day their teacher holds the class competition. They have no preparation other than what knowledge they have retained on their own. These students have little chance of winning the school competition, let alone passing the written test to qualify for the state Geography Bee. You should not only prepare your students by teaching them geography but also hold practice geography bees.

At least once before the actual classroom competition, put together a practice bee. Write your own questions, or use questions from past geography bees, from the Internet, or even from this book. Run the practice bee just as you would the real thing. This will give your students experience in this type of competition and teach them to listen carefully to the questions as they are asked.

Form Geography Clubs

Many schools around the nation have begun to form geography clubs. Their purpose is to help students prepare for the Geography Bee. One or two teachers usually sponsor the club, which meets regularly after school. Within the club, students can share information they have found on the various topics covered by the Bee and quiz each other with sample questions. Club meetings are also excellent times to have practice bees to prepare students for actual competition. If your school does not already have such a club, talk to your principal about starting one. Some geography clubs raise money to go on field trips to museums and other educational exhibits and promote the Geography Bee around the campus.

Worldly Tip

For more tips and ideas on teaching geography in the classroom, check out the National Geographic Society's Web site (www.nationalgeographic.com). It has a complete section on this topic.

Encourage Individual Preparation

There is no way teachers alone can prepare students for the Geography Bee. Success, especially at the state and national levels, requires hard work by the individual students. If you have some students who are really excited about the Geography Bee and want to do well, give them some pointers about what they need to do. Share some of the ideas in this book as well as tips from your own experience. You can also suggest resources for them to study. Above all else, encourage them to do their best and to work hard.

Part Four

1,001 Sample Questions

12

United States

This chapter and the ones that follow are sample questions of the type found in the National Geographic Bee. Since the questions at the Bee are read orally, we strongly recommend that the student preparing for the Bee have someone read these questions to them. Also, don't attempt all the questions in one sitting. It would be best to be tested on approximately twenty of the questions at a time. This allows the student to remain focused and to research the questions that were answered incorrectly. Remember that at the Geography Bee, the student will generally only have to answer seven questions, each about a different topic, to advance to the final round.

The questions in this chapter are about the geography of the United States and include a choice of two answers. Hint: If you don't know the answer immediately, try to determine which of the answer choices is definitely incorrect.

If you happen to find these questions too easy or simply want a greater challenge, some of these questions can be asked open-ended.

1. In the southwestern United States, a region called the Sunbelt includes which state—Indiana or New Mexico?
New Mexico

2. Which state borders the Atlantic Ocean—South Carolina or South Dakota?
South Carolina

3. Which state borders the Gulf of Mexico—Alabama or Arizona?
Alabama

4. Which capital city lies east of the Rocky Mountains—Sacramento or Columbus?
Columbus

5. Which mountains have the higher elevation—the Sierra Nevada or the Ozark Mountains?
The Sierra Nevada

6. Death Valley, which contains the lowest point in the United States, is located in which state—Ohio or California?
California

7. Which city is the largest city in Kentucky and the home of the Kentucky Derby—Louisville or Knoxville?
Louisville

8. The second-largest state in area in the United States is which state—Texas or California?
Texas

9. The smallest state in area in the United States is which state—Connecticut or Rhode Island?
Rhode Island

10. Which state is located between Kansas and Texas—Oklahoma or Arizona?
Oklahoma

11. Located in Alaska, which mountain peak is the tallest in the United States—Mount McKinley or Mount Rainier?
Mount McKinley

12. Which of the Great Lakes is the largest—Lake Michigan or Lake Superior?
Lake Superior

13. Lake Tahoe lies on the border of California and which other state—Nevada or New Mexico?
Nevada

14. The junction of the Mississippi and Ohio Rivers form the southern boundary of which state—Illinois or Idaho?
Illinois

15. Lake Okeechobee, the largest lake in the southern United States, is located in which state—Kansas or Florida?
Florida

16. Which state is the westernmost in longitude—Hawaii or Alaska?
Alaska

17. Lake Ontario borders which state—New York or Delaware?
New York

18. Lake Powell and Lake Mead are located on which major river— the Missouri River or the Colorado River?
The Colorado River

19. The Columbia River forms part of the southern boundary of Washington and which state—Oregon or Montana?
Oregon

20. Which state is located along the Appalachian Mountains—Virginia or Nevada?
Virginia

21. The city of New Orleans lies along the delta of which major river—the Colorado River or the Mississippi River?

The Mississippi River

22. Which coastal New Jersey city is known for its casinos—Atlantic City or Pittsburgh?

Atlantic City

23. In which southern state did President George W. Bush serve as governor—Texas or West Virginia?

Texas

24. Which major lake is located in Utah—Lake Winnipeg or Great Salt Lake?

Great Salt Lake

25. Which large lake is adjacent to the city of New Orleans—Lake Erie or Lake Pontchartrain?

Lake Pontchartrain

26. Which state borders four of the five Great Lakes—Michigan or New York?

Michigan

27. Which state has more people per square mile—Montana or Massachusetts?

Massachusetts

28. Which state is located in the region known as the Great Plains—Iowa or Ohio?

Iowa

29. Which state has the capital of Bismark and is located east of Montana—North Dakota or Washington?

North Dakota

30. Which state is located in the region known as New England—Indiana or Vermont?

Vermont

31. Which region is an elevated area between the Wasatch Range and the Sierra Nevada—the Great Plains or the Great Basin?

The Great Basin

32. Which elevated region lies east of the Blue Ridge and the Appalachian Mountains—Piedmont or Tidewater?

Piedmont

33. The region known as Acadia is located in which state—Louisiana or Idaho?

Louisiana

34. Which river forms the boundary between Texas and Mexico—the Rio Grande or the Missouri River?

The Rio Grande

35. The Mesabi Range, known for its deposits of iron ore, is located in which state—New Mexico or Minnesota?

Minnesota

36. Which state is one of the country's major producers of oil—Michigan or Texas?

Texas

37. Which national park is located in northwestern Wyoming and was the first national park established in the United States—Yellowstone National Park or Mammoth Cave National Park?

Yellowstone National Park

38. Which state is a major producer of dairy products—Wisconsin or Mississippi?

Wisconsin

39. Nantucket Island is part of which state—Pennsylvania or Massachusetts?
Massachusetts

40. The leading producer of uranium in the United States is which state—Alabama or Wyoming?
Wyoming

41. The population center of the United States is located in which state—Missouri or Florida?
Missouri

42. Which state produces a large amount of cotton—Montana or South Carolina?
South Carolina

43. Which state is famous for its apples—Washington or Oklahoma?
Washington

44. Spanish missions were established in the eighteenth century in which state—California or Maryland?
California

45. Which California valley is responsible for most of the nation's grapes—Death Valley or Central Valley?
Central Valley

46. Which state leads the country in the number of clothing manufacturers—Georgia or New York?
New York

47. Which state is home to the Winter Wheat Belt—Hawaii or Kansas?
Kansas

48. Which state has Columbia as its capital city and lies along the Atlantic Ocean—South Carolina or Ohio?
South Carolina

49. Which state's capital is Lansing and is known as the Wolverine State—Michigan or Connecticut?
Michigan

50. Which territory is not part of any state and is located between Maryland and Virginia—Puerto Rico or Washington, D.C.?
Washington, D.C.

51. Pensacola and Tampa can be found in which state—Florida or Rhode Island?
Florida

52. Which city is the capital of Illinois and the burial place of Abraham Lincoln—Springfield or Nashville?
Springfield

53. Which city is the capital of New Mexico and is also the oldest capital city in the United States—Santa Fe or Atlanta?
Santa Fe

54. Which U.S. state is composed only of islands—Alaska or Hawaii?
Hawaii

55. The cities Mobile and Montgomery can be found in which state—Minnesota or Alabama?
Alabama

56. In which state can you find the largest county, San Bernardino—Pennsylvania or California?
California

57. The northernmost point of the United States is located in which state—Alaska or Montana?
Alaska

58. Which is the easternmost of the forty-eight contiguous states—Tennessee or Maine?
Maine

59. Crater Lake, the deepest lake in the United States, can be found in which state—Oregon or Arizona?
Oregon

60. In which state could you find the country's tallest building, the Sears Tower—Illinois or New York?
Illinois

61. Which state has the longest coastline—Florida or Alaska?
Alaska

62. The Ohio River forms the boundary between Indiana and which state to the south—Missouri or Kentucky?
Kentucky

63. The Savannah River forms the boundary between South Carolina and which state to the southwest—Tennessee or Georgia?
Georgia

64. Which river forms the boundary between Vermont and New Hampshire—the Connecticut River or the Red River?
The Connecticut River

65. The latitude 42° North represents the northern boundary of California, Utah, and which other state—Nevada or Iowa?
Nevada

66. Which lake lies between Vermont and New York—Lake Havasu or Lake Champlain?
Lake Champlain

67. Which region contains the states of Washington and Oregon and is known for receiving a lot of rain—the Pacific Northwest or New England?
The Pacific Northwest

68. The Golden Gate Bridge and the Bay Bridge are located in which city—San Francisco or New York?
San Francisco

69. Which state is the most populous in the United States—California or New York?
California

70. Which state is located between Georgia and Mississippi—Kentucky or Alabama?
Alabama

71. Which mountain range is located farther west—the Catskill Mountains or the Cascade Range?
The Cascade Range

72. Which national park is located in South Dakota and is known for its fossils—Badlands National Park or Crater Lake National Park?
Badlands National Park

73. The Navajo Reservation lies primarily within which state—Arizona or Kansas?
Arizona

74. Active volcanoes Kilauea and Mauna Loa are located in which national park—Lassen Volcanic National Park or Hawaii Volcanoes National Park?
Hawaii Volcanoes National Park

75. In which state can you find the Valley of Ten Thousand Smokes, located in Katmai National Park—Montana or Alaska?
Alaska

76. Which state is one of the country's major producers of corn—Illinois or Florida?
Illinois

77. Which city lies on the opposite side of the Mississippi River from Minneapolis—St. Paul or Chicago?
St. Paul

78. By area, which is the largest city in the United States—Juneau or New York City?
Juneau

79. Which state is the leading producer of cranberries—Florida or Massachusetts?
Massachusetts

80. Large underground caverns form Carlsbad Caverns in which state—New Mexico or Kentucky?
New Mexico

81. Theodore Roosevelt's ranch forms much of Theodore Roosevelt National Park in which state—New York or North Dakota?
North Dakota

82. In which state can you find the Golden Spike National Historic Site, which commemorates the completion of the transcontinental railroad—Utah or Nebraska?
Utah

83. Which state increased in size due to the Gadsden Purchase in 1853—Washington or New Mexico?
New Mexico

84. During the Civil War, the Battle of Vicksburg was a major turning point. This town is located in which state along the Mississippi River—Alabama or Mississippi?
Mississippi

85. Active volcanoes are associated with which western mountain range—the Cascade Range or the Adirondack Mountains?
The Cascade Range

86. Which state would be most likely to experience a hurricane—
Idaho or Texas?

Texas

87. The Gateway Arch is a major monument in which Midwestern
city—St. Louis or Boise?

St. Louis

88. Which state would be most likely to experience a tsunami—
Hawaii or Wisconsin?

Hawaii

89. Which state is bordered by the Arctic Ocean—Alaska or Maine?

Alaska

90. Which mountain range lies directly east of Salt Lake City—the Coast
Range or the Wasatch Range?

The Wasatch Range

91. The border between Montana and Idaho lies along which mountain
range—the White Mountains or the Bitterroot Range?

The Bitterroot Range

92. In which mountain chain would you find the Allegheny
Mountains—the Appalachian Mountains or the Rocky Mountains?

The Appalachian Mountains

93. Though Anchorage is the largest city in Alaska by population, which
city is Alaska's capital—Fairbanks or Juneau?

Juneau

94. The Black Hills lie along the border of Wyoming and which other
state—Missouri or South Dakota?

South Dakota

95. Which city is the capital of Maryland and the location of the United
States Naval Academy—Annapolis or Raleigh?

Annapolis

96. Near which lake would you find the northernmost point in the lower forty-eight states—Shasta Lake or Lake of the Woods?
Lake of the Woods

97. In which state are you more likely to find a bayou, a small, swampy body of water—Louisiana or Montana?
Louisiana

98. The Mall of America, the largest shopping center in the United States, is located in which state—Utah or Minnesota?
Minnesota

99. Early settlers traveled through the Cumberland Gap, a pass through the Cumberland Mountains connecting Kentucky, Tennessee, and which state—Virginia or Indiana?
Virginia

100. For more than a century, people immigrating to the United States arrived at Ellis Island, located in the harbor of which city—New York City or San Francisco?
New York City

101. The Bonneville Speedway, where many land speed records have been set, is located in which state—Utah or Indiana?
Utah

102. Mount Whitney, the tallest mountain in the lower forty-eight states, is located in which state—Washington or California?
California

103. The first oil well in the world was drilled in which state—Texas or Pennsylvania?
Pennsylvania

104. In which state can you find Hartsfield Atlanta International Airport, one of the world's busiest airports—Georgia or Illinois?
Georgia

105. Walt Disney World is located near which large Florida city—
Orlando or Anaheim?

Orlando

106. In which state is Mount Rushmore located—New Mexico or South
Dakota?

South Dakota

107. Phoenix, located on the Salt River, is the capital of which state—
Arizona or Iowa?

Arizona

108. In which state is Mount St. Helens located—Colorado or Washington?

Washington

109. Which state has the capital of Montpelier and is located east of New
Hampshire—Vermont or Pennsylvania?

Vermont

110. The Mississippi River ends at which body of water—the Bering Sea
or the Gulf of Mexico?

The Gulf of Mexico

111. The Kennedy Space Center and Cape Canaveral are located in which
state—Florida or Colorado?

Florida

112. Which city is the capital of Connecticut and a major insurance headquarters—Pierre or Hartford?

Hartford

113. The Platte River flows through which state—Nebraska or Kentucky?

Nebraska

114. The Finger Lakes can be found in which state—New York or
Wyoming?

New York

115. Which city is the capital of Louisiana and means "red stick" in French—Des Moines or Baton Rouge?

Baton Rouge

116. Which waterfall is located on the border of Canada and New York—Niagara Falls or Bridalveil Falls?

Niagara Falls

117. Which city is home to Harvard University—Providence or Cambridge?

Cambridge

118. The Declaration of Independence was signed in Independence Hall, located in which city—Cleveland or Philadelphia?

Philadelphia

119. Which city, known for its automobile manufacturing, is the largest in Michigan—Detroit or Richmond?

Detroit

120. Which Alaskan national park was formally known as Mount McKinley National Park—Denali National Park or Zion National Park?

Denali National Park

121. Kansas City can be found in both Kansas and which other state—Nevada or Missouri?

Missouri

122. Which state has interstate highways named H1, H2, and H3—Oklahoma or Hawaii?

Hawaii

123. Which state lies within the region known as Tornado Alley—Oklahoma or Oregon?

Oklahoma

124. Omaha is the largest city in which state—Iowa or Nebraska?
Nebraska

125. The world's first atomic bomb was detonated near Truth or
Consequences in which southwestern state—New Hampshire or
New Mexico?
New Mexico

126. The pilgrims landed on Plymouth Rock in which New England
state—North Carolina or Massachusetts?
Massachusetts

127. Which state borders eight others—Tennessee or Nevada?
Tennessee

128. Which state is the largest in area east of the Mississippi—Georgia or
Montana?
Georgia

129. Which city is the most populous in Colorado and is also known as
the "Mile High City,"—Aspen or Denver?
Denver

130. With the Louisiana Purchase in 1803, the United States bought from
France all of the territory drained by which river—the Hudson or
the Mississippi?
The Mississippi

131. Which state has the lower average elevation—Wyoming or
Louisiana?
Louisiana

132. Which state's economy would suffer more if tobacco were made
illegal—North Carolina or Illinois?
North Carolina

133. Which U.S. city is adjacent to Windsor, Ontario, in Canada—Detroit or Rochester?
Detroit

134. The highest settlement in the United States is in which state—West Virginia or Colorado?
Colorado

135. In which California national park will you find the country's highest waterfall and El Capitan—Yosemite National Park or Glacier National Park?
Yosemite National Park

136. Russia, Spain, and England have all claimed parts of which state—California or Florida?
California

137. Which state does not meet at Four Corners—Colorado or Wyoming?
Wyoming

138. The headwaters of which major river is located in Montana—the Colorado River or the Missouri River?
The Missouri River

139. Which state includes the Providence Plantations within its borders—Rhode Island or Virginia?
Rhode Island

140. Which state has more lakes—Minnesota or Alaska?
Alaska

141. In which Texas city would you find the Alamo—San Antonio or Albuquerque?
San Antonio

142. Which state is the principal source of oranges in the United States—Florida or West Virginia?
Florida

143. Which state is a major source of sugarcane in the United States—Idaho or Louisiana?
Louisiana

144. Which state is the southernmost—Florida or Hawaii?
Hawaii

145. Which southern state was the first to secede from the Union and began the Civil War—South Carolina or Maryland?
South Carolina

146. Which state was organized as Indian Territory—Indiana or Oklahoma?
Oklahoma

147. Leif Eriksson allegedly landed on the shores of which state more than a thousand years ago—Maine or Florida?
Maine

148. Which site in Kentucky has the U.S. Gold Bullion Depository—Fort Leavenworth or Fort Knox?
Fort Knox

149. The deepest gorge in North America, Hells Canyon, is located in which state—Arizona or Idaho?
Idaho

150. Which city was the first capital of the United States—Philadelphia or New York City?
New York City

151. New London and the River Thames are in which state—New York or Connecticut?
Connecticut

152. Which river forms the border between California and Arizona—the Colorado River or the Snake River?
The Colorado River

153. Which mountain range runs through West Virginia—the Blue Ridge Mountains or the Tetons?

The Blue Ridge Mountains

154. Which Missouri city is a country music resort—Branson or Beaumont?

Branson

155. Cleveland, Ohio, lies along which Great Lake—Lake Huron or Lake Erie?

Lake Erie

156. Which Virginia city was the capital of the Confederacy—Richmond or Norfolk?

Richmond

157. Which state seceded from another state during the Civil War—North Carolina or West Virginia?

West Virginia

158. Which mountain range runs along the California and Nevada border—the Rocky Mountains or the Sierra Nevada Mountains?

The Sierra Nevada Mountains

159. Pioneers headed west followed which major river across Nebraska—the Platte River or the Mississippi River?

The Platte River

160. Kellogg's cereal began in which Michigan town—Lansing or Battle Creek?

Battle Creek

161. Which of the following states was included as part of the Louisiana Purchase—Iowa or Illinois?

Iowa

162. Alaska was purchased from which country—Great Britain or Russia?

Russia

163. Cheyenne Mountain, the home of the North American Air Defense Command, is located in which state—Colorado or Montana?
Colorado

164. Arkansas is the only state in the United States to mine which type of mineral—plutonium or diamonds?
Diamonds

165. The 1993 Midwest Floods affected which state—West Virginia or Missouri?
Missouri

166. Charleston is a port city in which Atlantic state—Louisiana or South Carolina?
South Carolina

167. On Christmas 1776, George Washington crossed which river that serves as the border between New Jersey and Pennsylvania—the Allegheny or the Delaware?
The Delaware

168. The Mojave Desert can be found in which state—California or New Mexico?
California

169. The Laramie Mountains and the Bighorn Mountains can be found in which state—Wyoming or Minnesota?
Wyoming

170. The Sacramento Mountains lie in which southwestern state—Idaho or New Mexico?
New Mexico

171. The Appalachian Mountains are which direction from the Mississippi River—east or west?
East

172. The Everglades, a vast tract of marshland, is located in which state—Tennessee or Florida?
Florida

173. Madison is the capital of which state—North Dakota or Wisconsin?
Wisconsin

174. Which state ceded land to the federal government to create Washington, D.C.—Maryland or Pennsylvania?
Maryland

175. Which city in Missouri was the start of both the Oregon and Santa Fe Trails—Kansas City or Independence?
Independence

176. The Colorado River flows through which national park—Grand Canyon National Park or Death Valley National Park?
Grand Canyon National Park

177. The most productive gold mine in the United States, the Homestake Mine, can be found in which state—California or South Dakota?
South Dakota

178. Which state lies directly south of South Dakota—Kansas or Nebraska?
Nebraska

179. Which state has only three counties—Delaware or Maine?
Delaware

180. Earthquakes are commonly associated with the San Andreas Fault, which lies in which state—California or Alaska?
California

181. Dodge City and Wichita can be found in which state—Kansas or Oklahoma?
Kansas

182. Eastport is the easternmost city in the United States and is located in which state—Massachusetts or Maine?
Maine

183. Which city is the capital of Indiana and also home to a famous car race—Indianapolis or Harrisburg?
Indianapolis

184. Islands within which state's boundaries were captured by the Japanese during World War II—Hawaii or Alaska?
Alaska (The Aleutians)

185. Which state does not border the Gulf of Mexico—Arkansas or Alabama?
Arkansas

186. Chesapeake Bay is fed by which major river—the Hudson River or the Potomac River?
The Potomac River

187. Considered the computer capital of the world, the Silicon Valley is in which state—California or Washington?
California

188. Which state was the first to ratify the Constitution and is now the Chemical Capital of the World—Delaware or Connecticut?
Delaware

189. Which state was the last admitted to the Union, in 1959—Alaska or Hawaii?
Hawaii

190. One of the largest bird refuges in the United States, the Okefenokee Swamp, is located in which state—Florida or Georgia?
Georgia

191. Which New England state borders Long Island Sound—Connecticut or Maryland?
Connecticut

192. Which state has parishes rather than counties—Rhode Island or Louisiana?
Louisiana

193. In which state will you find Mesa Verde National Park, home of prehistoric cliff dwellings—Colorado or Arkansas?
Colorado

194. Which state was ceded to the United States by Spain—California or Florida?
Florida

195. Which territory of the United States was purchased from Denmark in 1917—the Northern Mariana Islands or the Virgin Islands?
The Virgin Islands

196. Which U.S. territory is larger in area—Puerto Rico or Guam?
Puerto Rico

197. Graceland, Elvis Presley's estate located in Memphis, can be found in which state—Kentucky or Tennessee?
Tennessee

198. The United Nations is headquartered in which city—Washington, D.C., or New York City?
New York City

199. In which state is gambling the leading industry—Oklahoma or Nevada?
Nevada

200. George Armstrong Custer made his last stand at the Little Bighorn in which state—Montana or North Dakota?
Montana

13

World

The questions in this chapter are about the geography of the world and include a choice of two answers. Usually, the first two to three rounds of a Bee provide a choice of two answers. Hint: You can often answer these questions by picturing the locations in your mind.

If you find these questions too easy or want a greater challenge, some of these questions can be asked open-ended rather than multiple-choice.

201. The Rio Hondo forms a boundary between Mexico and which other country—Belize or the United States?
Belize

202. Which lake is on the border between Chad and Cameroon—Lake Chad or Lake Victoria?
Lake Chad

203. St. George's Channel divides the United Kingdom from which nation—France or Ireland?
Ireland

204. Which country is the largest trading partner with the United States—Japan or Canada?
Canada

205. While La Paz is the administrative capital of Bolivia, what is the constitutional capital—Sucre or Lima?
Sucre

206. Which mountain range is the traditional division between Europe and Asia—the Hindu Kush Mountains or the Ural Mountains?
The Ural Mountains

207. Which river forms part of the border between Costa Rica and Nicaragua—the San Juan River or the Rio Grande?
The San Juan River

208. Which country is the most populous in the world—China or Russia?
China

209. Bikini Atoll, where the United States tested nuclear weapons, is located in which country—the Marshall Islands or the Solomon Islands?
The Marshall Islands

210. The Nordic Council is composed of Sweden, Norway, Denmark, Finland, and which other country—Iceland or Russia?
Iceland

211. Gibraltar is controlled by which country—Spain or the United Kingdom?
The United Kingdom

212. What is the most commonly spoken language in the world—Spanish or Mandarin?
Mandarin

213. What is the largest desert in the world—the Sahara or the Kalahari?
The Sahara

214. Which is the only English-speaking country in Central America—Belize or Panama?
Belize

215. The Forbidden City is located in which Asian capital—Beijing or Phnom Penh?
Beijing

216. Which country lies to the west of Austria—Slovenia or Switzerland?
Switzerland

217. Denmark lies on which peninsula—Jutland or Iberia?
Jutland

218. Which country controls more area of the island of Hispaniola—Barbados or the Dominican Republic?
The Dominican Republic

219. The source of the Danube River is in which forest—the Black Forest or the Forest of Ardennes?
The Black Forest

220. Located within Tanzania, which is Africa's tallest mountain—K2 or Kilimanjaro?

Kilimanjaro

221. Which country controls the European exclave of Kaliningrad—Russia or Germany?

Russia

222. Which country is located northwest of Nicaragua—Costa Rica or Honduras?

Honduras

223. The United States mined Baker and Howland Islands in the Pacific for what—uranium or guano?

Guano

224. The Roman emperor Hadrian had a wall built in which country—the United Kingdom or Italy?

The United Kingdom

225. Mosquito Coast is located in which country—Venezuela or Nicaragua?

Nicaragua

226. Polders, which are lands reclaimed from the sea by using dikes and pumping, can be found in which country—the Netherlands or Norway?

The Netherlands

227. Which is the largest lake in Africa—Lake Victoria or Lake Volta?

Lake Victoria

228. Which is the largest lake in Central America—Lake Nicaragua or Gatun Lake?

Lake Nicaragua

229. Which country annexed Tibet in 1950—China or India?

China

230. Where did Fletcher Christian and the rest of the HMS *Bounty* mutineers settle—Easter Island or Pitcairn Island?
Pitcairn Island

231. The first major city in the Western Hemisphere was located in which country—Brazil or Mexico?
Mexico

232. Walloons and Flemings are the two cultural groups of which country—Belgium or Bangladesh?
Belgium

233. Hernán Cortés defeated the Aztec Empire, which was located in which modern country—Peru or Mexico?
Mexico

234. The Great Rift Valley is located on which continent—Africa or North America?
Africa

235. Which country includes Caprivi's Finger—Namibia or Niger?
Namibia

236. Where did Charles Darwin observe different types of animals and develop his theory of natural selection—the Canary Islands or the Galapagos Islands?
The Galapagos Islands

237. Which country includes Anatolia—Turkey or Ukraine?
Turkey

238. In 1707, England and Wales formally united with which other territory to form Great Britain—Scotland or Ireland?
Scotland

239. What is the least densely populated country in the world—Saudi Arabia or Mongolia?
Mongolia

240. Which country, along with Colombia, forms the border of North and South America—Ecuador or Panama?
Panama

241. Which country has the world's highest minimum elevation—Nepal or Lesotho?
Lesotho

242. The International Court of Justice and the headquarters of Europol are located in which European city—Zurich or The Hague?
The Hague

243. What are the natives of Australia called—Aborigines or Pygmies?
Aborigines

244. How many capital cities does South Africa have—two or three?
Three (Pretoria, Cape Town, Bloemfontein)

245. A ship sailing from the Atlantic Ocean to the Pacific Ocean through the Panama Canal would mostly travel in which direction—south or west?
South

246. Which country invaded Afghanistan in 1979—Iraq or Russia?
Russia

247. Mount Everest, the world's tallest mountain, is located along the border of Nepal and which other country—China or India?
China

248. What is the smallest autonomous state in the world—Monaco or Vatican City?
Vatican City

249. Which country has the higher per capita income—China or the United States?
The United States

250. Which country is located on the Horn of Africa—South Africa or Somalia?

Somalia

251. The Barbary Coast of Africa is located along which body of water—the Indian Ocean or the Mediterranean Sea?

The Mediterranean Sea

252. Basque separatists desire independence from which country—Turkey or Spain?

Spain

253. Which country was the first modern democracy—France or the United States?

The United States

254. The French Riviera contains which small country—Monaco or San Marino?

Monaco

255. The Taj Mahal, the mausoleum of Arjuman Banu Bagam, is located in which country—Bangladesh or India?

India

256. The sacred Muslim city of Mecca can be found in which country—Jordan or Saudi Arabia?

Saudi Arabia

257. France and Spain jointly rule which country—Andorra or Luxembourg?

Andorra

258. Which country controls the Caribbean island of Montserrat—France or the United Kingdom?

The United Kingdom

259. Which country claims to be Europe's oldest republic—Greece or San Marino?

San Marino

260. Which country lies completely within South Africa—Lesotho or Swaziland?

Lesotho

261. Which country relies more on nuclear power—France or Romania?

France

262. The majority of the border between Canada and the United States runs along which parallel of latitude—49° or 54°40'?

49°

263. In which African country are the native people of Indonesian descent—Madagascar or Eritrea?

Madagascar

264. The world's tallest building is in which country—Malaysia or the United States?

Malaysia

265. The world's largest monolith, Uluru, is located in which country—Australia or China?

Australia

266. Which country has the highest mountain outside of Central Asia—Argentina or Switzerland?

Argentina

267. Which is the largest country in the world, by area—Brazil or Russia?

Russia

268. In addition to French, Italian, and Romansch, which is an official language of Switzerland—German or Dutch?

German

269. The Blue Nile and White Nile combine to form the Nile at which capital city—Cairo or Khartoum?
Khartoum

270. Which country is the world's leading producer of both bauxite and wool—Australia or the United States?
Australia

271. Which country produces the largest number of motion pictures each year—India or the United States?
India

272. Which country controls Western Sahara—Algeria or Morocco?
Morocco

273. Which river flows through Venezuela—the Amazon or the Orinoco?
The Orinoco

274. Cape Morris Jesup, the northernmost point of land, is located where—Alaska or Greenland?
Greenland

275. Which is the longest railroad line in the world—the Transcontinental Railroad or the Trans-Siberian Railroad?
The Trans-Siberian Railroad

276. In which country are humans outnumbered by sheep more than ten to one—India or New Zealand?
New Zealand

277. Which West African country's north and south boundaries parallel a river—Gambia or Togo?
Gambia

278. The Kashmir region is disputed by India and which other country—Bangladesh or Pakistan?
Pakistan

279. How many provinces does Canada have—ten or thirteen?
Ten

280. Which country is the world's leading banana exporter—Ecuador or Chile?
Ecuador

281. Which capital city is east of Warsaw—Prague or Minsk?
Minsk

282. The mouth of which major river is located in Mozambique—the Niger or the Zambezi?
The Zambezi

283. Which country is located west of Haiti—Cuba or the Dominican Republic?
Cuba

284. Which is the longest freshwater lake in the world—Lake Superior or Lake Tanganyika?
Lake Tanganyika

285. Which is the longest river in Europe—the Danube or the Volga?
The Volga

286. K2, the second highest mountain in the world, is located along the border of China and which other country—Nepal or Pakistan?
Pakistan

287. On which Japanese island is Tokyo located—Hokkaido or Honshu?
Honshu

288. The Rio de la Plata is located along the border of which country—Peru or Uruguay?
Uruguay

289. What is the name of Canada's newest territory (1999)—Nunavut or Inuit?

Nunavut

290. What is the deepest lake in the world—Lake Superior or Lake Baikal?

Lake Baikal

291. Which African country is located the closest to Spain—Morocco or Tunisia?

Morocco

292. Which African country is the only one in which Spanish is the official language—Sierra Leone or Equatorial Guinea?

Equatorial Guinea

293. Machu Picchu is located in which country—Brazil or Peru?

Peru

294. Which city is the capital of the Republic of Ireland—Belfast or Dublin?

Dublin

295. The Rub' al Khali, or Empty Quarter, is located within which country—Saudi Arabia or Sudan?

Saudi Arabia

296. Which territory has desired to leave the Republic of Yugoslavia—Croatia or Montenegro?

Montenegro

297. Which Indian Ocean country of islands has its own continental shelf—Cape Verde or Seychelles?

Seychelles

298. In which country would you find the Southern Alps—New Zealand or South Africa?

New Zealand

299. What is the world's most visited mountain—Mount Everest or
Mount Fuji?
Mount Fuji

300. Mexico is divided into how many states—nineteen or thirty-one?
Thirty-one

301. The Tyrrhenian Sea is surrounded by the territory of which country—
Greece or Italy?
Italy

302. Lake Nyasa forms part of the border between Tanzania and what
other African country—Kenya or Malawi?
Malawi

303. Which former Yugoslav republic's name caused trouble because it was
the same as one of the provinces of Greece—Albania or Macedonia?
Macedonia

304. Which country is the world's leader in cocoa bean production—Côte
d'Ivoire or Colombia?
Côte d'Ivoire

305. Which Canadian province is predominately French—Nova Scotia or
Quebec?
Quebec

306. Which African country was settled by freed slaves—Liberia or Libya?
Liberia

307. The Suez Canal connects the Mediterranean Sea to which body of
water—the Red Sea or the Persian Gulf?
The Red Sea

308. Amelia Earhart was on her way to which island in the Pacific when
she disappeared—Howland Island or Wake Island?
Howland Island

309. Transylvania, the home of Count Dracula, is in which country—Romania or Slovenia?
Romania

310. The world's southernmost city, Ushuaia, is located in which country—Argentina or New Zealand?
Argentina

311. Japan has yet to sign a peace treaty ending World War II with Russia because Russia has refused to return which islands to Japan—the Aleutian Islands or the Kuril Islands?
The Kuril Islands

312. Which country is located west of Sweden—Finland or Norway?
Norway

313. St. Helena, the British-controlled island where Napoleon was exiled until his death, is located in which body of water—the Mediterranean Sea or the Atlantic Ocean?
The Atlantic Ocean

314. The deepest lake in North America, the Great Slave Lake, is located in which country—Canada or the United States?
Canada

315. Myanmar was formerly known by what name—Tibet or Burma?
Burma

316. Which river touches more countries than any other—the Danube or the Nile?
The Danube

317. Which mountain range runs through Austria—the Alps or the Pyrenees?
The Alps

318. Bougainville and the Bismarck Archipelago are controlled by which country—Germany or Papua New Guinea?
Papua New Guinea

319. If you travel east from Slovakia, which country will you enter—the Czech Republic or Ukraine?
Ukraine

320. Which continent contains the most countries—Africa or South America?
Africa

321. Which is the world's largest gulf—the Gulf of Mexico or the Persian Gulf?
Gulf of Mexico

322. Which Southeast Asian country is one of the world's richest countries—Brunei or South Korea?
Brunei

323. Which Pacific island country has a large population of Hindus—Fiji or Micronesia?
Fiji

324. Which country gained independence from Brazil in 1825—Argentina or Uruguay?
Uruguay

325. The Crimean Peninsula juts into which body of water—the Black Sea or the Mediterranean Sea?
The Black Sea

326. Which is the only Catholic country in Asia—Indonesia or the Philippines?
The Philippines

327. Lake Volta is located in which African country—Ghana or Zimbabwe?
Ghana

328. Which country is located west of Thailand—Cambodia or Myanmar?
Myanmar

329. Which country attempted to adjust the International Date Line so that the entire country would have the same day—Kiribati or the Philippines?
Kiribati

330. Bohemia and Moravia are regions of which country—Germany or the Czech Republic?
The Czech Republic

331. Which country has the lowest maximum elevation in the world—Sri Lanka or the Maldives?
The Maldives

332. What is the world's most densely populated island—Java or Taiwan?
Java

333. The Gulf of Bothnia is located off of the coast of which country—Finland or Norway?
Finland

334. Savaii and Upolu are the two largest islands of which country—Micronesia or Samoa?
Samoa

335. The Aswan High Dam controls the flooding of which major river—the Nile or the Yellow?
The Nile

336. East Timor recently gained independence from which country—Indonesia or Malaysia?
Indonesia

337. Suriname was formerly a colony of which European country—Portugal or the Netherlands?
The Netherlands

338. Guadalcanal, the site of bloody fighting during World War II, is part of which country—Marshall Islands or Solomon Islands?
Solomon Islands

339. Which river divides Paris into the Left and Right Banks—the Meuse or the Seine?
The Seine

340. Which salty body of water is the lowest land elevation on Earth—the Dead Sea or the Salton Sea?
The Dead Sea

341. What is the title of the leader of the Vatican City—pope or mayor?
Pope

342. The Sakhalin Peninsula is part of which country—Russia or Italy?
Russia

343. The Acropolis is located in which city—Athens or Rome?
Athens

344. Which modern country contains most of ancient Mesopotamia—Afghanistan or Iraq?
Iraq

345. Which country is crossed by both the equator as well as the Tropic of Capricorn—Brazil or India?
Brazil

346. The Coral Sea is located between Australia and which other country—Papua New Guinea or New Zealand?
Papua New Guinea

347. The Gulf of Aden is bordered by Somalia and what other country—Yemen or Mozambique?
Yemen

348. Which country, with a capital city of Bishkek, lies between China and Kazakhstan—Kyrgyzstan or Azerbaijan?
Kyrgyzstan

349. Which mountain range runs through Italy—the Carpathian Mountains or the Apennines?
The Apennines

350. Guam is a territory of which country—the United Kingdom or the United States?
The United States

351. What holiday brings a great number of tourists to Rio de Janeiro—Christmas or Carnival?
Carnival

352. Which country recently returned control of the Panama Canal to Panama—Spain or the United States?
The United States

353. Which is the smallest country in the Western Hemisphere—Grenada or St. Lucia?
Grenada

354. Which country is divided into Turkish and Greek sectors with United Nations peacekeeping forces monitoring a cease-fire line—Georgia or Cyprus?
Cyprus

355. The Gobi Desert runs through which country—Morocco or Mongolia?
Mongolia

356. Which Pacific island country has a constitutional monarchy—Malta or Tonga?
Tonga

357. What Southeast Asian communist state has the capital city Vientiane—Laos or Myanmar?
Laos

358. A region called Punjab can be found both in India and which other country—Bhutan or Pakistan?
Pakistan

359. China, Malaysia, the Philippines, Taiwan, and Vietnam all claim one or more of which groups of islands—the Spratly Islands or the Palau Islands?
The Spratly Islands

360. What is the highest capital city in the world—Kathmandu or La Paz?
La Paz

361. Which country was formerly known as the New Hebrides before it became independent from France and the United Kingdom—Tonga or Vanuatu?
Vanuatu

362. The Persian Gulf War (1990–1991) was fought by a coalition of countries to liberate which country—Saudi Arabia or Kuwait?
Kuwait

363. Which African country separated from Ethiopia in 1993, causing Ethiopia to become landlocked—Eritrea or Malawi?
Eritrea

364. The statue *Christ the Redeemer* stands overlooking which Brazilian city—Buenos Aires or Rio de Janeiro?
Rio de Janeiro

365. Which Japanese city was the second to be devastated by an atomic bomb—Kyoto or Nagasaki?
Nagasaki

366. Where is the launch site for the European Space Agency—French Guiana or Tahiti?

French Guiana

367. The ancient city of Carthage can be found in which modern country—Tunisia or Greece?

Tunisia

368. Which country is considered one of the Baltic States—Estonia or Slovenia?

Estonia

369. In which South African country can you find the Makgadikgadi Salt Pans, home to many flamingos—Niger or Botswana?

Botswana

370. Which island country can you drive to from Saudi Arabia—Bahrain or Seychelles?

Bahrain

371. Okinawa is part of which country—Japan or South Korea?

Japan

372. Brazil was a colony of which country—Portugal or Spain?

Portugal

373. The polluted Gulf of Riga is off the coast of which country—Latvia or Ukraine?

Latvia

374. Which country is the world's second most populous and leads the world in tea production—India or the United Kingdom?

India

375. The Sinai Peninsula and the Qattara Depression can be found in which country—Egypt or Chad?

Egypt

376. Cuba, Hispaniola, Puerto Rico, and Jamaica are all part of which island group—Greater Antilles or Lesser Antilles?
Greater Antilles

377. Manila, the capital of the Philippines, is located on which island—Luzon or Mindanao?
Luzon

378. Which Latin American country declared independence from Spain—Benin or Venezuela?
Venezuela

379. Which country lies between Benin and Ghana—Togo or Burkina Faso?
Togo

380. The Maginot Line was built in the 1930s to protect which country's eastern border—Poland or France?
France

381. Zero degrees longitude passes through which African country—Mali or Burundi?
Mali

382. The Kattegat separates Denmark from which Scandinavian country—Finland or Sweden?
Sweden

383. Which country used Devil's Island, off the coast of South America, as a penal colony—France or the United Kingdom?
France

384. Which major mountain range runs through Bhutan—the Himalaya or the Atlas Mountains?
The Himalaya

385. Which country was the first to give women the right to vote—New Zealand or Brazil?
New Zealand

386. What is the capital of Morocco—Rabat or Casablanca?
Rabat

387. The Bay of Pigs is located in which country—Cuba or Liberia?
Cuba

388. The Baykonur Cosmodrome is located in which country—Russia or Kazakhstan?
Kazakhstan

389. Which South American country is a member of OPEC—Uruguay or Venezuela?
Venezuela

390. The invasion by Germany of which country began World War II—France or Poland?
Poland

391. Which country is north of Brazil—Bolivia or Guyana?
Guyana

392. Which body of water is located off the coast of Vietnam—the Bay of Bengal or the Gulf of Tonkin?
The Gulf of Tonkin

393. Macao, a colony of which country, was returned to China in 1999—the United Kingdom or Portugal?
Portugal

394. The Mozambique Channel separates Mozambique and what other country—Madagascar or Liberia?
Madagascar

395. The three corners of the Bermuda Triangle are Bermuda; Miami, Florida; and which other island—Trinidad or Puerto Rico?
Puerto Rico

396. Mumbai was previously known by what name—Calcutta or Bombay?
Bombay

397. Which small country lies between Switzerland and Germany—Liechtenstein or Luxembourg?
Liechtenstein

398. Which country is located immediately west of Ethiopia—Sudan or Zambia?
Sudan

399. Which country controls the province of Cabinda, located between Congo and the Democratic Republic of the Congo—Angola or Rwanda?
Angola

400. Which country is located immediately north of Burkina Faso—Angola or Mali?
Mali

401. Lake Geneva is located in which country—Austria or Switzerland?
Switzerland

402. Which volcanic country is home to the world's oldest parliament, the Althing—Iceland or New Zealand?
Iceland

403. The Atacama Desert, one of the driest in the world, is located on which continent—Asia or South America?
South America

404. The Cambrian Mountains can be found in which country—Romania or the United Kingdom?
The United Kingdom

405. Which mountain range is located in Iran—the Kunlun Shan Mountains or the Zagros Mountains?
The Zagros Mountains

406. What is the name of the narrow waterway that connects the Persian Gulf to the Arabian Sea—the Strait of Hormuz or the Suez Canal?
The Strait of Hormuz

407. The Falkland Islands are controlled by which country—Argentina or the United Kingdom?
The United Kingdom

408. Which Scandinavian country was invaded by Russia in 1939—Finland or Sweden?
Finland

409. Which African country borders the Mediterranean Sea and has a purely green national flag—Mauritania or Libya?
Libya

410. Turkmenistan borders which body of water—the Caspian Sea or the Black Sea?
The Caspian Sea

411. The world's first and longest subway system is located in which city—New York City or London?
London

412. The Strait of Magellan is located in which country—Peru or Chile?
Chile

413. The Rio Bravo in Mexico is known by what name in the United States—the Rio Grande or the Rio Brazos?
The Rio Grande

414. Jakarta is the capital of which Islamic country—Kuwait or Indonesia?
Indonesia

415. Which is the world's busiest seaport—Rotterdam, Netherlands, or Shanghai, China?
Rotterdam, Netherlands

416. Which indigenous people are found in New Zealand—the Maori or the Melanesians?

The Maori

417. Which country is composed of seven sheikdoms—Saudi Arabia or United Arab Emirates?

United Arab Emirates

418. The Gaza Strip lies along which body of water—the Dead Sea or the Mediterranean Sea?

The Mediterranean Sea

419. Which country is home to Mount Kosciusko and the Great Victoria Desert—Canada or Australia?

Australia

420. U.S. Armed Forces invaded which country in 1983 to prevent a coup—Grenada or Kuwait?

Grenada

421. Which country had a policy of apartheid—Somalia or South Africa?

South Africa

422. You can drive on the Autobahn while in which country—Italy or Germany?

Germany

423. In which country can you find the Bekaa Valley and Beirut—Lebanon or Oman?

Lebanon

424. The island of Tasmania is a part of which country—Australia or New Zealand?

Australia

425. Which river flows through Rome—the Rhone or the Tiber?

The Tiber

426. Which country is farther north—Algeria or Bolivia?
Algeria

427. The delta of which major river can be found in southern Vietnam—the Mekong River or the Ganges River?
The Mekong River

428. Which country is the world's leading coffee producer—Brazil or Colombia?
Brazil

429. The Bosporus in Turkey is a strait connecting the Mediterranean Sea to which body of water—the Red Sea or the Black Sea?
The Black Sea

430. Which European country has a capital city that was formerly the towns of Pest and Buda on opposite sides of the Danube—Hungary or Norway?
Hungary

431. Which city is Russia's Pacific Ocean port—Vladivostok or St. Petersburg?
Vladivostok

432. Which Canadian province was formerly known as Acadia—British Columbia or Nova Scotia?
Nova Scotia

433. What is the only Southeast Asian country never to have been colonized—Laos or Thailand?
Thailand

434. Where is Angel Falls, the world's tallest waterfall, located—Venezuela or Zimbabwe?
Venezuela

435. Which island nation seceded from Malaysia in 1965—Sri Lanka or Singapore?
Singapore

436. The Mayan civilization was centered in which country—Mexico or Brazil?
Mexico

437. The Tower of London overlooks which river—the Thames or the Severn?
The Thames

438. Which country is located due west of Iran—Yemen or Iraq?
Iraq

439. The Indus River flows primarily through and reaches the Arabian Sea in which country—India or Pakistan?
Pakistan

440. Which natural disaster is a greater threat to the people of New Zealand—volcanic eruptions or blizzards?
Volcanic eruptions

441. Which mountains run through South America—the Andes or the Sangre de Cristo?
The Andes

442. Which country is located south of Mongolia—China or Kazakhstan?
China

443. Tegucigalpa is the capital of which country—Honduras or Bolivia?
Honduras

444. Which country is run by a one-man dictatorship—Turkey or North Korea?
North Korea

445. Which river carries the most water in the world—the Amazon or the Congo?
The Amazon

446. Which body of water is located on the border of Israel and Syria—the Sea of Tiberias or the Sea of Galilee?
The Sea of Galilee

447. Which former Soviet republic rejected unification with Romania in 1994—Moldova or Hungary?
Moldova

448. In which Australian city were the 2000 Summer Olympic games held—Melbourne or Sydney?
Sydney

449. Which ancient civilization was centered in Peru—the Inca or the Olmec?
The Inca

450. Which former European country located east of Germany split into two separate countries in 1993—Austria-Hungary or Czechoslovakia?
Czechoslovakia

14

Physical Geography

This is a very difficult chapter. The questions are open-ended and are about all aspects of physical geography. Unfortunately, unlike most other types of questions in the Geography Bee, you must know the subject matter, rather than rely on hints, to get the answer correct. Fortunately, usually only one round of physical geography is in any Bee competition.

451. The gaseous layer surrounding the Earth is known as what?
The atmosphere

452. The reflectivity of a surface, such as the ground or a cloud, is known as what?
Albedo

453. The circumference of the Earth is largest at which imaginary line?
The equator

454. What is the name of the outer layer of the lithosphere?
The crust

455. What is the name for a rocky desert?
Reg

456. What large U.S. lake is the remains of Pleistocene Lake Bonneville?
The Great Salt Lake

457. What is the most abundant element, by weight, in the Earth's crust?
Oxygen

458. Approximately how long does it take for the Earth to rotate once?
One day, or about twenty-four hours

459. The tilt of the Earth's axis is responsible for what changes during a year?
The seasons

460. What is the name of the lowest layer of the atmosphere?
The troposphere

461. The sun is directly over the Tropic of Cancer at which time of the year?
June solstice (also acceptable: June 21 or 22)

462. The North Pole is dark twenty-four hours a day during which season in the Northern Hemisphere?
Winter

463. What term is used to describe crescent-shaped lakes, formed when a meander of a stream has been bypassed?
Oxbow lakes

464. Diverging winds have what affect on air pressure?
Lower or reduce

465. Earthquakes can cause large, damaging ocean waves known by what Japanese name?
Tsunamis

466. What is the name of bowl-like features cut into mountains or hills where glaciers form?
Cirques

467. Aeolian erosion is caused by what?
Wind

468. Smaller quakes that can follow for several days after an earthquake are known as what?
Aftershocks

469. A narrow strip of land (such as Panama) connecting two larger land-masses is called what?
An isthmus

470. What is the name of the "sea" in the North Atlantic Ocean that lies within the Gulf Stream and is named for the floating seaweed found there?
Sargasso Sea

471. The steep area between the continental shelf and the ocean floor is known as what?
The continental slope

472. Sand ridges that connect an offshore island to the mainland are called what?
Tombolos

473. What is the name of a narrow valley cut by a river so that the sides are steep?
Canyon (also acceptable: gorge)

474. The condition where the average temperature of the Earth is increasing, possibly due to an increase in greenhouse gases, is known as what?
Global warming

475. What three types of sediment are measured to obtain soil texture?
Sand, silt, and clay

476. Off the coast of which continent do most hurricanes that affect the United States form?
Africa

477. What is the name of the large flat areas along the deep ocean floor?
Abyssal plain

478. A funnel cloud that touches down on the ground is called what?
A tornado

479. Ozone is made up of three atoms of which important element?
Oxygen

480. What is the longest river in the world?
The Nile

481. The horse latitudes are found near which two imaginary lines on the Earth?
Tropics of Cancer and Capricorn

482. The inner core of the Earth consists primarily of which element?
Iron

483. What is the name for the calm center of a hurricane?
The eye

484. What is the name of the supercontinent from which all the present continents separated more than two hundred million years ago?
Pangaea

485. Heat index is calculated using temperature and which other measurement?
Humidity

486. What term is used to describe a spring that intermittently spurts hot water or steam into the air?
Geyser

487. What is the name of the sun's radiation that reaches the Earth?
Insolation

488. What is the area surrounding a river that would be covered by water during a flood called?
Floodplain

489. The measurement of kinetic, or thermal, energy is known as what?
Temperature

490. Gases such as carbon dioxide and ozone, which absorb heat released by the Earth's surface rather than letting it pass back into space, are called what?
Greenhouse gases

491. What valley in California subsided by as much as 28 feet during the 1900s due to the removal of a large amount of groundwater?
The San Joaquin Valley

492. What instrument measures air pressure?
Barometer

493. The percentage of the maximum amount of water vapor the air can hold is known by what name?
Relative humidity

494. The temperature at which air becomes saturated with water vapor as it cools is known as what?
The dew point

495. What is the name of the process of warm air rising?
Convection

496. What is the name of soil that is frozen permanently for most of the year?
Permafrost

497. Orographic precipitation can be found near what type of terrain?
Mountains

498. What is the name of magma that cools beneath the surface in chambers?
Plutons

499. Which tall and dark type of cloud is typical of thunderstorms?
Cumulonimbus

500. What is the largest inland body of water in the world?
Caspian Sea

501. Which wispy type of cloud can be found at high altitudes?
Cirrus

502. Which two waves from an earthquake can be used to triangulate the epicenter?
P and S waves (primary and secondary)

503. Which type of winds, converging or diverging, characterize an anticyclone?
Diverging

504. Rapid flows of water that quickly fill dry streambeds of a desert during thunderstorms are known as what?
Flash floods

505. In which type of front is a warm air mass forced up by two converging cold air masses?
Occluded front

506. Long ridges of sand, separated by troughs and created by the wind, are known as what type of dunes?
Transverse

507. Which mineral has the highest concentration within seawater?
Sodium chloride, or salt

508. Spherical pieces of ice falling from cumulonimbus clouds typically during storms are called what?
Hail

509. The boundary between drainage basins, such as the Continental Divide, is known as what?
A watershed

510. What is the name for a scientist who studies the weather?
Meteorologist

511. Washes, arroyos, and wadis are all names for what?
Dry streambeds

512. Barchan sand dunes are characterized by which shape?
Crescent

513. A fumarole is a volcanic vent in the ground that releases what?
Gas

514. What are the lines on a map that show areas of similar pressure called?
Isobars

515. Granite is an example of which type of rock?
Igneous

516. A vibration of the Earth caused by a rapid release of energy is known as what?
An earthquake

517. What effect causes free-moving objects in the Northern Hemisphere to be deflected in their motion to the right?
The Coriolis effect

518. When a small glacier flows into a large glacier with a deeper trough, what type of U-shaped valley remains when the glaciers recede?
A hanging valley

519. Which country has more tornadoes than any other?
United States

520. Which type of rock is created by volcanoes and volcanic action?
Igneous

521. What is the name given to dry, barren plains where the soil is mostly permafrost?
Tundra

522. Waterfalls consisting of several small steps are known as what?
Cascades

523. The difference in temperature between land and sea often causes what type of local wind?
Sea breeze or land breeze

524. Monsoons, which drop large amounts of rain in the summer, mostly affect which continent?
Asia

525. What type of feature is formed by lava that flows up into a fissure and then solidifies?
Dike

526. Off what layer of the atmosphere do AM radio waves bounce?
The ionosphere

527. What is the name for a landform created by till and deposited by glaciers?
Moraine

528. The intertropical convergence zone, or ITCZ, is a low-pressure band found where on the Earth?
Near the equator

529. Which scale is used by sailors to determine wind speed?
Beaufort scale

530. The point of elevation where trees can no longer grow due to cold temperatures and/or frozen soil is called what?
The tree line

531. Artesian springs that come up in the middle of deserts can create what?
Oases

532. Which sea was created by Arabia's movement away from Africa?
The Red Sea

533. In addition to thunder, what is another feature of thunderstorms?
Lightning

534. Large clumps of magma that cool and then rise to the surface to form mountain ranges, such as the Sierra Nevadas, are called what?
Batholiths

535. Large storms with winds over 74 miles per hour are called what?
Hurricanes

536. S-shaped curves in a stream or river are also called by what name?
Meanders

537. The powderlike particles of rock that spew from an erupting volcano are called what?
Ash

538. In which zone of a glacier would you find an area of growth?
Zone of accumulation

539. What is the name of the organic component of soil formed from plant and animal litter?
Humus

540. Most of the energy on Earth ultimately comes from what source?
The sun

541. Deposits of calcite that form on the roof of caverns into icicle-looking structures are called what?
Stalactites

542. The largest and most destructive tornadoes have what rating on the Fujita scale?
F5

543. Marble and asbestos are examples of which type of rock?
Metamorphic

544. In what form can most of the Earth's fresh water be found?
Ice

545. What is the name for the point at which the Earth is nearest the sun during its revolution?
Perihelion

546. In the Western Pacific and Indian Oceans, hurricane-like storms are called what?
Typhoons

547. What is the name of the large crater in a volcano?
Caldera

548. What type of precipitation consists of a mixture of rain and snow?
Sleet

549. The slope of a stream is known as what?
The gradient

550. What type of fault is the San Andreas Fault in California, where the North American plate and the Pacific plate slide past each other?
Transform

551. The boundary between the warm surface water and the colder deep water in the ocean is known as what?
The thermocline

552. Which waterfall has the largest flow of water in the world?
Niagara Falls

553. What happens to the perceived temperature when wind speed increases?
It decreases

554. Coal is an example of which type of rock?
Sedimentary

555. Why is the salinity of seawater often highest near the surface?
Evaporation

556. What agent plays the most important role in erosion?
Water

557. What term describes the largest type of glacier that covers large areas of land and sea?
Ice sheets or continental glaciers

558. The process by which layers of sediment are cemented together to form rock is called what?
Lithification

559. Volcanic eruptions combined with rainstorms can cause deadly mudflows called what?
Lahars

560. The period when glaciers covered all of Canada and parts of the United States was known as what?
The Ice Age

561. The Bergeron process is used to explain what weather-related action?
Precipitation

562. What term is used to describe a river dragging stones along its bed, wearing them away?
Abrasion

563. The average temperature and precipitation for an area determine what?
The climate

564. What term is used to describe air that is holding its maximum amount of water vapor?
Saturated

565. When a small stream flows into a river, like the Kaskaskia River into the Mississippi, the small stream is known as what?
A tributary

566. The point where the energy of an earthquake is released is known as what?
Focus or hypocenter

567. What are thermal springs called when their temperature is above human body temperature?
Hot springs

568. What term is used to describe a mountain valley carved by fast-moving water?
A V-shaped valley

569. What is the term used to describe the series of rapids along the Nile River?
Cataracts

570. As a stream curves, where is the velocity of the water, as well as the erosion, the greatest?
On the outside of the curve

571. What is the name of the process where cold, nutrient-rich water rises from the deep?
Upwelling

572. What term is used to describe a layer of rock containing water that can often be pumped from the ground?
An aquifer

573. How many high tides are there usually during a twenty-four-hour period?
Two

574. The ozone layer plays an important role by blocking which type of radiation from the sun?
Ultraviolet

575. What term is used to describe water naturally seeping from the ground?
A spring

576. Ring-shaped islands, created by coral, with a central lagoon are called what?
Atolls

577. Named for a river in Mississippi, what term is used to describe a river that runs parallel to another river until it can find a break in a natural levee?
A Yazoo tributary

578. What celestial body is primarily responsible for the Earth's tides?
The moon

579. During ebb tide, which way does the water flow?
Away from the shore

580. When a warm air mass comes in contact with a cold air mass, which is forced upward?
The warm air mass

581. What instrument records the intensity of an earthquake?
A seismograph

582. What Hawaiian term is used to describe lava with a smooth, glassy surface?
Pahoehoe

583. What is the name of the warm surface current in the North Atlantic that moderates Great Britain's climate?
The Gulf Stream

584. When the water table drops in Florida, some homes are destroyed when they fall into a depression in the ground known as what?
A sinkhole

585. During the 1930s, the Dust Bowl was created by a prolonged period of dry weather called what?
A drought

586. Water falling from clouds as rain, snow, or sleet is known as what?
Precipitation

587. What percentage of land is covered by glaciers?
10 percent

588. What is the name of the process when chunks of a glacier break off into the sea to form icebergs?
Calving

589. What is the name of the deepest ocean trench on Earth?
The Mariana Trench

590. An artificial lake, created by damming a river, is called what?
A reservoir

591. The valley between diverging plates where magma is forced up to create new crust is known as what?
A rift valley

592. The process of mountain building is known by what scientific term?
Orogeny or orogenesis

593. Where is the Earth's crust the thinnest?
Under the oceans

594. On a map, lines of equal temperature are known as what?
Isotherms

595. A body of water, larger than a bay and surrounded partially by land, is called what?
A gulf

596. What is the Spanish name for a dry lakebed in a desert?
Playa

597. Areas of low pressure where the pressure decreases toward the center are known as what?
Cyclones

598. The Richter scale is used to measure the intensity of what?
Earthquakes

599. Warm and dry winter winds along the eastern slopes of the Rockies are called what?
Chinooks

600. Within a straight stream, where does the water flow the fastest?
In the center

601. Which natural phenomenon caused by thunderstorms causes more deaths in the United States than any other natural hazard?
Lightning

602. The semiarid climate that often borders a desert is known by what name?
Steppe

603. What is the most common gas found in the atmosphere?
Nitrogen

604. The continental shelf is wider along which coast of North America?
The Atlantic or East

605. What types of climates are found in the rainshadow of mountains?
Dry, arid, or desert

606. What is the main source of erosion in a desert?
Water

607. Clouds and precipitation are caused as air rises or falls?
Rises

608. What causes surface currents?
Wind

609. What is the name of the condition where water-saturated soil loses its ability to bear weight due to the vibrations of an earthquake?
Liquefaction

610. What happened to the level of the oceans at the end of the Ice Age?
They rose

611. What is the name of a sandy desert?
Erg

612. A tablelike plateau, surrounded on all sides by scarps, is known as what?
A mesa

613. What is the name of the thin, linear clouds created by airplanes?
Contrails or condensation trails

614. Currents in the Northern Hemisphere circle around in which direction?
Clockwise

615. Molten rock under the surface of the Earth is called what?
Magma

616. What two things do deserts lack sufficient amounts of to help prevent erosion?
Water and vegetation

617. Name one of the two elements of which mafic rocks have high concentrations.
Iron or magnesium

618. Loess deposits of silt around the Yellow River in China were transported and deposited by what agent?
Wind

619. As altitude increases, air pressure does what?
It decreases

620. What is the primary cause of earthquakes?
Plate tectonics, or movement of tectonic plates

621. What is the name of the boundaries between plates, where most earthquakes occur?
Faults

622. What are the three different types of rocks?
Igneous, sedimentary, and metamorphic

623. The condensation of water in the air near the surface of the Earth creates a cloudlike effect called what?

Fog

624. Named for the shape of a Greek letter, what is the area where a river reaches the ocean and deposits its load of sediment?

A delta

625. What causes waves?

The wind

626. Minerals containing both oxygen and silicon are known by which classification?

Silicates

627. What is the name of the theory that holds that the continents are slowly moving apart?

Continental drift

628. What is the name of ridges of sand that collect several miles off the coast parallel to the mainland?

Barrier islands

629. What type of tectonic plate boundary formed the Mid-Atlantic Ridge?

Diverging or divergent

630. What is the term for the surface of water you must reach if you are digging for a well?

The water table

631. Which type of cloud is puffy and cottonlike?

Cumulus

632. What is formed when an oceanic plate is forced down by a continental plate?

An ocean trench or subduction zone

633. The ozone layer can be found in which atmospheric layer?
The stratosphere

634. What type of topography is characterized by subterranean limestone caverns carved by groundwater?
Karst topography

635. What is the top of a wave called?
The crest

636. The low pressure of a hurricane creates a dome of elevated water that is called what when it hits shore, often causing flooding?
A storm surge

637. Glaciers on their way to the sea caused what landform commonly found in Norway?
Fjords

638. The movement of air from a high-pressure area to a low-pressure area causes what?
Wind

639. What force causes water to flow from a higher elevation to a lower elevation?
Gravity

640. A deadly volcanic release, which flows on top of superheated gases and can reach high speeds, is known as what?
A nuée ardente

15

Human Geography

Questions in this chapter have been divided into four key areas of human geography: historical, cultural, economic, and political. They are all open-ended questions. At the Geography Bee, these types of questions may appear in rounds exclusively devoted to that topic or may appear intermixed in other rounds.

Historical Geography

641. It was said that the sun never set on which empire?
The British Empire

642. Which Aztec emperor was killed by Cortez and his conquistadors?
Montezuma

643. Who was the commander of the first expedition to circumnavigate the globe?
Ferdinand Magellan

644. A 1982 dispute over which islands caused Argentina and the United Kingdom to go to war?
Falkland Islands

645. Which two neighboring Asian countries both conducted testing of nuclear weapons for the first time in 1998?
India and Pakistan

646. Which sixteenth-century empire stretched from the Balkans, through Turkey, and into Arabia and the Barbary States?
The Ottoman Empire (also acceptable: Turkish Empire)

647. Which Southern Hemisphere country was founded as a British penal colony in the eighteenth century?
Australia

648. The first atomic bomb used for war was dropped on which Japanese city?
Hiroshima

649. Which North American colony became part of the British Empire at the end of the Seven Years' War in 1763?
Canada

650. The Bolsheviks, under the leadership of Vladimir Lenin, overthrew the government of which country?
Russia

651. Cleopatra was the queen of which ancient empire?
The Egyptian Empire

652. The storming of the Bastille in Paris was the beginning of what major event?
The French Revolution

653. In which U.S. state did the hydrogen-filled *Hindenburg* explode in 1937?
New Jersey

654. What was the name of the Spanish conquistador who plundered the Incan Empire?
Francisco Pizarro

655. The Jones Act of 1917 granted U.S. citizenship to residents in which territory?
Puerto Rico

656. The Cold War was a standoff between which two superpowers?
The United States and the USSR (or Russia)

657. Which European country invaded Ethiopia in 1935?
Italy

658. The Minoan civilization was centered on which island?
Crete

659. Mao Tse-tung was the first leader of which country?
People's Republic of China (if answer is China, ask to be more specific)

660. Which Mesoamerican civilization followed the Olmec?
The Mayan

661. Which country did the USSR invade in 1968 to end liberalization?
Czechoslovakia

662. What did Winston Churchill name the divide between free and communist Europe in a famous 1946 speech?
The Iron Curtain

663. During the Holocaust in Europe, which religious group faced genocide?
The Jews

664. Nuclear missiles on which Caribbean island created a crisis in 1962?
Cuba

665. A war broke out following the World Cup soccer match in 1969 between Honduras and which neighboring country?
El Salvador

666. What event brought hundreds of thousands of people to California in 1848?
The Gold Rush

667. The period of peace within the Roman Empire during the first two centuries A.D. is referred to by what term?
Pax Romana

668. Which Egyptian city was famous for its lighthouse as well as its library during ancient times?
Alexandria

669. The CIS, or Commonwealth of Independent States, was formed from the remnants of which country in 1991?
The USSR (also acceptable: Russia)

670. The 1914 assassination of Archduke Franz Ferdinand in Sarajevo led to which conflict?
World War I

671. The Vietnam War spread into which two neighboring countries?
Laos and Cambodia

672. Jawaharlal Nehru became the first prime minister of which former British colony in 1947?
India

673. What Greek leader conquered the known world during the fourth century B.C.?
Alexander the Great

674. On June 6, 1944, Allied troops landed on the shores of Normandy in which country?
France

675. In 1997, China regained control of Hong Kong from which country?
The United Kingdom

676. The Khmer Rouge began a reign of terror in 1975 in which Southeast Asian country?
Cambodia

677. In which European city were the first modern Olympics held in 1876?
Athens

678. Which Italian civilization preceded and was absorbed by the Romans?
The Etruscans

679. The Zimmermann telegram was meant to persuade which country to ally with Germany against the United States during World War I?
Mexico

680. In 1961, a wall was built in which European city to divide east from west?
Berlin

681. What is the name of the treaty that ended World War I?
The Treaty of Versailles

682. Who became prime minister of the United Kingdom in 1940, after the start of World War II?

Winston Churchill

683. During the American War for Independence, which European country sided with the Americans against the British?

France

684. Which conflict began in 1950 when communist forces crossed the Thirty-eighth Parallel?

The Korean War

685. What was the first Sub-Saharan country to gain its independence in 1957?

Ghana

686. The Contras fought for democracy against the communist Sandinistas during the 1980s in which Central American country?

Nicaragua

687. What was the first country to put a man in space?

USSR (also acceptable: Russia)

688. In 1978, which two countries signed a peace treaty as a result of the Camp David Accords?

Israel and Egypt

689. Who invaded England in 1066?

The Normans (also acceptable: William the Conqueror, William I, or William of Normandy)

690. Which group, led by Genghis Khan, conquered much of Central Asia, from China to modern Russia?

The Mongols

Cultural Geography

691. What is the official language of the African nation of Algeria?
Arabic

692. Which cultural group, composed of the descendants of French who immigrated from Canada to Louisiana, is known for their music as well as their spicy food, including gumbo and jambalaya?
Cajun

693. What religion was founded in Saudi Arabia during the seventh century?
Islam

694. Which Middle Eastern city do Christians, Jews, and Muslims consider sacred?
Jerusalem

695. Which country has eleven official languages, including Afrikaans, English, Swazi, and Zulu?
South Africa

696. What is the fastest-growing religion worldwide?
Islam

697. The Coptic Church is native to which North African country?
Egypt

698. Which country is the most populous in Western Europe?
Germany

699. Shinto is the indigenous religion of what country?
Japan

700. What are the two official languages of Canada?
English and French

701. What is the primary religion of India?
Hinduism

702. Kazakh and what other language are the official languages of Kazakhstan?
Russian

703. What 984-foot-tall skeletal iron tower was built for the 1889 exposition in France?
The Eiffel Tower

704. Which country, north of Australia, has more than seven hundred indigenous dialects spoken there?
Papua New Guinea

705. What are the names of the towers from which Muslims are called to prayer?
Minarets

706. The combination of trade, colonial conquest, and indigenous people developed what East African language?
Swahili

707. The Brandenburg Gate, once stranded in No Man's Land behind a very long wall, is now open in which European city?
Berlin

708. What is the official language of the South American country of Suriname?
Dutch

709. A famous opera house is an icon of which Australian city?
Sydney

710. The Kaaba is a holy Islamic site located in which city?
Mecca

711. Which nomadic culture lives in tents and travels with their herds throughout the Middle East?
The Bedouins

712. In 1958, the government of which country replaced its transliteration system Wade-Giles with Pinyin?
China

713. What is the second-most common language spoken in the United States?
Spanish

714. What structure is the only remaining wonder of the ancient world?
The Great Pyramid of Giza

715. What is the largest sect of Christianity, comprising about half of the total?
Roman Catholic

716. Members of which ethnic group born in the United States were made U.S. citizens in 1924?
Native Americans

717. The followers of what religion, common in Botswana, Zimbabwe, and Mozambique, believe that natural objects such as rocks and trees have souls that interact with humans?
Animism

718. In which city can the cathedral of Notre Dame be found?
Paris

719. What U.S.-based religion forbids the consumption of caffeine, tobacco, and alcohol?
The Church of Jesus Christ of Latter-day Saints (Mormon)

720. The Zionist movement sought to establish a homeland for which religious and cultural group?
The Jews

721. Which ethnic group makes up a vast majority of the population of China?
Han Chinese

722. A mestizo is a combination of which two ethnic groups?
Spanish and American Indian

723. Traditional Hinduism divides society into various social classes, with the lowest level being the untouchables. What is this system called in India?
The caste system

724. What are the two main sects of Islam?
Sunni and Shiite

725. Which minority ethnic group desires to create a state independent from both Turkey and Iraq?
The Kurds

726. The Pashtun are the largest ethnic group in which Asian country?
Afghanistan

727. What region of the United States is home to the legendary forest-dwelling creature known as Bigfoot?
The Pacific Northwest (also acceptable: Northwest)

728. In an attempt to control population growth, which country instituted a one-child policy in 1979?
China

729. Which major Christian sect broke away from the Roman Catholic Church during the Great Schism and had its center at Constantinople?
Eastern Orthodox

730. Along with Jews, which other group of people is also considered Semitic?
Arabs

731. In which tiny country are the main languages Italian and Latin?
Vatican City (also acceptable: the Holy See)

732. While Hindi is the official language of India, what is the most important language for political and economic communication?
English

733. So that traders in ancient Mediterranean ports could understand each other, a new language, "Frankish language," was created from a mixture of French, Greek, Italian, and Spanish. What is this type of language called?
Lingua franca

734. For most of the twentieth century, South Africa practiced a policy of racial segregation known by what Afrikaans term meaning "apartness"?
Apartheid

735. Sephardim, who settled in Northern Africa and the Iberian Peninsula, is one of the two main branches of what religion?
Judaism

736. What type of tourism is pursued by those interested in visiting preserved environmental areas without impacting those sites?
Ecotourism

737. Which religion found in Haiti as well as other places combines Roman Catholicism with West African tribal traditions?
Voodoo

738. Some pregnant women in the southern United States and in Africa practice geophagy, which means they eat what?
Earth or clay

739. What is the most popular sport in the world?
Soccer

740. The north coast of Africa was historically referred to as the Barbary Coast, named after what group of people who lived there?
The Berbers

741. St. Basil's Cathedral in Red Square, known for its colorful onion-shaped domes, is located in which capital city?
Moscow

Economic Geography

742. What was completed in 1914 and created a shortcut between the Atlantic and Pacific Oceans?
The Panama Canal

743. Spain, Italy, and what other country lead the world in olive production?
Greece

744. What term is used to describe factories in northern Mexico that assemble products for American and Japanese companies?
Maquiladoras

745. What type of crops are luxuries grown solely for profit, like tobacco in the United States?
Cash crops

746. What country is well known for its export of hand-woven, woolen blankets called Afghans?
Afghanistan

747. NAFTA was a free trade agreement created in 1994 among which three countries?
The United States, Canada, and Mexico

748. Half the world's emeralds come from a mine in Muzo in what South American country?
Colombia

749. What Caribbean country relied on the Soviet Union for foreign aid until the USSR's collapse but continues to suffer economically due to an embargo by the United States?
Cuba

750. A new bridge crosses the Koge Bay to connect Copenhagen with Malmö, thus linking Denmark to which other country?
Sweden

751. Which small, European country exports printed religious material and imports almost all of its necessities?
Vatican City (also acceptable: the Holy See)

752. What railway corridor opened in 1994 to connect Folkstone, England, to Sangatte, France?
The Channel Tunnel (also acceptable: Chunnel)

753. Although 40 percent of Egypt's workforce is engaged in agriculture, food must be imported because of the extensive farming of what cash crop?
Cotton

754. Odessa was important as the USSR's warm-water port on which sea?
The Black Sea

755. What Southeast Asian city-state is considered one of the Four Tigers because of its strength in trade and industry?
Singapore

756. Which West African country, with Conakry as its capital city, is the world's second-leading producer of bauxite?
Guinea

757. Which country controls the Suez Canal?
Egypt

758. Which South American country lost its Pacific Ocean corridor in a war with Chile in 1884?
Bolivia

759. The Philippines is the world's leading producer of copra, which is used to make what cooking oil?
Coconut oil

760. In which country is the Witwatersrand, an extensive gold mine, located?
South Africa

761. What Caribbean island country has been called "Spice Island" because it leads the world in nutmeg production?
Granada

762. What sweet crop is extensively grown on Mauritius?
Sugarcane

763. What natural resource plays a major role in Oklahoma's economy?
Petroleum (also acceptable: oil)

764. Which product dominates Iceland's exports?
Fish

765. Which West African country, located between Senegal and Guinea, exports cashews as its primary product?
Guinea-Bissau

766. The Bab el Mandeb, which connects the Red Sea with the Gulf of Aden and is one of the world's busiest shipping lanes, is off the west coast of which country?
Yemen

767. Which peninsular European country has its industrial region in the north and its agricultural region in the south?
Italy

768. The headquarters of the European Union is located in which capital city?
Brussels

769. What does GNP stand for?
Gross national product

770. Due to its open registry policy, which African country has the largest merchant fleet in the world?
Liberia

771. What monetary unit of Panama is named after the explorer who established the first European settlement in the country?
The Balboa

772. The New York Stock Exchange is located along which well-known street?
Wall Street

773. Which European country, located east of Germany, is the world's leading producer of rye?
Poland

774. Which former Portuguese colony is the world's leading producer of citrus fruit?
Brazil

775. Which Roman Catholic European country is one of the world's leading apple exporters?
France

776. Which South American country is the world's leading producer of unrefined copper?
Chile

777. Which Asian country's sultan is considered one of the wealthiest men on Earth due to the country's extensive oil and gas production?
Brunei

778. Which river valley is home to *Cyperus papyrus*, a plant soaked and dried to make a paper that was commonly used by several ancient civilizations?

The Nile

779. Yaren is the capital city of which Pacific island country that relies on phosphate mining for its economy?

Nauru

780. Which country, known as Siam until 1939, was the only Southeast Asian country never colonized by a European country?

Thailand

781. Which country has the world's largest democracy and is the world's largest producer of tea and sugarcane?

India

782. Name one of Hawaii's two most important crops.

Pineapple or sugarcane

783. Which tiny Mediterranean country is known for its casinos, car races, and beaches?

Monaco

784. Shocked by Western advances in the 1850s, which country finally opened its doors to Western trade after the Meiji Restoration during the nineteenth century?

Japan

785. Which African country's Copperbelt is centered along its primary urban area of Kitwe?

Zambia

786. The Strait of Hormuz is the exit of which body of water that is important to the world's supply of oil?

The Persian Gulf

787. Along with Japan, the United States, and France, what other country is among the top four of the world's largest economies?
Germany

788. The Owen Falls Dam, just north of Lake Victoria and east of Kampala, produces electricity for which African country?
Uganda

789. Haneda, one of the world's busiest airports, is located near what Asian capital city?
Tokyo

790. What does IMF stand for?
International Monetary Fund

Political Geography

791. Rudolph Giuliani was the mayor of which major U.S. city?
New York City

792. What Asian country crosses five time zones but insists on using only one?
China

793. Which south Asian country was previously known as East Pakistan?
Bangladesh

794. The Golan Heights is a disputed territory between Israel and which other country?
Syria

795. Slobodan Milosevic was accused of crimes against humanity while president of which European country?
Serbia and Montenegro (also acceptable: Yugoslavia)

796. For many years, which country had Israeli troops occupying its south and Syrian troops its northeast?
Lebanon

797. Which European country was formerly known as Gaul and is predominantly Roman Catholic?
France

798. Which Middle Eastern country's government is a theocratic republic?
Iran

799. In addition to Libya and Algeria, which other African nation is a member of OPEC?
Nigeria

800. Yasir Arafat heads which Middle Eastern ethnic independence organization?
PLO, or Palestinian Liberation Organization

801. NATO is made up of European countries as well as what other two countries?
The United States and Canada

802. Who is the first and longtime leader of communist Cuba?
Fidel Castro

803. Which country is composed of over thirteen thousand islands, making it the most fragmented in the world?
Indonesia

804. Which type of government can be found in Saudi Arabia?
Monarchy

805. In which Latin American country was Ernesto Zedillo succeeded by Vincente Fox?
Mexico

806. Which country was formerly known as Zaire?
Democratic Republic of the Congo

807. Which military alliance, headed by the former Soviet Union, was dissolved in 1991?
The Warsaw Pact

808. In 1979, the Ayatollah Khomeini led the overthrow of the government of which country?
Iran

809. What city was the capital of Australia before Canberra?
Melbourne

810. Yemen was formerly composed of which two countries?
North Yemen and South Yemen

811. Which organization replaced the disbanded League of Nations following World War II?
The United Nations, or UN

812. What continent was declared a demilitarized zone in 1959?
Antarctica

813. What is the common name for the international organization that focuses on fighting crime?
Interpol

814. What three countries are members of ANZUS?
Australia, New Zealand, and the United States

815. In 1979, Margaret Thatcher became the first female prime minister of which country?
The United Kingdom

816. Which country is known as Suomi in its native language?
Finland

817. The region known as Andalucia can be found in which Mediterranean country?
Spain

818. Which country's name translates to "Ivory Coast"?
Côte d'Ivoire

819. The Dalai Lama, currently in exile, is the traditional and religious leader of which former country absorbed by China?
Tibet

820. Which country includes the provinces of Utrecht and Zeeland?
The Netherlands

821. Which country is known as Oesterreich in its native language?
Austria

822. The Tamil demand recognition in which teardrop-shaped country?
Sri Lanka

823. In the Boer War, which country fought against the Transvaal and the Orange Free State?
Great Britain

824. One hundred soldiers from which country are responsible for the security of the Vatican City?
Switzerland

825. Which country controls the island of Tahiti?
France

826. Greenland is a territory of which country?
Denmark

827. India and Pakistan are in dispute over which region?
Kashmir

828. Which country is known as Eire and uses the punt as its currency?
Ireland

829. The trade union Solidarity swept the government of which European country during the elections of 1990?
Poland

830. Where was the 1884 conference held to divide Africa among European colonial powers?
Berlin

831. Which two tribes have fought for control of the government of Rwanda?
The Hutu and the Tutsi

832. What is the capital city of Trinidad and Tobago?
Port-of-Spain

833. What was the capital of Brazil before it moved to Brasilia?
Rio de Janeiro

834. Wake Island, located near the Marshall Islands, is actually a territory of which country?
The United States

835. Which European confederation is composed of twenty-three cantons?
Switzerland

836. What country contains the states of Sabah and Sarawak?
Malaysia

837. Which country is known as Nippon in its native language?
Japan

838. The Windsor family has ruled which country since 1917?
Great Britain

839. The Netherlands, Luxembourg, and which other country are known as the Low Countries?

Belgium

840. What are the names of the three Baltic States that declared independence from the Soviet Union in 1991?

Estonia, Latvia, and Lithuania

16

The Environment

This chapter features open-ended questions about the environment. During the Geography Bee, entire rounds concerning
plants, animals, conservation, or the environment may appear. Hint:
Don't focus on an unfamiliar name or term, such as an exotic animal;
instead, pay attention to the geography behind the question.

841. Since the late 1980s, chlorofluorocarbons (CFCs) were banned to prevent further damage to what?
The ozone layer

842. Often called "sea cows," what endangered marine mammal can be found off the Florida coast as well as in South America and Africa?
Manatees

843. Tahrs, descendents of Himalayan mountain goats, are an invasive species causing problems with the ecosystem in Table Mountain Nature Reserve in which African country?
South Africa

844. The Chernobyl nuclear power plant, located in which current country, released radioactive material into the atmosphere in 1986?
Ukraine

845. Which island country, off the coast of Africa, was the home of the dodo bird before it was hunted to extinction?
Mauritania

846. The Great Smokey Mountains National Park, which preserves 130 species of trees and 26 species of salamander, is located in Kentucky and which other state?
Tennessee

847. The Serengeti National Park, home to lions, elephants, rhinos, zebras, and many other species of animals, is located in which African country?
Tanzania

848. The Great Barrier Reef Marine Park in the Coral Sea is located off the eastern coast of which country?
Australia

849. Gunung Mulu National Park, containing the world's most extensive cave system and tropical rain forests, is located in which Asian country?
Malaysia

850. In addition to the American alligator, which lives in the southeastern United States, a second species of alligator can be found in the Yangtze River Basin in which country?
China

851. What region south of the Sahara Desert is at risk of desertification?
Sahel

852. Parts of the Black Sea are covered by a toxic layer of hydrogen sulfide from untreated sewage and agricultural byproducts primarily from which country?
Russia

853. Around which sea has a region of more than 150,000 square miles been officially recognized as an Ecological Disaster Zone due to an 80 percent decrease in water volume caused by diversion of water?
The Aral Sea

854. Over 95 percent of the water in which European country's rivers and lakes is considered unfit for consumption?
Poland

855. The Asiatic lion, which was nearly brought to extinction due to hunting, lives on the Kathiawar Peninsula in which country?
India

856. The giant panda is native to the bamboo forests of which country?
China

857. Which large mammal, native to Africa, is being hunted into extinction for its horn?
Rhinoceros

858. Which is the only marsupial native to the United States?
The opossum (or Virginia opossum)

859. Which gas is responsible for approximately 75 percent of the green-house effect?
Carbon dioxide

860. Which country is the largest in Africa and has an ecosystem ranging from sparse animal and plant life in the deserts to equatorial areas and rivers with a variety of species, including tsetse flies?
Sudan

861. In which U.S. state would you find extremely water-tolerant cypress trees living in the Atchafalaya Swamp?
Louisiana

862. What is the largest rain forest in the world?
The Amazon rain forest

863. Over which continent is the hole in the ozone layer the largest?
Antarctica

864. Which U.S. state contains nearly 2,500 species of flora and few native mammals?
Hawaii

865. Which animal is the largest terrestrial animal in North America, found on the plains from Canada to Mexico, and was nearly hunted to extinction during the nineteenth century?
Bison (or buffalo)

866. Which islands, constituting a province of Ecuador, are home to giant tortoises, iguanas, and eighty-five species of birds?
The Galapagos Islands

867. The oldest public park in the United States is located in which New England capital city?
Boston

868. Which Latin American capital is known for its persistently hazardous air pollution?
Mexico City

869. What is the most important domestic animal of the Andes, used as a beast of burden as well as for its wool, milk, and meat?
The llama

870. The heaviest snake in the world, the anaconda, lives in the river systems on which continent?
South America

17

Current Events

For each National Geographic Bee, the current events questions are based on world events from the year preceding that of the Bee. To give you an example of the types of events that may appear, we have created these sample questions as if for a 2002 Geography Bee, thus using events that occurred in 2001. Notice that for most questions, you don't need to know the event because clues in the question lead you to the answer.

871. In June 2001, which South American country was rocked by an 8.4 earthquake that struck 370 miles southeast of Lima?
Peru

872. On September 11, 2001, which two major U.S. cities were the targets of terrorist attacks?
New York City and Washington, D.C.

873. In August 2001, thirty-six coal miners were killed in an explosion in the Donetsk region, near the Sea of Azov, of which former Soviet republic?
Ukraine

874. June 2001 was the twentieth anniversary of the recognition of which worldwide epidemic that is still devastating Africa?
AIDS

875. In October 2001, a coalition of countries, led by the United States, began air strikes against which Islamic country?
Afghanistan

876. In February 2001, which country elected Ariel Sharon, a former military commander, as prime minister?
Israel

877. In April 2001, sixteen people were killed in a helicopter crash 280 miles south of Hanoi while searching for U.S. soldiers missing in action in which country?
Vietnam

878. In October 2001, anthrax-tainted letters were mailed to Senator Thomas Daschle and Senator Patrick Leahy with a return address of Franklin Park and a postmark of Trenton from which state?
New Jersey

879. In March 2001, the Mir space station crashed back to Earth after fifteen years in orbit, splashing into what body of water?
Pacific Ocean

880. In April 2001, a U.S. surveillance plane collided with a fighter craft, forcing the U.S. plane to land on the island of Hainan in which Asian country?
China

881. In June 2001, former Yugoslav president Slobodan Milosevic was transferred to which city in the Netherlands to stand trial for war crimes?
The Hague

882. In July, the people of Vieques Island overwhelmingly voted to request that the United States Navy immediately stop all bombing exercises there. Vieques Island is part of what U.S. territory?
Puerto Rico

883. In September 2001, which Asian island was hit by Typhoon Nari, which dropped four months of rain in only two days and caused extensive damage to the Taipei subway?
Taiwan

884. Two towering figures of which religious holy person, carved in cliffs in Afghanistan, were destroyed by the Taliban regime in March 2001?
Buddha

885. In October 2001, the Russian nuclear submarine *Kursk*, which sunk with all its crew in 2000, was raised from which sea north of Norway and Russia?
The Barents Sea

886. In April 2001, which major U.S. river reached its highest level since 1965, flooding communities in Minnesota, Wisconsin, and Iowa?
The Mississippi River

887. In June 2001, dozens were killed and hundreds were injured when a passenger train plunged into the Kadalundi River, which flows from the Kerala state to the Arabian Sea, in which country?
India

888. In July 2001, the International Olympic Committee announced that the 2008 summer games will be held in which city?

Beijing

889. In October 2001, a deadly fire raged in Switzerland's Gotthard Tunnel, the second longest tunnel in the world, which runs through what mountain range?

The Alps

890. In February 2001, many countries banned the import of beef from which European country after the discovery and spread of foot-and-mouth disease from Northumberland?

United Kingdom (also acceptable: Great Britain)

891. In June 2001, Simeon II, the boy-king who was forced from Sofia into exile in 1946, was elected prime minister of his home country. Name his country.

Bulgaria

892. In April 2001, Dr. Robert Shemenski, a researcher at the Amundsen-Scott station, was rescued in extremely cold weather from what continent?

Antarctica

893. In June 2001, the king, queen, and numerous other members of the royal family of which Hindu country were massacred by Crown Prince Dipendra over his choice of a bride?

Nepal

894. In June 2001, Presidents Vladimir Putin and George W. Bush met for the first time at a summit held in Ljubljana in which European country?

Slovenia

895. In March 2001, roaming blackouts plagued the Golden State. Name this western U.S. state.

California

896. In July 2001, protesters demanding more rights for immigrants and refugees demonstrated outside the G-8 summit in Genoa in which country?
Italy

897. In October 2001, the prime minister of Japan visited which peninsular country bordering the Sea of Japan to apologize for mistreatment during its occupation from 1910 to 1945?
Korea (also acceptable: South Korea)

898. In January 2001, Laurent Kabila, the dictator of which African nation, was assassinated by his bodyguard in Kinshasa?
Democratic Republic of the Congo

899. In August 2001, a Palestinian suicide bomber killed fifteen people and wounded over a hundred more at a pizzeria in which capital city?
Jerusalem

900. In September 2001, elephants from Botswana and South Africa were airlifted over Namibia to which African country, whose wildlife had been devastated by more than twenty-five years of civil war?
Angola

901. In May 2001, the Zapatista rebel movement, angry about the passage of a weak indigenous rights law, led them to break negotiations over the state of Chiapas with the government of which country?
Mexico

902. Begun in August 2001, the UN World Conference Against Racism was held in Durban in which country?
South Africa

903. In March 2001, the United States expelled fifty diplomats suspected of being intelligence agents from which country, causing strain between the United States and its former Cold War enemy?
Russia

18

Map Reading

This chapter's questions test the student's ability to read a map. All of the open-ended questions relate to the map shown on the next page. In competition, the length of time in which you view the map may vary.

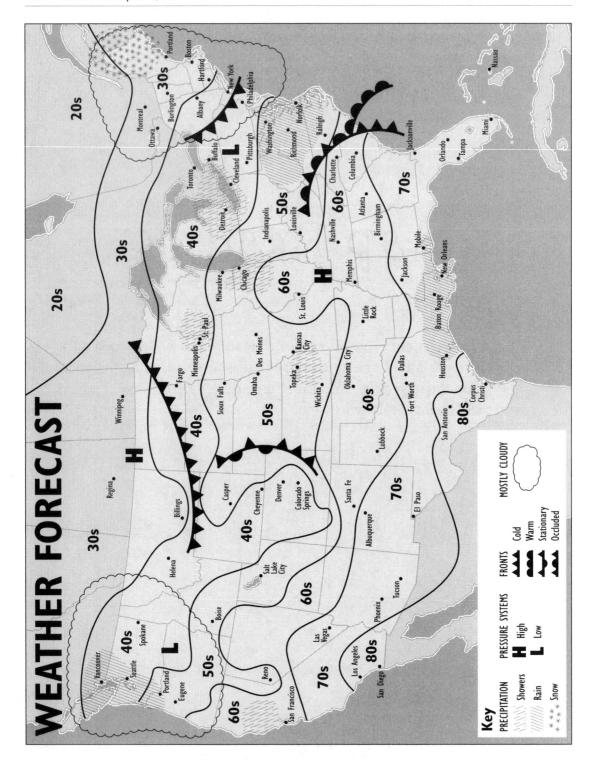

904. What type of front is centered over North Carolina?
Occluded front

905. Which western state is completely overcast?
Washington

906. What type of weather can New Orleans expect?
Rain

907. What type of front is moving across North Dakota?
Cold

908. What temperature can be expected in Little Rock?
60s

909. Which state is mostly covered by snow?
Maine

910. What type of front is centered over Nebraska?
Stationary

911. What type of weather could spectators at a Chicago Cubs home game expect?
Showers

912. What is the difference in temperature between Salt Lake City and Louisville?
There is none; they are in the same isotherm.

913. What will the temperature be like in Boston?
30s

914. What type of pressure system is located over Pennsylvania?
Low

915. What temperature can you expect in Canada's capital city?
30s

916. What temperature can Salt Lake City expect?

50s

917. Which state contains the largest variation in temperature?

California

918. What is the approximate difference in degrees of temperature between Los Angeles and San Francisco?

20 degrees

919. What geographical feature might explain the cooler temperatures around Reno?

Mountains

920. Which southern state can expect rain throughout almost most of the state?

Louisiana

921. Clouds can be expected over which country in addition to the United States?

Canada

922. What two cities are the warmest in the West?

Los Angeles and San Diego

923. What will probably happen to the temperature in Fargo in the next day or two?

Drop or get cooler

924. What weather would you expect if you were sailing on Lake Erie?

Showers

925. Will the weather be clear to go sailing on Lake Erie?

No

926. What temperature could you expect at the Four Corners?

50s

927. What is a probable reason for the clear skies over North Dakota?
The high-pressure system

928. What temperature is expected throughout Vermont?
30s

19

Potluck Geography

Potluck geography is a common round of questions at the Geography Bee. It consists of many open-ended questions about the world.

929. What percentage of the Earth is covered by oceans?
71 percent

930. Which country lies along the Mid-Atlantic Ridge and is partially covered by the Vatnajokull ice sheet?
Iceland

931. The Klondike region can be found in which Canadian province?
Yukon Territory

932. The ancient city Teotihuacán, containing the Pyramid of the Sun and the Temple of Quetzalcoatl, can be found in what modern Latin American country?
Mexico

933. Cook Strait separates the North Island and South Island of which country?
New Zealand

934. What major south Asian river contains more sediment than any other and merges with the Ganges in Bangladesh?
Brahmaputra

935. The capital of Lilongwe and the cities of Blantyre, Zomba, and Mzuzu are located in which small African country on the west side of Lake Nyasa?
Malawi

936. What South American country is 2,650 miles long and no more than 270 miles wide and includes hundreds of islands?
Chile

937. Which Western Hemisphere country leads the world in milk and butter production?
The United States

938. What is the name of the Alaskan sound that was devastated by the *Exxon Valdez* oil spill in 1989?
Prince William Sound

939. The country of Ecuador is named after which imaginary line?
Equator

940. What small country, with a capital of Mbabane, lies on the border of South Africa and Mozambique?
Swaziland

941. Near which pole can you find the Beaufort Sea?
The North Pole

942. The region of Inner Mongolia, also known as Nei Monggol, can be found in which country?
China

943. Ogallala, the largest aquifer in the United States, is a classic example of overextraction of groundwater. Ogallala lies under which region of the United States?
The Southwest (also acceptable: the Midwest)

944. Sulawesi and Halmahera Islands, separated by the Molucca Sea, are part of which country?
Indonesia

945. The Weddell Sea can be found off the western coast of which continent?
Antarctica

946. The twentieth century's deadliest earthquake, which struck in 1976 and killed 242,000 people, occurred in which country?
China

947. Cape Horn is located at the southern tip of which continent?
South America

948. Which European country contains a region of hills known as the Transdanubia, home to Balaton, the country's largest lake?
Hungary

949. The Johore Strait separates Malaysia from which city-state?
Singapore

950. West Edmonton Mall, North America's largest shopping mall, is located in which Canadian province?
Alberta

951. Located south of the Simpson Desert, Lake Eyre has a maximum depth of 4 feet and is the largest salt lake on which continent?
Australia

952. Which European capital city began as a dam across the Amstel River?
Amsterdam

953. What central Asian country is doubly landlocked, thus surrounded by landlocked countries?
Uzbekistan

954. The Grand Erg Occidental and the Grand Erg Oriental are large regions of what North African country?
Algeria

955. The Gulf of Bothnia is bounded on the west by Sweden and on the east by what country?
Finland

956. How many points are there on the Mercalli scale of earthquake intensity?
Twelve

957. Which New Hampshire location had the highest wind speed ever recorded—231 miles per hour?
Mount Washington

958. Godthaab is the capital city of which ice-covered territory?
Greenland

959. Which peninsula is located between the Gulf of Suez and the Gulf of 'Aqaba?
Sinai

960. What is the capital of the Mediterranean country of Malta?
Valletta

961. Australia and which subcontinent lie on the Indo-Australian plate?
India

962. From 1898 through World War II, the Philippines were a territory of which country?
The United States

963. Egypt and which other country united to form the United Arab Republic from 1958 to 1961?
Syria

964. From which direction does the sun appear to rise?
East

965. Venice lies along which sea east of Italy?
The Adriatic Sea

966. New World monkeys, most of which have prehensile tails capable of grasping, are native to which hemisphere?
The Western Hemisphere

967. What cold region extends from the Ural Mountains to the Pacific Ocean and has been used as a penal colony since the seventeenth century?
Siberia

968. Which Canadian province borders the Pacific Ocean?
British Columbia

969. Over one and a half million pilgrims visit what Saudi Arabian city annually?
Mecca

970. The city of Limerick, located at the mouth of the Shannon River, is on what island country?
Ireland

971. The Kalahari Desert is primarily located within Namibia and which country to its east?
Botswana

972. Melbourne is the capital of which Australian state?
Victoria

973. Petrograd and Leningrad are former names of what city?
St. Petersburg

974. The country Trinidad and Tobago lies off the coast of which South American country?
Venezuela

975. Cerro Aconcagua, at 22,834 feet, is the tallest mountain on which continent?
South America

976. Dictator Nicolae Ceauşescu ruled which country north of Bulgaria from 1965 to 1989?
Romania

977. In which Middle Eastern country would you find the sites of the ancient cities Babylon, Ur, and Nippur?
Iraq

978. The Forbidden City and adjacent Tiananmen Square can be found in which Asian city?
Beijing

979. The rocky Antipodes Islands, almost the exact antipode of London, are located off the coast of which Southern Hemisphere country?
New Zealand

980. In which Canadian city is the world's tallest freestanding tower, the CN Tower, located?
Toronto

981. What is the name of the line of longitude that passes through Greenwich, England?
The prime meridian

982. Which West African country has a capital city named after U.S. president James Monroe?
Liberia

983. South Korea has been attempting to change the name of which sea, located to its east, to the East Sea?
Sea of Japan

984. The largest number of immigrants to the United States from 1820 to 1990 came from what country?
Germany

985. The swampy Gran Chaco is composed of southern Paraguay and the northern portion of what country?
Argentina

986. Which of the Great Lakes is the farthest west?
Lake Superior

987. Which African country, south of Mali, has a capital city of Ouagadougou?
Burkina Faso

988. Approximately how many millions of miles is the Earth from the sun?
93,000,000

989. Palk Strait separates India from which country?
Sri Lanka

990. Qatar and which Persian Gulf island country declined to join the seven other states forming the United Arab Emirates?
Bahrain

991. What treelike plant of the grass family grows abundantly in Asia, where it is used for construction, paper, and even food?
Bamboo

992. Land's End is located at the tip of the Cornwall Peninsula in the southern portion of which European country?
The United Kingdom (also acceptable: Great Britain)

993. Easter Island, home to hundreds of ancient monolithic statues, is a territory of which South American country?
Chile

994. Which U.S. city is located at the confluence of the Missouri and Mississippi Rivers?
St. Louis

995. Corsica is a department of which European country?
France

996. Following Greenland, what is the largest island in North America, located in northern Canada?
Baffin Island

997. Following Asia, which continent is the most populated?
Africa

998. Which country's languages include Faeroese and Greenlandic?
Denmark

999. The Mouths of the Irrawaddy can be found just south of Rangoon in which country?
Myanmar

1,000. Azerbaijan and which other country border Russia in the Caucasus?
Georgia

1,001. The United Kingdom borders one country. Name this country.
Ireland

Appendix

What follows are basic reference maps of each continent and of the United States. The maps include many important features to memorize. However, they are definitely not all-inclusive. As we have said before, be sure to use a current atlas when studying.

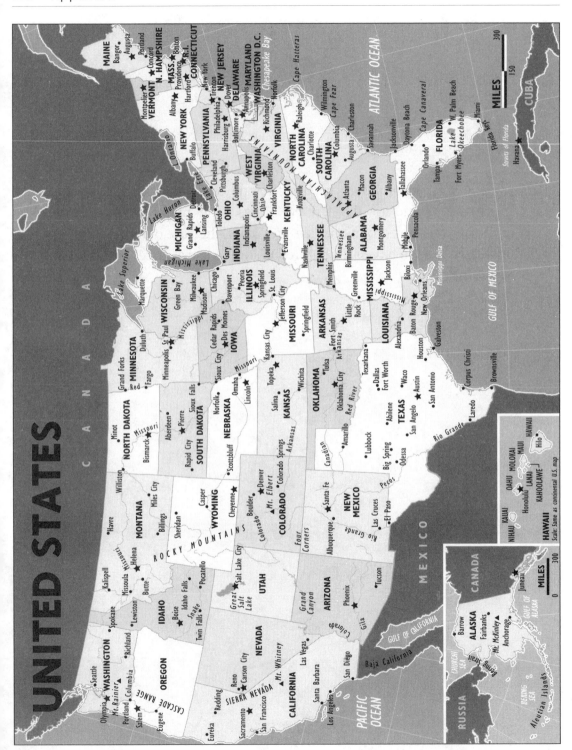

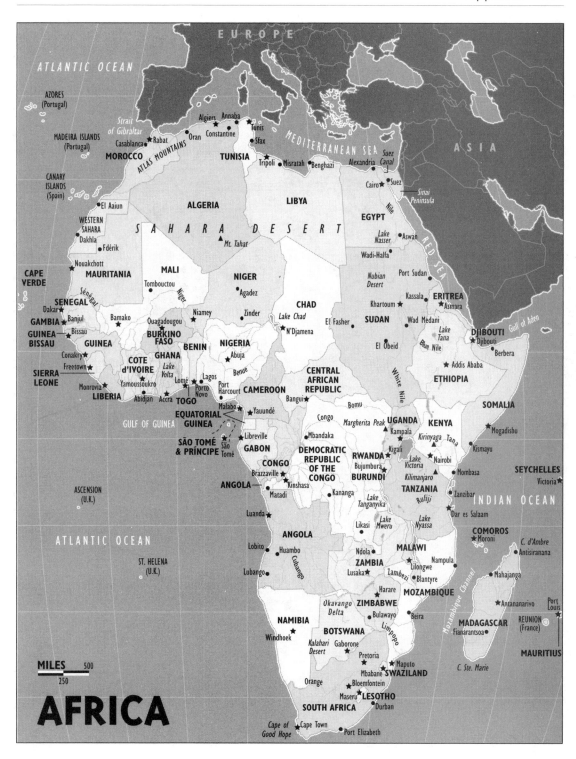

AFRICA

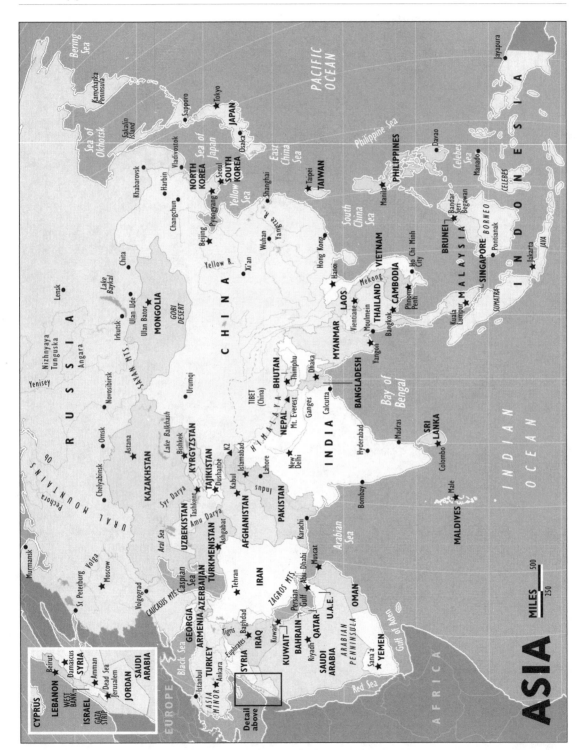

EUROPE

MILES 150 300

ARCTIC OCEAN

BARENTS SEA

GREENLAND SEA

Denmark Strait

Reykjavik ★ **ICELAND**

KOLA PENINSULA

• Murmansk

• Arkhangel'sk

NORWEGIAN SEA

S C A N D I N A V I A

FINLAND

SWEDEN

FAEROES (Demark)

SHETLAND IS.

NORWAY

Gulf of Bothnia

L. Onega

ATLANTIC OCEAN

HEBRIDES

ORKNEY IS.

SCOTLAND

• Edinburgh

NORTH SEA

Oslo ★ ●

Göteborg ★

Stockholm ●

Helsinki ★

L. Ladoga

St. Petersburg •

Tallinn ★

ESTONIA

L. Peipus

RUSSIA

Volga

Skagerrak

Gulf of Riga

BALTIC SEA

Riga ★ **LATVIA**

Moscow •

Belfast ★

Dublin ★

IRELAND

WALES

Cardiff •

UNITED KINGDOM

ENGLAND

London ★

DENMARK

Copenhagen ★

Kaliningrad •

LITHUANIA

Vilnius ★

RUSSIA

• Minsk

Hamburg •

BELARUS

English Channel

NETHERLANDS

★ Amsterdam

Berlin ★

Warsaw ★

Kiev •

BELGIUM

★ Brussels

GERMANY

POLAND

Seine

★ Luxembourg

Prague ★

★ **LUXEMBOURG**

U K R A I N E

Paris ★

Loire

Danube

Munich •

CZECH REP.

SLOVAKIA

Vienna ★ ★ Bratislava

Dnestr

CARPATHIANS

Dnipro

MOLDOVA

Chisinau ★

Zurich •

★ Budapest

FRANCE

Bay of Biscay

Bern ★

SWITZERLAND

Mont Blanc

AUSTRIA

HUNGARY

Prut

• Odessa

MASSIF CENTRAL

A L P S

Po

SLOVENIA

Ljubljana ★

Zagreb ★

ROMANIA

CROATIA

Sevastopol' •

Bilbao •

PYRENEES

MONACO ●

SAN MARINO

BALKAN PENINSULA

Bucharest ★

BLACK SEA

Porto •

ANDORRA ★

BOSNIA-HERZEGOVINA

Belgrade ★

PORTUGAL

SPAIN

Barcelona •

CORSICA (France)

ITALY

APENNINES MTS.

ADRIATIC SEA

Sarajevo •

YUGOSLAVIA

BULGARIA

Sofiya •

Bosporus

Istanbul •

Lisbon •

Madrid •

★ Rome

Skopje •

MACEDONIA

T U R K E Y

Sevilla •

SARDINIA (Italy)

VATICAN CITY

Naples •

Tirane •

A S I A

Malaga •

Gibraltar •

BALEARIC IS. (Spain)

M E D I T E R R A N E A N

ALBANIA

GREECE

Athens •

AEGEAN SEA

Strait of Gibraltar

SICILY

SEA

CRETE

A F R I C A

MALTA ★

Valletta

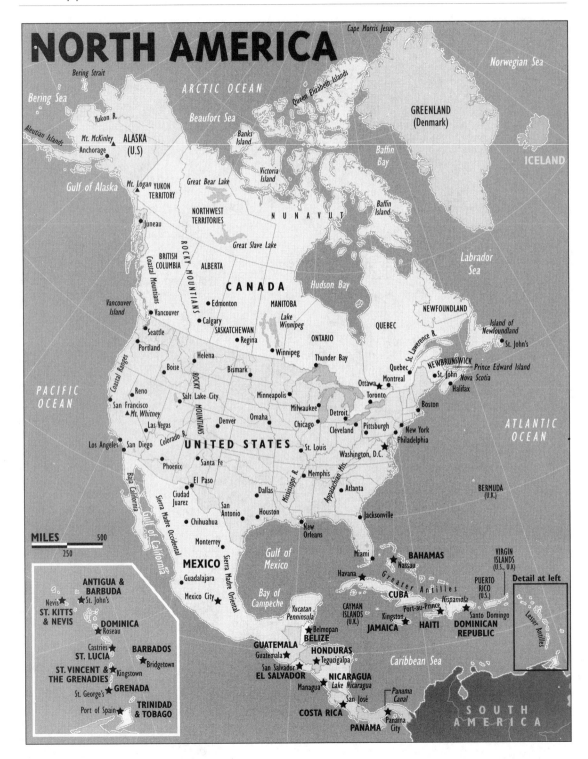

NORTH AMERICA

Cape Morris Jesup

Norwegian Sea

ARCTIC OCEAN

Bering Strait

Bering Sea

Aleutian Islands

Yukon R.

Mt. McKinley ▲ **ALASKA (U.S)**
Anchorage

Gulf of Alaska

Mt. Logan ▲ **YUKON TERRITORY**

Juneau

BRITISH COLUMBIA

Coastal Mountains

Vancouver Island

Vancouver

Seattle

Portland

Coastal Ranges

Reno

San Francisco
▲ Mt. Whitney

Los Angeles ● San Diego

Baja California

Sierra Madre Occidental

Gulf of California

PACIFIC OCEAN

Beaufort Sea

Banks Island

Great Bear Lake

NORTHWEST TERRITORIES

Victoria Island

Queen Elizabeth Islands

GREENLAND (Denmark)

ICELAND

Baffin Bay

Baffin Island

N U N A V U T

Great Slave Lake

ALBERTA

ROCKY MOUNTAINS

Edmonton

Calgary

SASKATCHEWAN

Regina

CANADA

MANITOBA

Lake Winnipeg

Winnipeg

Hudson Bay

ONTARIO

Thunder Bay

Labrador Sea

NEWFOUNDLAND

Island of Newfoundland

St. John's

Helena

Boise

Bismark

Salt Lake City

Denver

ROCKY MOUNTAINS

Colorado R.

Phoenix

Santa Fe

El Paso

Minneapolis

Omaha

Milwaukee

Chicago

St. Louis

Memphis

Appalachian Mts.

Mississippi R.

St. Lawerence R.

Quebec

Ottawa

Montreal

Toronto

Detroit

Cleveland

Pittsburgh

QUEBEC

NEW BRUNSWICK

St. John

Prince Edward Island

Nova Scotia

Halifax

Boston

New York

Philadelphia

Washington, D.C.

ATLANTIC OCEAN

UNITED STATES

Las Vegas

Dallas

San Antonio

Houston

Chihuahua

Monterrey

Atlanta

Jacksonville

BERMUDA (U.K.)

New Orleans

Miami

Gulf of Mexico

Bay of Campeche

MILES 500
250

Ciudad Juarez

Sierra Madre Oriental

MEXICO

Guadalajara

Mexico City

Yucatan Peninsula

Havana

Greater Antilles

Nassau

BAHAMAS

CUBA

Hispaniola

VIRGIN ISLANDS (U.S., U.K)

PUERTO RICO (U.S.)

Detail at left

Lesser Antilles

CAYMAN ISLANDS (U.K.)

Kingston

JAMAICA

Port-au-Prince

HAITI

Santo Domingo

DOMINICAN REPUBLIC

Belmopan

BELIZE

GUATEMALA

Guatemala

HONDURAS

Tegucigalpa

San Salvador

EL SALVADOR

Managua

NICARAGUA

Lake Nicaragua

San José

COSTA RICA

Panama Canal

PANAMA

Panama City

Caribbean Sea

SOUTH AMERICA

ANTIGUA & BARBUDA

Nevis ★ ● St. John's

ST. KITTS & NEVIS

DOMINICA

Roseau

Castries

ST. LUCIA

BARBADOS

Bridgetown

ST. VINCENT & THE GRENADIES

Kingstown

St. George's ● **GRENADA**

Port of Spain

TRINIDAD & TOBAGO

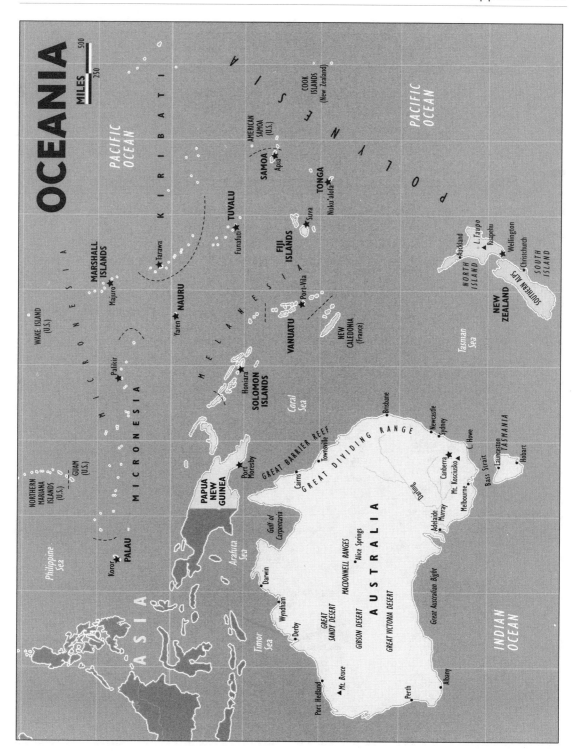

CARIBBEAN SEA

NORTH
AMERICA

Barranquilla•   •Maracaibo   ★Caracas
    Valencia•
    Lake
    Maracaibo
        VENEZUELA
•Medellín   Georgetown ★
                        GUYANA   ★
•Bogota   Paramaribo ★   FRENCH GUIANA
Cali•   SURINAM   Cayenne•   (France)
    COLOMBIA

ATLANTIC OCEAN

★Quito
Guayaquil•
    ECUADOR   Macapá•
                Negro   •Belém
            •Manaus   Amazon

                            Tocantins   •Fortaleza
        Juruá   Madeira   Tapajós
    PERU   Purus   Xingu   •Marabá
Turjillo•   Arinos   B R A Z I L   •Recife

    A   •Maceió
    N   ★Lima
    D   Mamoré   •Salvador
    E
    S   Lake
        Titicaca   ▲Nevado Ancohume   PLANALTO DO   ★Brasilia
                ★La Paz   BOLIVIA   MATO GROSSO   •Goiâna
                •Cochabamba

        ALTIPLANO   ★Sucre   G   Belo Horizonte•
                        R   Paraná
                        A   São Paulo•
Antofagasta•   CHILE   N   PARAGUAY   •Rio de Janeiro
            A   Pilcomayo   Asunción★
            N   C   Curitiba•
            D   H
            E   A   Uruguay R.
    PACIFIC OCEAN   S   C   Porto Alegre•   ATLANTIC OCEAN
                    O   ARGENTINA
                        •Córdoba

            Valparaíso•   Rosario•   URUGUAY
            Santiago★   Buenos Aires★ Montevideo★
            P   Mar de Plata•   Río de la Plata
            A
            M   Bahia Blanca•
            P
            A   Golfo San Matias
            S

        Isla de Chiloé

                Golfo de
                San Jorge

    Strait of   FALKLAND
    Magellan   Strait of Magellan   ISLANDS
        Punta Arenas• Tierra del Fuego   (U.K.)   SOUTH GEORGIA
                                (U.K.)

SOUTH
AMERICA
MILES _____ 500
    250

Index

About the Authors

Matthew T. Rosenberg is a geographer best known for his work as the Geography Guide for About.com, the Internet's most popular site devoted exclusively to geography (geography.about.com). Matt is the author of *The Handy Geography Answer Book.* He has also served as a judge at Geography Bees and has appeared in a PBS television special on geography. His geography articles are regularly published in the *Dallas Morning News.* Matt's full-time job is as a Director of Emergency Services for the American Red Cross, where he works to prepare and plan for disaster response.

Jennifer E. Rosenberg is a historian and writer who works as About.com's Guide to 20th Century History at history1900s.about .com. She most recently wrote the foreword for the *Idiot's Guide to the Great Depression* and an encyclopedia entry for the *Great Events of the Twentieth Century.* Jen's work has appeared in many other publications online and offline. Jen has a passion for places around the world and travels extensively.

Matt and Jen live with their two dogs in Southern California.